T0150057

DETROIT

{ A BIOGRAPHY }

SCOTT MARTELLE

CHICAGO
REVIEW
PRESS

The Library of Congress has cataloged the hardcover edition as follows:
Martelle, Scott, 1958-
 Detroit : a biography / Scott Martelle. — 1st ed.
     p. cm.
 Includes bibliographical references.
 ISBN 978-1-56976-526-5 (hardcover)
 1. Detroit (Mich.)—History. 2. Detroit (Mich.)—Economic conditions.
 3. Detroit (Mich.)—Population. 4. African Americans—Michigan—Detroit—
 History. I. Title.

 F574.D44M37 2011
 977.4'34—dc23

                                                        2011041173

Cover design: Natalya Balnova
Cover photo: Library of Congress (LC-DIG-PPMSCA-15308)
Interior design: Jonathan Hahn

Printed in the United States of America
5 4 3 2 1

For Margaret.

And for Detroiters, past and present, who are fighting for its future.

CONTENTS

Detroit is especially noted for its broad and cleanly streets, its wide and well-kept walks, its numerous and thrifty shade trees, its extensive and beautiful lawns and gardens, the number and attractiveness of its parks and public squares, the varied and tasteful architecture of its residences, the stability of its mercantile life, and the range and extent of its manufacturing interests.

—Guide to the Streets, Street Pavements, Street Car
Routes and House Numbers of Detroit, 1901

PREFACE

The grand dreams of Detroit's many pasts are clustered here in the heart of downtown, bookended by the termini of the John C. Lodge and Walter P. Chrysler Freeways. The roads end a half mile apart, the Lodge at West Jefferson Avenue and the Chrysler at East Jefferson Avenue, and for a couple of generations now they have linked the region's sprawling suburbs with the city's downtown heart. Given Detroit's economy, which has seized up like an engine run dry, it's hard not to see those worn and potholed freeways as metaphors. Arteries carrying shrinking loads. Aspirations that fell short. The distance between what is and what might be. Or what once was.

There's a history behind the names. Chrysler, of course, helped build Detroit into the center of the automotive world. The Lodge Freeway is named after a pre–Great Depression mayor who moved to politics from the city desk of the *Detroit Free Press* newspaper. Midway between them lies a parallel thoroughfare, Woodward Avenue, a psychological dividing line separating east from west while physically connecting the northern suburbs beyond Eight Mile Road to the riverfront. The avenue—a grand boulevard, really, at six lanes wide in places—is the legacy of Augustus B. Woodward, appointed in 1805 by his friend, President Thomas Jefferson, as the first chief justice of what was then the Michigan Territory.

The timing was crucial to creating the Detroit we know today. Woodward arrived in Detroit less than three weeks after most of the small frontier town had burned to the ground, and he assumed for himself the task of redesigning the city, the first of many attempts at a renaissance, by borrowing Pierre Charles L'Enfant's hub-and-spoke vision for the nation's capital. In a display of hubris, Woodward named Detroit's new central artery after himself, joking later that he intended nothing more than to reflect its direction from river to woods. Woodward also named the road running parallel to the river (and following an active Indian trail) after Jefferson, and over the next two centuries Woodward Avenue became the city's defining corridor while Jefferson Avenue gave rise to the early industries that defined Detroit's niche in the world.

These and other roadways, and the men after whom they are named—Chrysler, Ford, Fisher, Jeffries, Reuther—represent different slices of Detroit's past, and each in its way played a significant role in the city's evolution from forest to factory, boom to bust, and dawn to dusk. I lived in Detroit for a decade in the 1980s and 1990s, spending most of it as a staff writer for the *Detroit News*, whose offices still stand a few blocks northwest of the intersection of Woodward and Jefferson. And it was as a journalist that I first came to see this spot as the nexus of many things—past and present, river and land, wealth and poverty.

Just to the east of the intersection stands the Renaissance Center, the iconic vertical tubes that Henry Ford II had built in the 1970s hoping they would, indeed, spark another renaissance in this once-great city. The RenCen, as it's called, defines Detroit's skyline as much as the Empire State Building defines New York City's. Downriver, to the west, stands the Veterans Memorial Building at Hart Plaza, roughly on the site of the original 1701 French settlement that evolved into present-day Detroit. Nearby, on a traffic island at the intersection of Woodward and Jefferson, a twenty-four-foot-long arm ending in a giant clenched, black fist dangles horizontally from a four-legged pyramid frame, like those that backyard mechanics use to suspend engines they've lifted out of cars. Known locally as *The Fist*, the statue's formal name is the *Joe Louis Memorial*, recognizing the larger-than-life boxer who came of age in Detroit's old Black Bottom slum. Louis was a black hero in an era in which black heroes, and black celebrities, were forced into small orbits ancillary to most of American life. Louis, a punching machine, broke through that barrier, and it's fitting that a reproduction of a powerful and successful black man's fist stands here in the arrhythmic heart of the city. It was designed by Los Angeles sculptor Robert Graham, on commission from *Sports Illustrated*, as a gift to Detroit. Graham chose to cast a fist instead of the whole fighter because, he said, he wanted to focus on the core element of Louis's fame, and leave the monument open to interpretation. He never addressed whether he chose to leave the boxer's fist ungloved as a bit of artistic subterfuge, but that is how it has been taken—a play on the Black Power salute anchoring one of the city's key intersections.

In October 2009, just down the street from *The Fist*, the full weight of Detroit's modern decline played out in a moment of poignant drama. As the nation struggled with the worst financial crisis since the Great Depression, the City of Detroit decided to use $15.2 million in federal economic stimulus money to help 3,500 city residents stave off eviction or, if homeless, help them pay for housing. Given the city's pervasive poverty and the auto industry's financial crisis, city officials expected a lot of interest in the program. So they set up a room in Cobo Hall, the city's 2.4-million-square-foot riverfront convention center, to handle the rush for applications. Still, they weren't prepared for the flood of desperation. Propelled by false rumors of a cash handout, some fifty thousand people showed up looking for help, many spending the night on the sidewalk in a sprawling, brawling mass.[1]

That outpouring of need, and the boiling-over frustrations that led to fistfights in the waiting crowd, illustrate the raw and deep economic devastation that has slowly crumbled Detroit. Just two generations ago the city was the healthy, beating heart of the American economy, with the auto industry accounting for one in six jobs across the nation. Now, the auto industry is a shell of itself. General Motors—as in, "What's good for General Motors is good for America"—was trading as a penny stock before it slipped into bankruptcy in 2009. It has since emerged after sloughing off its worthless assets into the Motors Liquidation Company in hopes of selling off the properties that had been a drain on GM itself.

Chrysler also needed a federal bailout to survive. Ford managed to skirt bankruptcy and federal bailout funds, but just barely. By mid-2011, GM and Chrysler had emerged from bankruptcy and all three were reporting profits, but the industry was a shadow of its former self. In 2007, there were 10.8 million cars and trucks produced in the United States. That was nearly halved to 5.7 million in 2009 before rebounding to just under 7.8 million in 2010.

The effect of the automakers' collapse on Detroit, already battered by decades of deindustrialization, was brutal. In March 2011, the US Census reported that the population of Detroit, once the nation's fourth-largest city, had dropped to 714,000 people, down by a quarter-million since 2000 and by more than 1.1 million people from its peak of 1.8 million residents in 1950 (Note: Unless otherwise specified, when I say Detroit in this book, I mean the city itself, not the sprawling metropolitan region). No other major American city has been gutted so deeply. Chicago has lost about 964,000 people since 1950, but it still holds about 2.7 million residents, down 25 percent from its peak of 3.62 million in 1950. Detroit's loss amounts to a staggering 60 percent of the city's peak population. It is now smaller than Charlotte, North Carolina, or Fort Worth, Texas. More people have left Detroit since 1950 than live in San Francisco; more people have left in the last decade than live in Saint Petersburg, Florida.

While many of the problems that have led Detroit to this point are specific to the place itself, many are also linked to the fates of other American cities. It's unclear when we look at Detroit today whether we're seeing the last spasms of America's industrial past, or a harbinger of the nation's urban future. But what is clear is that this is what the abject collapse of an industrial society looks like. Massive iconic factories stand silent and cold. Blocks of commercial districts are vacant and open to the elements, many burned by fires that seemed to spread like a virus. Housing prices have fallen so far that it is cheaper to buy a home in Detroit than a new car. Once-vital neighborhoods have been bulldozed and reverted to urban meadows; in places, wild pheasants and the occasional fox roam freely. Even Detroit's murder rate, which for years was the worst among the nation's big cities, has dropped considerably, prompting

2009 mayoral candidate Stanley Christmas to say, "I don't mean to be sarcastic, but there just isn't anyone left to kill."[2]

Present-day Detroit challenges our comprehension of what an American city is. Where most cities have a few "bad" neighborhoods, Detroit has a few "good" areas. Artists and photographers chronicling Detroit's demise focus on the hard-to-resist images of the vast urban decay, capturing ancient ruins in the making. But the true loss, and damage, is to the people of Detroit, particularly those without resources— financial, educational, and vocational—to make an economy hum. Or, for that matter, the personal resources to leave. Many of those left behind face personal ruin as surely as the abandoned buildings that have come to frame our perceptions of modern Detroit.

The middle and upper classes have effectively abandoned the city, and statistical measures of life in Detroit are mind-boggling. Official unemployment peaked at 27.4 percent in July 2009, and remained above 20 percent through the first half of 2011. But the true jobless rate for working-age Detroiters, where chronic unemployment and underemployment is endemic, is much higher. In 2010, of 468,000 adults between the ages of 16 and 65, only 138,000 were employed—less than a third. Obviously, not all of those in their working years were employable, or wished to work, but the gap between those in their working years and those with jobs is sobering—especially compared with a national rate of about 60 percent of work-age Americans who held jobs.[3]

The effect on wealth in Detroit is staggering. In 2010, nearly four in ten Detroiters overall, and more than half of Detroit's children, were living below the federal poverty line, making Detroit the poorest of the nation's big cities. And it's a stingy threshold: poverty is defined as a family of four living on less than $20,650 a year. Per capita income in Detroit for 2009 was estimated at $15,310, just over half the national rate of $27,041. Significantly, there were nearly twice as many families consisting of single mothers with minor children than there were two-parent families.[4]

Lack of education is a significant compounding factor in the relentless poverty. One in four Detroiters over age twenty-five hasn't finished high school (the current graduation rate is worse—three out of four students drop or flunk out), compared with a national average of 8 percent of adults between the ages of sixteen and twenty-four.[5] Women in Detroit outnumber men 53 percent to 47 percent against a national ratio of 51 percent to 49 percent. The average family size is much higher than elsewhere in the country, and from 2005 to 2009, more than two of every three children born in Detroit were to unmarried mothers, many of whom pass their responsibility on to their own parents. Significantly, the median age for all Detroiters, at 33.2 years, is a full three years lower than the national median—a massive statistical variance that, when matched against the other stats, means Detroit's population skews younger, poorer, and less-educated than the rest of the nation's big cities. It is a lost generation in the making. A recent study published in the American Sociological Review charted the progress of more than four thousand children into adulthood, and concluded that those raised in poverty had a significantly lower chance of graduating high school, and, by extension, of reaching long-term financial stability.[6]

Underlying all of this is a dearth of ways to earn a living. In 1970, there were 735,000 jobs in the city of Detroit; in 2000, there were 345,000 jobs; in 2005, there were 279,000 jobs. That's a 62 percent decline in a generation, and jobs have continued to evaporate. Yet, during the same time span the number of jobs in Southeast Michigan, which covers Detroit and its sprawling suburbs, grew by more than 600,000. Detroit is the flotsam of that tidal economic shift. In human terms, the numbers mean Detroit is now largely composed of fractured families led by young, uneducated single mothers lucky to find minimum-wage jobs in a political environment in which aid programs have been slashed. These are not the seeds of a stable community.

How Detroit got to this juncture is the subject of this book. As the title reflects, this is a biography of a place, but it is not an exhaustive look at the entire history of the city. Such an undertaking would far exceed the limits of a single book. In fact, the histories of the auto industry and of the United Auto Workers union alone have spun off enough books to fill their own libraries. So, as one does when looking at the life of a person, I've sought to focus on some of the key events in the city's evolution, exploring the major forces that have shaped Detroit into its adulthood. I've left out cultural touchstones, such as the rise of Motown and other slices of Detroit's influential music history and the city's much-loved sports franchises, to focus on the economic and population changes from which the culture has sprung. And I've omitted such demographic developments as the influx of Arab Americans, Mexican Americans, Jews, Italians, and other ethnic groups, since they primarily came to Detroit for the same reasons everyone else did: to make cars, and to make money. But one cannot write about Detroit without exploring the roots of its black population, which now accounts for more than four of every five Detroiters.

Despite the current devastation, Detroit remains a place of tremendous resilience, with generations carving out lives and livelihoods alongside—and often outside—the roller coaster of the auto industry. I hope this work captures that aspect of Detroit, too.

This also is not an argument for specific policies, nor does it end with an obligatory chapter of rosy suggestions for solutions. There are no handy answers. It took decades of government, corporate, and personal decisions, social pressures and fractures, and global economic shifts, to make Detroit what it is. To think there might be a menu of simple solutions is naive at best. But key to finding any sort of plan for fixing Detroit, and, perhaps, to prevent what has happened here from afflicting other cities, is to fully understand what Detroit once was, and how it came to be what it is.

There is widespread confusion and ignorance outside Detroit about the broad forces that have eroded it away. In March 2011, after the 2010 census reported Detroit's surprisingly low 714,000 population, I wrote an opinion piece for the *Los Angeles Times* touching on some of this history, and, after arguing that as a society we owe a moral debt to the city that helped propel the rise of the nation's middle class, asked an open-ended question: What is the nation going to do about Detroit? The online comments were chilling in their thinly veiled racism, their angry and deep antiunion sentiments, their opportunistic attempts to blame Democrats (Detroit began shrinking under a Republican pro-development mayor, with Eisenhower in the White House), and their generally harsh and coldhearted outlook. "Detroit has no future because it had no vision of a future," wrote one anonymous commenter. "All it cared about were freebees from government, and took no responsibility for its own future. It should be left to rot as an example of failed leadership at the local and even state levels!!! It will happen in other places—Chicago—for the same reasons!!!! LET THEM ROT!!!!"[7] My hope is this book might push back some at that kind of vicious dismissiveness.

The tendency in looking at Detroit is to break its history in two: before the rise of the auto industry, and after. It is a history spiced with the well-known, from Ossian Sweet's defiant defense of his right, as a black man, to move into a white neighborhood in 1925, to the Depression-era auto plant sit-down strikes that gave rise to the United Auto Workers union and the American middle class, to the names we see on the roadways every day—Dodge, Olds, Chrysler, and, of course, Ford. But it also harbors compelling stories of everyday lives, their dramas and comedies, their successes and failures. This is a place and a community that has been buffeted by government failure and corporate hubris, but also by racism, fear, greed, and avarice. Some have soared and some have fallen. As a whole, they are the story of Detroit. While this book is a history of a place, it is also a book about life and human nature, and about a city as a living and breathing thing. And, naturally, it begins with a birth.

1

A DIFFICULT CHILDHOOD

Detroit is, in many ways, the result of a planned birth. The details of the day, July 24, 1701, a Thursday, are lost to time, but it was the peak of summer, so it may well have been one of those sultry afternoons on the Great Lakes when the sky washes white with haze. Or maybe mugginess had settled in, with thunderheads billowing majestically on the updrafts. What is certain is that given the personal drive of Antoine Laumet de la Mothe, sieur de Cadillac, not even a drenching summer downpour would have kept him from beaching his canoe on the north bank of the Detroit River that day, the culmination of more than two years of lobbying and preparations.

Cadillac, a magistrate's son from southwest France's mid-Pyrenees region, had been in the Americas since 1683. An officer in the French navy with strong connections in the court of Louis XIV, Cadillac had made himself something of an expert on the geography of present-day New England and the Great Lakes. His knowledge won him an appointment in 1694 as commandant of the frontier fort at Michillimackinac, which gave him military authority over the trading post and lands surrounding the Straits of Mackinac—where Lakes Michigan and Huron come together at the five-mile gap between Michigan's Upper and Lower Peninsulas. Cadillac's mission there was to provide security for French fur traders, roust English interlopers, and try to bring the local tribes—mostly Chippewa—under French rule while maintaining peace with the ferocious Iroquois confederacy to the east.

The best way to win the loyalty of the local tribes, Cadillac thought, was to establish tribal villages near the fort where they would be easier to monitor and trade with, and where they could be offered medical treatment, "for there is nothing more urgent for gaining their friendship than the care taken of them in their illnesses." And Cadillac believed—he was French, after all—that love might be part of the answer. "It would be absolutely necessary also to allow the soldiers and Canadians to marry the savage maidens when they have been instructed in religion and know the French language, which they will learn all the more eagerly (provided we labor carefully to that end) because they always prefer a Frenchman for a husband to any savage whatever." The shape of the idea was drawn from history. "Marriages of this kind will strengthen the friendship of these tribes, as the alliances of the Romans perpetuated peace with the Sabines through the intervention of the women."[1]

Cadillac's plan appalled the Jesuit missionaries in Quebec and at Fort Michillimackinac, as did his advocacy of trading furs for alcohol with the natives. But he was sure about his strategy. He also realized that the thin, rocky soil around the post at Michillimackinac was poor for farming, which made it harder to persuade the native tribes to settle into villages. And given how far west into the Great Lakes the post was established, it was ineffective at monitoring who was moving along the main travel routes.

Cadillac rolled the problem around in his mind and reasoned that the French would have better luck if they abandoned the post at Mackinac and moved the garrison south to the much narrower and more easily defended river that drained the upper lakes into Lake Erie. And he knew just the spot, a bend in the narrows where the river flowed temporarily from east to west, making the northern bank a perfect place to monitor traffic, control passage, and keep the British from moving in on French trade with the native tribes.[2]

In 1699, Cadillac asked to be relieved of his command so he could return to Quebec, then sail for Paris to make his proposal to his patron—Louis Phélypeaux, le comte de Pontchartrain, and chancellor of France—and, through him, to King Louis XIV. Both men saw the logic in Cadillac's plan and, over the bitter objections of the Jesuits, Louis XIV approved the new settlement.

Cadillac made the return trip across the Atlantic, stopped in Montreal to put his expedition together, and on June 7, 1701, struck out with twenty-five large canoes bearing fifty blue-coated French soldiers, another fifty settlers (assorted artisans), two priests (one a Jesuit missionary, the other a Franciscan Recollet chaplain), and enough supplies to last two months. They paddled up the Rivière des Outaouais—Ottawa River, which separates the present Quebec and Ontario provinces—nearly to its source, then portaged westward to Lake Nipissing, then down the pine-shrouded Rivière des Français—French River—to Georgian Bay, the northeastern lobe of Lake Huron. It was a long, difficult route, but necessary to avoid the escarpment at Niagara, which created the massive waterfalls and gorge on the river that drained Lake Erie into Lake Ontario. (Cadillac, in fact, dreamed of a day when French engineers would build a canal around the falls, something businessman William Hamilton Merritt finally did in 1824.) As difficult as the trek was, the route through Lake Nipissing was something of an early explorers' highway, which the bulk of the French fur traders, soldiers, and priests followed to get to the northern reaches of the Great Lakes.[3]

Instead of continuing west from Georgian Bay along the established trade route, Cadillac and his party paddled southwest until they reached the Saint Clair River, then followed the shore of Lake Saint Clair into the straits. They maneuvered past a large island, about two and a half miles long (eventually named Belle Isle, it is the largest island park in the nation) then, a few hundred yards downstream, drifted to the north, where they beached the canoes. Cadillac, in letters to his superiors, described his landing site as a meadow rimmed by fruit trees leading into a dense forest of walnut, white and red oak, ash, and cottonwoods, all entwined with thick vines that provided cover for turkey, pheasant, and quail. Deer grazed at the edges and nibbled on fallen apples, plums, and other fruits, the streams and the river itself teemed with fish, and the reeds along the bank hid flocks of swans, geese, and ducks. But it was the open space that drew Cadillac's closest interest. "There the hand of the pitiless mower has never shorn the juicy grass on which bisons of enormous height and size fatten." Cadillac likely was overselling a bit in his reports back to his patrons, but not by much—his group killed both a deer and a bear the first day.

With the harsh winter only a few months away, Cadillac wasted no time turning the meadow into a frontier outpost. He ordered the band of soldiers and settlers to craft a storage building, then a stockade around it, on the first rise of land. It was a modest but effective enclosure of sharpened fifteen-foot-high oak trunks driven four to five feet into the ground. Within those walls, beneath present-day Hart Plaza and nearby buildings roughly at the feet of Griswold and Shelby streets, the settlers built grass-roofed log houses and barracks. Over time, more buildings were added outside the stockade, and more settlers arrived— including Cadillac's wife, who would give birth to the first child in the settlement.

Cadillac named the place Fort Pontchartrain, after his boss, but it didn't have the immediate effect of pacification that Cadillac had hoped. Two groups from regional tribes—the Ottawas and the Miamis—did settle near the fort. But it was an uneasy existence, marked by petty jealousies, including the belief by the Ottawas that the Miamis were getting better treatment and trading terms from the French.

In 1703, a disgruntled Ottawa set one of the external storage buildings on fire. The flames spread to the adjacent fort, heavily damaging part of the wall, the church, the homes of Cadillac (burning many of his papers) and one of his top lieutenants, and the House of the Recollets (home of the Franciscan priests).

To assuage the angry French, other Ottawas helped them rebuild, but the peace was short-lived. In 1706, while Cadillac was away, the dog of the officer he left in charge, a man named Bourgmont, bit an Ottawa tribesman, who in response beat the dog, which led Bourgmont to beat the tribesman, killing him. The Ottawas took their revenge by ambushing a group of six Miamis, killing five, and also taking hostage Father Nicholas Constantine del Halle while he was walking in his garden outside the fort. The Recollet priest was released a short time later, but just as he reached the gate, a musket-toting Ottawa fired a single shot and killed him. Bourgmont ordered the fort sealed, aligned his soldiers in the battlements, and told them to open fire. Some thirty Ottawas fell dead.[4]

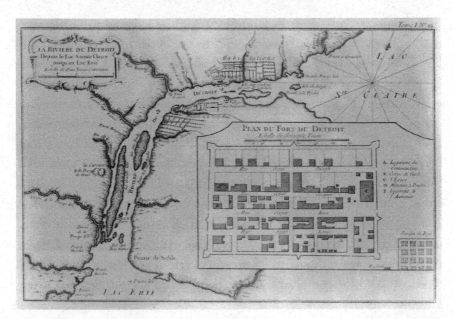

Bellin Atlas map of Detroit, 1763. COURTESY OF THE BURTON HISTORICAL COLLECTION, DETROIT PUBLIC LIBRARY

The French settlers knew they could not live by hunting and trading alone and began establishing private farms outside the stockade on long, narrow plots—three hundred to nine hundred feet wide—stretching northward from the river. Those early farms form the skeleton for present-day Detroit. Saint Antoine Street marks the edge of the original Saint Antoine family land grant and farm, as do Beaubien, Rivard, Chene, Moran, and other streets that begin at or near the river and run perpendicular, at a cant slightly west of north. Other, smaller farms similarly stretched back from the Rivière Parent, a large stream flowing southward into the Detroit River near the west end of Belle Isle, a stream long since buried by urban development.

In a sense, three hundred years ago the rivers and navigable streams were the roads joining the farms, and the Detroit River was the major thoroughfare. The houses were built close to the water's edge, and behind them invariably stood an orchard, after which came the cleared fields for corn, wheat, and other staples. It was an inefficient design; the layout was adopted for safety. Each farmer would have plenty of land to tend to, and space to grow crops. But their houses would be close enough together that they could easily reach each other in the event of emergency, from health troubles to raids by the natives.

Where land ownership is involved, squabbles soon follow, and the early years of Detroit were no different. For half a century claims and counterclaims were made over property rights, and even Cadillac's initial land grant from Louis XIV came under challenge in a legal battle that lasted long after his death in 1730. (He left Detroit in 1710 to govern the new Louisiana territories, but returned to France in 1717 under a cloud concerning his management of the colony, which included violent showdowns with Natchez tribesmen. A rather intemperate man, upon his arrival in France, Cadillac was thrown into the Bastille for five months for harsh comments about his overlords in letters and official reports.[5]) And, of course, the native tribes, who were there first, were given no say.

The early houses were drawn from the rough-hewn frontier, walled with oak or cedar logs beneath roofs of thatch or grass. Until 1750 or so, when the first brick kilns were built in Detroit, stones for the chimneys were brought in from Stony and Monguagon Islands, barren outcroppings downriver near Lake Erie. Over time the stockade itself was enlarged to incorporate the new houses, numbering around one hundred by mid-century.

During the first couple of decades, Detroit remained a mixed, though strictly segregated, settlement (a legacy that continues, though in decidedly less formal arrangements). The French had their safe houses within the stockade. Their farms and orchards were outside, where the local natives also settled. In 1705, several hundred Native Americans inhabited encampments on both sides of the river, all invited by Cadillac—and all seeking some protection from the Iroquois tribes to the east. Thirty Hurons lived in wigwams just outside the stockade, and a Potawatomi village arose farther to the west. Ottawas and Hurons also settled across the river, in what became present-day Windsor.

Still, Detroit remained a frontier outpost, and by mid-century had only grown to around twenty-five hundred settlers. The population began dwindling after silk hats replaced beaver hats as the high fashion in Paris and London, cutting demand and prices for beaver pelts and collapsing the fur trade, in what would become a familiar pattern for Detroit.

War between the royal houses of England and France was something of a national pastime for each, and the rivalry extended to the New World. The Seven Years' War began in 1754 in Europe and quickly spread across the Atlantic, pitting the French and their tribal allies against the British and their tribal allies in what became known as the French and Indian War—in essence, America's first involvement in a world war. And it was a war of marked atrocities: the targeting of settlers, the paying of bounties by both the French and English to scalp-bearing Native Americans, and a "scorched-earth" policy toward overrun settlements, leaving nothing in their wakes but ashes.

Detroit, as a distant settlement, remained outside most of the fray. In fact, displaced French fighters from captured forts eventually made their way to Detroit, which became the base for eastward sorties. Still, there was some fighting in the area, and one notable attack planned by Iroquois warriors was thwarted when a tipster let the French garrison at Detroit know what was coming.

But the British were winning more of those fights than the French, and in 1763 the fighting ended with the Treaty of Paris, which assigned to England all of France's claims east of the Mississippi. By then Detroit had long been in British hands, with the first British troops displacing the French garrison on November 29, 1760, granting the vanquished safe passage to Philadelphia, and on to France. As they left, the French promised their allies among the native tribes that they would return. But it was a hollow—and unfulfilled—promise, something to which Detroiters would become accustomed.

2

THE BRITISH DECADES

The outpost the British took over on the banks of the Detroit River was a rough-hewn frontier garrison measuring one hundred *toises* wide by sixty *toises* deep—about 213 yards by 127 yards, or a little bigger than five football fields. The stockade held four streets running east-west, or parallel to the river, with Saint Louis closest, then Saint Anne, Saint Jacques, and Saint Joseph, all cut north-south by two unnamed alleys. The compact settlement contained the commandant's lodgings, the munitions building, a small church, and a few dozen houses.[1] "The fort is very large and in good repair; there are two bastions toward the water and a large bastion toward the inland," Capt. Donald Campbell, the first British commandant of Detroit, wrote in a 1771 report to his superiors.

> The point of the bastion is a cavalier of wood, on which there are mounted the three pounders [light cannons] and the three small mortars, or coehorns. The palisades are in good repair. There is scaffolding around the whole, which is floored only toward the land for want of plank; it is by way of a banquette. There are seventy or eighty houses in the forest; laid out in regular streets. The country is inhabited ten miles on each side of the river and is a most beautiful country. The river here is about nine hundred

yards over and very deep. Around the whole village, just within the palisades, was a road which was called the "*Chemin de Ronde*."[2]

The British, more militarily focused than the French, upgraded the fort and replaced the French ten-foot pickets with fifteen-footers and over the next few years would continue to tinker with and expand the fort.[3]

Detroit's main function was as a military outpost, but it was established to foment trade, particularly in pelts, from beaver to buffalo. Fur trapping was an individualistic business, and even after demand collapsed for hat-caliber beaver pelts, the river was plied by swift-moving and brightly painted canoes paddled by native trappers as well as the French frontiersmen, who would beach and sleep under their dugouts at night.

By the time the English took over, trade with the native tribes had evolved from a system through which French fur traders gathered pelts (mainly beaver) to ship to Europe into a regular conduit of European goods to the Native Americans, who developed a key dependency on outposts like Detroit. In the early going, metal ax heads, to replace the natives' stone ones, were in high demand. But eventually the most yearned-for European staple was gunpowder. The tribesmen had learned to repair their guns and make their own ammunition, but they lacked the equipment and material to make gunpowder.

Detroit also was a source of power for tribal leaders. Within the tribes, particularly among the Ottawa, political power was built on a culture of shared largesse. As Gregory Evans Dowd points out in his fine history of that period, *War Under Heaven*, the Ottawas looked at trade not as a means to acquire individual wealth, but as a mechanism for controlling personal loyalties. "A successful Ottawa trader . . . amassed no fortune and sought no propertied independence; instead he carefully gave away his goods to acquire both socially indebted followers and personal prestige. He forged alliances, personal, familial and diplomatic. The system worked because trade, rather than being a way to wealth, was an avenue to the authority achieved through the generous distribution of goods and services. . . . Trade relations were, then, a way to power." Most of the gifts bestowed by French military commanders on the tribal chiefs were in turn passed out to lower-level members of the tribes. In a sense, the chiefs' relationships with the French were the wellsprings of tribal patronage.

For six decades, the French had treated the natives relatively gently— as gently as a land-grabbing imperial force can be expected to behave. But under the British, who held a much darker view of the natives than the French, conditions changed radically. The British saw the natives as savages, rather than trading partners, and as a vanquished people whom they were intent on driving from the territory.

General Jeffery Amherst, who was overseeing the extension of British control, was under orders from London to cut expenses, and among the first to go were the gifts to the natives as rewards for good behavior. "If they do not behave properly they are to be punished," Amherst wrote to one underling in February 1673. When the gifts dried up, the tribal leaders became vulnerable to challenges from within, destabilizing the political relations within the tribes. And while the French soldiers tended to be polite and effusive with the tribal leaders, the British soldiers "were often brutal and uncivil. With oaths, menaces and sometimes blows, the Indians were kept at a safe distance."

The arrival of the British troops also heralded a rise in the number of British traders, and within a few years the British so dominated fur trading that most of the French settlers gave up the business and turned primarily to farming. The British traders' "unscrupulous" behavior and "methods in business soon aroused the hatred and ire" of the tribes, according to Clarence M. Burton, an early Detroit historian. The traders themselves were seen as a problem by the military leaders, who recognized that many had been failures in their homelands who had escaped to the frontier as a last chance to make a living. The traders cheated with abandon, using false weights on scales, watering down rum sold to the natives, and charging exorbitant prices. Under the French, for instance, four raccoon pelts were equal in value to one beaver pelt. Under the British, that "exchange rate" rose to six raccoon pelts, arbitrarily driving down the value of the more easily caught raccoon pelts. The British would rule Detroit for less than forty years, but their treatment of the native tribes set the tone for the next century or more.[4]

The native people did not go quietly. And they found an able leader in an Ottawa chief named Pontiac, who was vested with a keen sense of the geopolitics of his world. The British move west across North America had displaced many of the Native American societies along the East Coast, most notably the Delaware. Those tribes in turn moved westward through Pennsylvania and into Ohio, where the shifting territorial claims roiled intertribal politics. Pontiac and other chiefs knew full well how the Delaware had been treated and how the British had stolen their lands in the East. Pontiac expected the same would happen to his people.

In April 1763, after weeks of quiet outreach to tribal leaders around present-day Michigan, Ohio, Indiana, and Ontario, Pontiac convened a gathering of tribal leaders at his village about ten miles southwest of Detroit and laid out his list of grievances against the new British regime. Some were broad, such as the threat to their lands. Some were more personal, including a long list of slights and insults. Pontiac argued that if the tribal leaders didn't band together and force the British out of their territory, they risked losing everything.

He was persuasive. On May 1, Pontiac and some fifty warriors arrived at Fort Detroit and gained entrance by telling the British they wanted to perform a dance for them. While the garrison was distracted by the performance, Pontiac and several others cased the layout of the fort, including the location of powder storehouses. At the end, Pontiac talked the fort's commander, Henry Gladwin, into hosting a council a week later, a gathering that Pontiac planned to use to launch a surprise attack from inside the fort.

The gathering was set for May 7, a Saturday. Pontiac and other tribal leaders arrived, and upward of three hundred warriors, some traveling across the river by canoe, converged on the fort. Pontiac had laid out a plan under which, at the right moment, he would flip over a wampum belt he was carrying to signal the warriors to launch a surprise attack. But a spy had betrayed Pontiac—the identity was never revealed, but speculation centered on a tribeswoman with whom Gladwin was sleeping. As Pontiac and the others gathered on the parade ground, they were surrounded by an array of soldiers, weapons at the ready, along the scaffolding of the stockade and at critical spots on the parade ground and guarding the storehouses. Pontiac never gave the signal, and the warriors left after what had to have been one of history's most awkward meetings.

Pontiac eventually launched his war anyway, though in truth he was but one of several tribal leaders working to try to oust the British. Most of the forts throughout the upper Great Lakes were overrun. Detroit was laid siege to but never taken. Hundreds of settlers and British soldiers, as well as an uncertain number of natives, died before the tribes slowly gave up. They failed, obviously, to drive the British from the region, but they did manage to scuttle trade and usurp farm life for two years as settlers abandoned their remote farms for the relative safety of forts, many of which were in turn abandoned under the onslaught. By late 1764, the fighting had all but ended, Pontiac and his fellow chiefs defeated.[5]

The British had nearly as much disdain for the French settlers in Detroit as they did for the Native Americans, and frictions seemed to arise with every contact. The "cruel and tyrannical disposition[s]" of both the British commander, Lieutenant-Governor Henry Hamilton, and justice of the peace Philippe Dejean, a French businessman from Quebec, didn't help.[6] The transition from French to British rule led to confusion in everything from property rights and deeds to the criminal justice process itself. The Quebec Act of 1774 essentially erased the French legal traditions in criminal matters and replaced them with British law, but the representatives of the Crown in the various colonies had wide latitude.

The setting was ripe for abuse, particularly by those with a predisposition for autocracy. Hamilton and Dejean were quick with the noose, sparking complaints to the British territorial government center in Montreal. One letter came from John Dodge, who had been weighted with irons and held in frigid isolation on Dejean's order for infractions that are murky. In his letter, Dodge cited two other cases in which criminals had been summarily hanged on orders of Hamilton and Dejean. "You'll readily allow that these criminals deserve death, but how dared Lieutenant-Governor Hamilton, and an infamous judge of his own making, take upon them to try them and execute them without authority?" Dodge wrote that other officials with whom he had corresponded believed Hamilton and DeJean "were both liable to be prosecuted for

murder. I beg you may make these things known in England, that we
may be freed from usurpation, tyranny, and oppression."

Hamilton was eventually indicted for letting Dejean wield too free
and arbitrary a hand. The Montreal jury accused Dejean of acting without authority when, in December 1775, he arrested Joseph Hecker, a
furrier, after Hecker's brother-in-law, Charles Moran, was found stabbed
to death. Hecker was quickly convicted and hanged, though the garrison
had no legal authority to do so. A few months later, Dejean arrested John
Coutincinau and a black slave named Ann Wyley and accused them of
stealing money and pelts from the Abbott & Finchley fur-trading store
(it also had a steady side business selling liquor), and then trying to burn
the structure down to cover up the thefts. Both were ordered hanged.
Dejean, facing growing opposition to his capriciousness, couldn't find
anyone in Detroit to perform the execution. So, he struck a deal with
Wyley, telling her that if she hanged Coutincinau, Dejean would pardon
her. Wyley did the deed on March 26, 1777, but then Dejean hanged
her anyway.[7]

The hangings of Coutincinau and Wyley came in the midst of the
Revolutionary War, in which Detroit played a minimal role. The British turned over their claims on the region to the nascent United States
under the 1783 Treaty of Paris, formally ending the war, but the British
were slow to leave and controlled the garrison at Detroit until 1796.
They briefly reoccupied Detroit during the War of 1812—US brigadier general William Hull infamously was hoodwinked into turning the
fort and city over to a much smaller British detachment commanded
by Major General Isaac Brock. But at war's end, Detroit was solidly in
American hands.

Little of Detroit's early days—its childhood, if you will—has left a
mark on the present-day Detroit beyond some street names and the lin-
eage of a few old families. In fact, the first event that has left a mark on
the current city didn't come until 1805. And it nearly killed off the city.

Frontier towns were of necessity built mainly of wood. And given their
largely informal births, little attention was paid to planning. Thus in the

core of the settlement at Detroit, wooden cabins and shanties—some of them decades old—lined up in tight proximity, which made the early leaders worry about fire. On June 3, 1805, the city trustees ordered a weekly inspection of the village to ensure that fireplaces were properly maintained and that fire buckets were in good repair, filled with water, and at the ready. It's unclear whether the first inspection was actually carried out, but eight days later fear turned into reality.[8]

A little before 9 AM on June 11, baker John Harvey sent a worker to a nearby stable at Saint Anne's Street (the north side of present day Jefferson, just west of Shelby), to harness his horses for some deliveries. The man was a pipe smoker, and in the process of tending to the horses, some hay caught fire. The stable was quickly engulfed. The fire crew responded with the water pump. Given the distance from the river, the firefighters decided to use water from a furrier's vat to extinguish the blaze. But loose bits of fur in the water clogged the pump, rendering it useless. A fire bucket brigade also formed, but the roaring flames spread too quickly, routing the firefighters and leading to a mass and frantic evacuation. People darted in and out of houses removing whatever possessions they could. Some loaded up stocks of furs and household items in canoes and *bateaux* and paddled them out on the river, out of the fire's reach.

Father Jean Dilhet was talking with a parishioner in Saint Anne's Church when someone ran in to say that three buildings were on fire "and that there was no hope for saving the rest." Dilhet told all within earshot to go try to help put out the fire "and immediately commenced the celebration of a low Mass, after which we barely had time to remove the vestments and furniture of the church" and adjoining residence before the flames swept through. Smoke plumes had risen high into the sky "giving the city the appearance of an immense funeral pile," Dilhet wrote. "It was the most majestic, and at the same time the most frightful spectacle I ever witnessed."

By 1 PM, some four hours later, the fire had burned itself out. No one was killed, but several people were reported injured and one young boy was described as "crippled" by the fire. Of some two hundred buildings within the stockade, only a single structure was left standing. Scores more to the east of the stockade were also damaged or destroyed by the windblown flames, though the buildings downriver, to the west, escaped damage. "Nothing was to be seen of the city except a mass of burning coals, and chimney-tops stretching like pyramids into the air," Dilhet wrote.

There was little to be done with so many homeless. "The situation of the inhabitants is deplorable beyond description," wrote Robert Munro, a store manager, to his bosses back east. "Dependence, want, and misery is the situation of the former inhabitants of the town of Detroit. Provisions are furnished by contributions, but houses cannot be obtained. Mr. Dodemead lives in a corner of the public storehouse at the ship yard; Mr. Donovan with his family have gone to Sandwich [across the river]; and Mr. Audrain, with many others, occupy the small house below Mr. May's. A number of families are scattered over the commons without any protection or shelter. I have been very much bruised by my exertion to save the property. My right arm particularly is so much swelled that I can hardly hold the pen to write these few lines, and my mind is equally affected with the distressing scenes I have witnessed for the last three days."

Detroiters were quick to see skullduggery behind the apparently accidental, or negligent, start of the fire. To rebuild would require a huge store of lumber, and so the lumbermen—who began offering supplies on credit—were suspected of setting the fire to gin up their business, though the historical records offer no evidence of a sound base to the rumors. What the fire did, though, was present Detroit with a tabula rasa for its reconstruction. Or, to move forward several generations, for its first renaissance.

Six months before the fire, the young US government had renamed a portion of the Indiana Territory, including Detroit, the Michigan Territory, one of several jurisdictional incarnations before the region qualified for statehood (for a while, under the British, it had been the rather drab sounding Western District of the Province of Quebec). In January 1805, Congress established the new territorial government effective in June 1805, and President Thomas Jefferson appointed a governor, William Hull (who, as a brigadier general, would give up the city seven years later to the British), and three judges, Augustus Brevoort Woodward, Frederick Bates, and John Griffin (replacing Samuel Huntington, who had turned down the job).

Hull and Woodward arrived June 12, the day after the fire, to find the place in charred shambles and likely still smoldering. Woodward, though without explicit authorization, quickly took command of the effort to rebuild the city and drew up plans that created the core of the downtown street layout that exists today. He adapted his "spoke-and-hub" layout from Pierre Charles L'Enfant's design for the District of Columbia, establishing small parks as hubs from which streets would radiate as spokes. As the city grew, new hubs would be added, sending off new spokes to establish yet more hubs, like a hens and chickens plant.

In Detroit, Woodward established Campus Martius as the base park, connecting with Grand Circus Park just to the north. The connecting "spoke" was the grand boulevard he named after himself. Woodward's plans didn't get very far. The design was soon abandoned for the more conventional grid of streets on compass-point axes, north–south crossing east–west. In fact, only the southern half of Grand Circus Park and the main spokes—Fort, Grand River, Woodward, and Gratiot, most following old Native American trails—survived, and they formed the spines of the city's eventual sprawl.

But in the early 1800s, as the new city was rebuilding, Detroit was still a western frontier outpost. It would take a project to the east, in upstate New York, to give Detroit its first major trade connection to the world and establish it as an economic engine.

DETROITERS I

THE MORANS

Mike Moran sits at the dining table in his comfortable ranch-style house in Pasadena, a few miles from downtown Los Angeles, with a small portion of his extensive family history collection scattered before him. He has old newspaper clippings and government records, books and photographs, the physical evidence of a long family line. Moran was born and raised here in Southern California, but his roots tie directly back to the early decades of Detroit, and in many ways his family connections trace the trajectory of Detroit itself—early dreams, then wealth, then abandonment.

Moran has limited personal memories of Detroit from long-ago family visits. Yet, the connections fascinate him. The first of the family line to settle in Detroit arrived from Quebec City in 1750. He was a trader named Claude Charles Morand, though later generations would drop the "d" from the family name to conform to a misspelling on an 1818 deed signed by President James Monroe affirming old French land grants. In that era of hard travel and slow communications, it was easier to change the family name, Moran says, than to change the deed.

A year after he arrived in Detroit, Claude Moran married Marie Anne Belleperche, a shirttail relative of Cadillac (her grandmother was

a cousin of Cadillac's wife), which tied him to the early upper echelon
of the settlement. And that, of course, meant owning a farm (he apparently bought some existing claims). The original Moran property began,
as did all the ribbon farms, at the river and stretched northward several
thousand yards. It was to the east of the fort, and as the city grew and
farms were subdivided into urban tracts, the original farmhouse became
an address on Woodbridge Street between Saint Antoine and Hastings
Streets. The site now is covered by a bend in East Jefferson Avenue near
the Renaissance Center.[1]

Moran quickly began adding to his farm holdings and over time was
among the city's largest landholders. A versatile trader (mostly in furs),
he became one of Detroit's wealthiest businessmen, which brought with
it the expectation of generosity. In 1768 he helped shoulder the cost of
rebuilding the deteriorating wooden stockade, an act likely as rooted
in self-preservation as it was in a sense of duty to his less well-to-do
neighbors.

Moran also had the dubious distinction of becoming one of Detroit's
earliest high-profile murder victims—he was stabbed by his brother-
in-law Joseph Hecker. History didn't record many details of the murder, other than that Hecker stabbed Moran around three o'clock in the
morning on December 9, 1775. A listing in the Saint Anne Parish Register noting the burial two days later described his death from "several knife wounds received treacherously at the hands of a man named
Hecker, and with circumstances which were horrible on the part of the
assassin." Hecker was hanged a few days later.

Moran's son, Charles, continued the farming business, and his grandson, also named Charles, eventually became a local judge—but not until
after witnessing Detroit's humiliating defeat in the War of 1812. When
the younger Moran was fifteen he was pressed into service as a sentry
at Fort Detroit, just as American general William Hull, who had fallen
back to the fort after forays into Ohio and then Ontario, was confronted
with what he thought was a vastly larger force of British troops and
native tribesmen. But Hull was duped. He had more men and weapons
than the attackers, but he let himself be hoodwinked by the tribal leader
Tecumseh, who marched about four hundred warriors through the same

clearings several times, making it seem as though he had more than a thousand men. The British had set up cannons within range of the fort. As the cannonballs flew and the warriors whooped, Hull—who feared a massacre—surrendered.

After the war, Charles Moran prospered from the family landholdings. In the mid-1800s, Jefferson Avenue and Fort Street were extended eastward through his land, a development that angered Moran and others of the old guard whose farms were similarly bisected. But it also made them wealthy by opening their farms for land speculation.

Eventually Moran's farm was subdivided and new streets laid out, including Hastings Street, which would become the heart of African American life in Detroit. Farther east, Moran Street was laid out, stretching from the river northward. Moran, though, didn't sell the land—he maintained ownership and collected rent from those who built houses and commercial buildings on it. A map of the subdivided farm recorded December 6, 1869, shows 409 buildable lots just east of present-day downtown north and south of Gratiot and roughly lying beneath the Interstate 375 freeway—the old Hastings Street neighborhood.[2] By the time Moran died in 1876, Detroit was a thriving industrial city of some 100,000 residents, and Moran's estate was worth several million dollars.

Moran was married twice and fathered eleven children, a generational explosion of sons who became entrepreneurs and daughters who, not surprisingly, married well. John Vallee Moran was the ninth of Charles Moran's brood, born in 1846. As an adult, he became a partner in a successful grocery wholesaler, part-owner of a bank that went bust in the 1890s depression, and an investor in a series of businesses, including the Ward Steamship Line that sailed a small fleet on the Great Lakes.

One of the rewards of his professional success was gaining memberships in the local clubs of the upper crust, including the Detroit Boat Club. He also had a farm on Lake Saint Clair, an area that eventually would become the Detroit region's most formidable mansion row. Moran's children lived there during the summer and ate the cheeses, milk, and eggs that it produced during the non-growing season. One of those children was John Bell Moran—the grandfather of Mike Moran, the Pasadena retiree.

J. Bell Moran embraced the family's legacy of entrepreneurship. After leaving the University of Notre Dame in 1906 he worked for a couple of years for a western Michigan railroad, then for the Interstate Telephone Company, and eventually the Detroit United Railways before striking out on his own around 1910 as a real estate investor and developer on Detroit's west side. He was trained as a tank commander in World War I, though it's unclear whether he was deployed to Europe. At war's end, he returned to his real estate development work in Detroit and eventually became a city planning commissioner. But the biggest key to his eventual success came in whom he married: Serena K. Murphy, the granddaughter of Simon J. Murphy, a native of Maine who managed to parlay early work cutting lumber along the Penobscot River into a national financial empire.

Murphy's story is that of the classic American capitalist done good. He spent about a decade working in the lumberyards and mills, then formed a series of small logging companies with some colleagues. Success begat success and by 1866, the Civil War over and Maine already heavily logged, Murphy moved to Michigan, settling in Detroit. He continued to amass his fortune through lumbering enterprises in the northern woods and on the Upper Peninsula. He eventually took over Pacific Lumber Co., a main harvester of northern California's majestic redwoods, and through his wealth built the first section of the Penobscot Building, one of Detroit's downtown anchors. Murphy also invested heavily in the Union Trust Company bank, which built the Guardian Building, an architectural gem a stone's throw from the Penobscot Building.

The Murphys' son, Charles H. Murphy, continued the family business and was one of four investors in Henry Ford's first and ill-fated foray into automobile making, the Detroit Automobile Company. He also was an avid patron of the arts, particularly music, and despite the onset of deafness was a key figure in the development of the Detroit Symphony Orchestra and helped draw its first celebrity conductor, Ossip Gabrilowitsch (who was married to Samuel Clemens's daughter, Clara). The younger Murphy had two children of his own, a son, Charles V., and daughter Serena.

It was Murphy's Pacific Lumber Co. that began the exodus of Morans from Detroit some two hundred years after Claude Charles Moran settled in the frontier trading village. When J. Bell and Serena Moran's eldest son, Charles V. Moran, was ready to strike out on his own, the Murphy family company—with the boss's son-in-law, J. Bell Moran, now a top executive—sent him to Scotia, California. He met and married a local girl, Sarah Lorene Grove, in June 1941, and moved a short time later to the Los Angeles area, where his father helped set him up in a car dealership in San Moreno, Moran Motors, which he ran with his son Mike until the late 1990s.

J. Bell Moran's other children also left Detroit once they reached adulthood. As he neared retirement age, he and his wife decided to pull up their stakes, too. The couple owned a summer home in Bel Air, near Santa Monica, and around 1948 they moved there permanently to be near the bulk of their adult children and grandchildren—including Mike Moran.

Most of the original Morans might be gone from Detroit, but the family name still shows up on signposts on the near east side where Moran Street appears and disappears along the ribbon that was once the edge of the family farm. In 2007, the local alternative weekly newspaper, *Metro Times*, decreed Moran Street Detroit's Best Urban Prairie, marked by "long stretches . . . in various stages of wilderness. Some are mowed regularly, looking like parks. Some are mowed seasonally, looking like lush prairie. Some blocks have stands of ailanthus, the tree of heaven, with the faint smell of burnt peanut butter wafting from them in the summertime. Biking through the narrow streets, it's almost like the city in the country, and often more restful for the soul than many of our crowded public parks."[3]

3

DETROIT AND THE
CANAL OF RICHES

A crowd began gathering early on Thursday morning, October 26, 1825, at the newly built courthouse in Buffalo, New York, and one can presume a certain buzz of excitement. It was to be a day of celebration and pageantry, marking a technological achievement that would change the course of the nation—the opening of the Erie Canal. And it would signal something of a rebirth for Buffalo, a lakeside village of some twenty-five hundred people that was still recovering from being burned to the ground by marauding British troops twelve years earlier. Buffalo was the easternmost settlement of any size on the four upper Great Lakes, and its location was significant. Just to the north, Lake Erie funnels into the Niagara River, which, a few miles beyond, flows over that great blockage of Great Lakes transportation, Niagara Falls. Forming the boundary between the United States and Canada, the Niagara River flows into the western end of the fifth Great Lake, Ontario, which in turn drains into the Saint Lawrence River, at the time navigable as far as the portage around Montreal's Lachine Rapids. From there, it was a straight sail past Quebec City to the North Atlantic.[1]

At the time, the three middle Great Lakes—Michigan, Huron, and Erie—formed a massive, but closed, waterway. It was separated from

Lake Superior to the north by Saint Mary's Falls at Sault Sainte Marie, a twenty-one-foot drop that forced a short portage. And it was separated downstream from Lake Ontario, the easternmost of the lakes, by 176-foot-high Niagara Falls, which, with its sheer-sided gorge, made for a very difficult portage.

But the falls had been tamed. Or at least, for transportation purposes, it had been trumped by engineering. Over the previous eight years, work crews had scattered across some 360 miles of western, central, and upstate New York to create a canal connecting the middle three Great Lakes to the Atlantic Ocean. The workers carved away hillsides in some places, filled low spots in others, and built aqueducts over rivers to create a navigable waterway linking Lake Erie at Buffalo to the Hudson River at Albany, which connected with the markets of New York City, and then the Atlantic Ocean beyond. Relying on a series of more than eighty locks, the new Erie Canal rose some six hundred feet, an expensive marvel of engineering designed to open central and western New York to development. Farm produce that once rotted before it could reach New York City by land could now get from Buffalo to Manhattan in four days. And goods that formerly cost a fortune to ship to distant markets would now cost pennies to move. The opening of the canal also gave the young American nation an alternative to the often dangerous voyage over Lake Ontario to the Saint Lawrence River—controlled by the British—and then on to the North Atlantic for the long sail southwest along New England to New York.

The celebrations in Buffalo that morning were full of pomp and circumstance, and, one imagines, visions of wealth dancing in the heads of Buffalo's small mercantile class. The opening of the canal would indeed make Buffalo one of the nation's fastest-growing cities of the mid-1800s. At nine o'clock, several hundred people left the courthouse in a parade through the streets to where the canal connected with Lake Erie, and where a packet boat called the *Seneca Chief* was docked. The procession included the luminaries of the state, led by Governor DeWitt Clinton, whose early support for the controversial canal earned it the nickname "Clinton's Ditch" by political adversaries who thought the project too expensive, and too ambitious, to be feasible. In a sense, Clinton was about to begin his victory lap, riding the *Seneca Chief* from the canal's western end to the edge of the Atlantic.

After a series of speeches, a cannon tender lit the fuse of a thirty-two-pounder (named for the size of the cannon ball it could propel) confiscated from the British fleet during the 1813 Battle of Lake Erie. The boom echoed across the countryside. In rapid succession, scores more cannons—most, like the first, the spoils of war—were fired off, each blast a cue to the next eastward along the length of the canal, then the Mohawk River and then down the Hudson River to Sandy Hook, New Jersey, where New York Harbor gives way to the open Atlantic.

It's unclear whose idea it was to establish a cannon communications network, but it was ingenious. A little more than an hour passed between that first blast in Buffalo and the last at Sandy Hook. Then the daisy chain of salvos reversed itself, taking another hour or so until the thirty-two-pounder that fired the first shot in Buffalo fired the last. Clinton had hoped to use the stunt to measure the speed of sound, an idea that collapsed under what now seem clear logistical and control issues. But it was a moment of great symbolism, using the spoils of the War of 1812 to herald the opening of a trade route between the Great Lakes and the Eastern Seaboard, and the world beyond, signaling that the still-young United States was stepping out of the shadow of its European forebears. And the speed of those blasts heralded the boon of the Erie Canal itself.

By the time the last cannon boom had died away, the *Seneca Chief*, drawn by four parade-dressed gray horses, was already moving eastward along the canal, a narrow and shallow channel (four feet deep in most places) that, in eight short years, managed to solve a transportation problem that had been eons in the making. The rest of the convoy followed: the *Superior*, then the *Commodore Perry* (a freight boat), and finally the *Buffalo*. Lagging behind those ceremonial packet boats came a line of working freight boats; the canal was open for business.

The flotilla would spend the next nine days in a leisurely cruise along the Erie Canal, then the Mohawk and Hudson Rivers, where the horses were replaced by steamboats with tow ropes, before reaching Manhattan. In each town, the travelers were feted as heroes and greeted with rifle volleys and picnics, parades and speeches. In New York, the packet boats were towed to Sandy Hook, where with great ceremony Clinton tapped a keg filled with Lake Erie water and poured it into the Atlantic Ocean.

After a whirlwind of parades, balls, and other celebrations in New York, the *Seneca Chief* began the return voyage to Buffalo, a cask of ocean water stashed away for a bookended celebratory dumping of salt-water into the freshwater Lake Erie, which took place November 23, the weather already turned raw as winter settled in.

The opening of the canal—the "Wedding of the Waters," as it was called—was a defining moment for New York State. It made the central and western portions more valuable for agriculture and, in the coming decades, for heavy industry. Settlers poured in from the east, some stay-ing in New York State and others moving on to Ohio, Michigan, and beyond.

At the western tip of the canal, Buffalo thrived. Five years after Clin-ton's Ditch had opened, Buffalo had grown from some two thousand residents to nearly nine thousand. By the 1840 census, it had grown to eighteen thousand people. Other canal cities also flourished, from Rochester to Syracuse to Albany. And the terminus helped cement New York City as the nation's financial capital.

But the benefits of the Erie Canal were not New York State's alone. At the western end of Lake Erie, the opening of a water route connect-ing the heartland to the Eastern Seaboard turned dangerous weeks of travel into a sailing excursion of a matter of days. And it fertilized yet another flower of capitalism: Detroit.

In the years leading up to the opening of the Erie Canal, Detroit was evolving into a regional commercial center and, if the words of booster-ish travelers of the time can be counted, was rather pretty. One anon-ymous traveler reported in the *Pittsburgh Gazette* in May 1819 about his experience coming upon Detroit by boat after sailing west along Lake Erie, "subject to frequent and heavy squalls of wind." Entering the Detroit River became a moment of relief "after suffering, as you frequently do, in a boisterous and unpleasant passage of six or seven days in a small but dirty vessel" from Erie, Pennsylvania. As he sailed upriver, passing the Canadian settlements of Malden—"a small, dirty town, of a few houses, and a British garrison"—and then the "small but handsome" Sandwich, Detroit began appearing on the left. "This view, of a clear day, is extremely picturesque and beautiful: as the wind gently wafts you up the river, its green banks, fine farms, covered with orchards, and their houses of a singular order of architecture, which you can but discern through the trees planted around it, or various fruit, or in full bloom." Rises in the land were topped with "the large wings of a wind mill, attached to a neat round white building, cutting the air."[2]

It had only been four years since the War of 1812 had ended. To reward veteran soldiers for their service and help settle the countryside, the US government hatched a plan to provide them with tillable land. In 1815, it deployed surveyor Edward Tiffin to report on what lands would be most suitable for farming. In modern parlance, he blew the call, describing Michigan as too swampy and the soil too thin to be of much value. (He apparently relied on earlier erroneous descriptions without surveying the land himself.) Tiffin deemed the region unlikely to support a large enough population for the Michigan Territory to eventually qualify for statehood. As a result, the federal government gave the first wave of ex-soldiers land in Ohio, Indiana, and Illinois instead.

So even in its infancy, Detroit suffered from a bad reputation and misperceptions from the outside. For years, schoolbook maps dismissed the interior of the state with the label, "Interminable Swamp." Still, soldiers who had served in Michigan saw through the erroneous reports and decided on their own to settle there. And other, more curious travelers reported in books and articles that Michigan was more than the government surveyor made it out to be.

Lewis Cass, a brigadier general during the war, was named Michigan's territorial governor at war's end, and in 1820 he led a surveying expedition into the northern territories (which also helped establish the source of the Mississippi River, then in dispute). He "warmly criticized" the Tiffin report about inhospitable lands, and his more accurate description of virgin forests covering arable land helped turn the flow of settlement from Illinois, Indiana, and Ohio toward Michigan.[3]

By then, fire-ravaged Detroit was expanding under Woodward's hub-and-spoke design, but its full form had yet to take shape. Detroit was still a riverside city, much as the French had developed it. "It has two streets running parallel with the river, and intersected by two other streets and two alleys at right angles. The main or second street, from the river, is remarkably broad, and having a sandy or gravelly soil, is seldom muddy." Only a short section was paved with stones. The homes were "built of frame or logs, of one low story, and, as they are frequently on a large ground plot, with high roofs, you would frequently imagine the garret to be the larger part of the house." In a decision destined to inform the city's long-term disregard for the river, "the beauty of the place is much injured by the want of a street on the river bank, where the houses have been built so close as to destroy all passage betwixt them and the water." And there were no water wells; all residents carried water from the river or traveled three miles west from town to "the Spring Wells, where all classes and fashions resort to, on parties of pleasure."[4]

It was a bustling place for a small frontier town. A June 1819 list of 232 Detroit businesses included twenty-four dry goods and grocery merchants, twelve shoemakers, eighteen tailors, six hat makers, and, in a harbinger of the future, a "coach and chaise maker." By 1836, more than a decade after the Erie Canal opened, Detroit was in the throes of a wave of massive business speculation and growth. Detroit also had a new connection to the West. A road cut through the wilderness, around the southern tip of Lake Michigan and into Chicago, which was undergoing its own boom as one of the launching places for settlers moving into the upper plains. Other roads radiated outward from Detroit: the northwestward Grand River Road to Lake Michigan's eastern shore, ending at the mouth of the Grand River at present-day Grand Haven; the Saginaw Road north to the lower edge of Lake Huron's Saginaw Bay; the Fort Gratiot Road cut to the northeast to where Lake Huron itself flowed; and a fifth road cut south to Ohio. All those roads supplanted wilderness trails carved out over generations by the local tribes, so the settlers not only took the land, they neatly slipped into the native peoples' transportation network.[5]

Even the land grab was tenuous at first. Until laws changed in 1820, squatters in the wilderness had no mechanism for making a legal claim for the farmland they had carved out, nor the houses and farm buildings they put up. Many of the early settlers were gambling their time and meager savings, and many lost out when the land was surveyed. Land offices finally opened in the 1820s to process legal sales, and much of the land was divided into large-scale sections too expensive for a small farmer to buy. Speculation was rampant, and an epidemic of cholera and the short-lived Black Hawk's War with native tribesmen dampened demand in the 1830s.

But the siren call of open land was persistent, and the settling of Michigan picked up pace from 1834 to 1836. The Depression of 1837 to 1844 stifled Detroit, as elsewhere, but with the recovery came more expansion and more settlers with fresh investments. Detroit was the anchor settlement for all of it. "It became a rendezvous for settlers and a clearing-house of ideas about the interior," according to one history. "Frequently settlers who intended to go to the interior or further west to Wisconsin and Illinois made only tentative plans until they should reach Detroit, where many were induced to settle within its limits or its vicinity . . . which in turn would put new life currents circulating through the rural districts."[6]

Accurate counts of the population are hard to come by, since different census takers defined Detroit differently, some counting all heads in the general region and others limiting their tally to those within the settlement proper. By the latter method, an 1834 Detroit census counted 4,973 residents in 477 dwellings with 64 stores and warehouses. By 1837, the population had jumped to 9,763, with more than 1,300 stores and dwellings, and the city built its first stone-lined "Grand Sewer," ten feet deep, more than four feet wide, and covered above ground with arched brick. It cost $22,607 to build, and supplanted the small Savoyard River, which angled from Beaubien Street to the west through the heart of town southwest to First Street, and then emptied into the river. Other sewers followed, many privately financed, designed, and built, until 1857, when the city government centralized the system. Waterworks were similarly begun around the same time, and both systems grew from primitive networks—the first water pipes were, in fact, hollowed out logs—into intricate systems, constantly being changed, added to, and upgraded.[7]

H. Massey, who grew up in central New York, was part of the westward flood. He and some young friends decided to make their fortune
in "this new and beautiful city of the west." They struck out on the last
day of August 1828, journeying to Syracuse, where they booked passage on a packet boat to Buffalo because it was cheaper, faster, and had
"greater social advantages" than taking the overland coach. Three days
later, they alit in Buffalo, "then only a good sized village," and boarded
the *Niagara* steamship the next morning for the lake voyage to Detroit.

Lake Erie, as modern sailors know, can be a difficult body of water to
navigate. Shallow on the western end, deepening out on the east (imagine a massive spoon), strong winds have a tendency to create inconsistent
and cross-cutting waves, and has been likened to trying to sail on a giant
tea cup as someone is shaking it. There are few natural harbors for sanc-
tuary. Most of the landings consisted of maneuvering the steamer close
to shore then offloading passengers via skiffs.

On Massey's journey, the *Niagara* hugged the southern shore of Lake
Erie and was able to put in at Dunkirk, New York; Erie, Pennsylvania; and Ashtabula, Ohio, before encountering rough waters near the
Cuyahoga River (Cleveland), and at Huron and Black River (Lorain),
in Ohio. "The consequence was that passengers were obliged to remain
on board, trusting to have better luck on the downward voyage." They
had boarded the ship on a Friday morning, and Sunday morning, when
the *Niagara* was still a mile downriver from Detroit, the captain fired off
a cannon as a signal to the port that it was approaching. "All the other
boats of the line made their landing at the up-town docks, mostly New-
berry's, but the *Niagara* came to at a new wharf which had recently been
built about a mile further down the river, where extensive improvements were being made, among them a hotel more spacious and elegant
than any previously existing in the city, known as the Mansion House,
kept by a New York landlord by the name of Alman." The name actually was Isaac J. Ullman, one of a series of owners of the building, which
was located near where the foot of Cass Avenue would reach the river.
The building had previously been a British military barracks, a jail, and
courthouse. It was eventually torn down around 1836.[8]

Despite the rapid developments in Detroit, construction couldn't
keep up with the demand, and new arrivals often as not had to sleep

aboard the steamships that brought them. An average of six boats arrived daily and over the course of the year deposited some 200,000 travelers, the vast majority of whom moved on into the wilderness. "So rapid is the increase of this number, that in all probability, it will be doubled in less than four years," read the breathless accounting in the city directory for 1837, the year Michigan joined the union. That boosterish prognosis didn't pan out, though, as an international economic depression hit that same year, driving banks out of business and freezing economic expansion for nearly a decade.

By 1840, Detroit had dropped to about 9,100 people. But it was a temporary ebb tide. Drawn by farming, lumbering, and mining, the pace of settlement in Michigan began to pick up. The extension of rail lines in 1838 to Saint Joseph on Lake Michigan—envisioned as a transshipment hub to Chicago—and over the next few years northward to Bay City helped propel the growth of settlements along the rail lines. Daily mail delivery by lake steamers solidified the city's role as the regional economic and business center. By 1850, Detroit had passed twenty-one thousand residents. A decade later, on the eve of the Civil War, it had doubled again to more than forty thousand residents, lodging it between Milwaukee, Wisconsin, and Rochester, New York, as the nation's nineteenth largest city.[9]

The post-fur economic engine across the Great Lakes area was agriculture, and Detroit became a major collection point for grains, especially. Mills were busy grinding it into flour to be shipped using a growing network of Great Lakes steamers along Lake Erie to Buffalo, and then over the canal to New York City. Michigan-grown wheat was valued for its texture and color, and rivaled that from California for most desirable, according to an overview of US industry from later in the century. "The flour made from the best California or amber Michigan wheat is of a very delicate creamy tint, just turned from white, and if pressed firmly in the hand will remain in a ball, retaining the impress of the fingers. When spread evenly in the hand, and smoothed with an ivory spatula, it presents a uniform and polished surface."[10]

Riches, though, didn't mean Detroit was turning into a showboat town. By 1855 the city was "both a harbor and a depot," but one that didn't invest much in itself. The main settlement covered some three

miles of riverfront, but it "is no credit to the city," according to James
Dale Johnston, whose publishing company printed an 1855 city directory. The river's edge properties were privately owned, in many places
built up so tightly that access to the river was blocked from city streets.
It's not as though there was much to see, though. "The state of the docks
are, with few exceptions, wholly out of repair, and accidents and loss of
life are not uncommon." Johnston called on local officials to use public funds to build a public wharf out into the river, though it's unclear
whether anyone heeded him.[11]

Despite the disrepair, Detroit was a vibrant town geared toward serving its regional population, with a healthy export business to the East,
primarily, but also westward to Chicago. Johnston's directory included
a list of building uses compiled for 1854 by the Board of Water Com-
missioners, which had been busy emplacing a network of iron pipes to
move water from the river and new wells to dwellings and businesses.
There were more than 5,700 family homes, 120 boarding houses, and
348 stores. There were also 50 taverns and 17 breweries, 166 offices, and
27 churches. Most tellingly for the city's future, Detroit was also home
to 264 "mechanic" shops.[12]

Detroit was still, at heart, a small and agriculturally focused town.
In 1860, parts of the original Cass Farm were still being farmed. "Only
a few leading thoroughfares were paved," according to an 1875 directory comparing the city's growth over fifteen years. "There were neither
street railways nor omnibus lines. Old-fashioned drays did the hauling.
There were no public street lamps except in the central part of the city.
. . . There were but three stone business fronts, and all these old fashioned
two-storied structures on Jefferson Avenue."[13]

But it was also a city on the verge of great and radical change.

4

THE CIVIL WAR AND
RACIAL FLASHPOINTS

You can't write about nineteenth-century America without discussing slavery. And you can't write about Detroit without writing about race, which has influenced the city's evolution as much as the city's shifting economic fortunes.

Slavery was integral to the early settler culture in Detroit, though it never came close to the economic and cultural influence it established in the Deep South. The natives kept slaves, usually captured from vanquished villages. When the French controlled the region, they allowed slavery (the victims were blacks, Native Americans, and occasionally whites), and the practice continued under the British.

In 1773, 96 slaves were counted in Detroit, and by 1778—as the Revolutionary War was raging—there were 127. By 1782, there were 179 slaves.[1] Slavery in the territory ebbed a bit after the Revolutionary War. When Michigan achieved statehood in 1837, the practice was abolished even though there were no slaves reported held at the time (technically barred in the Michigan Territory, the 1830 census nonetheless recorded 32 slaves; by 1836 they had all either died or been freed). But that didn't mean blacks were granted equal citizenship with whites.

Only white males could vote, serve on juries, join the militia—and marry white women.

In fact, white Michiganders worked hard to keep black people out of the region. The 1827 law "An Act to Regulate Blacks and Mulattoes, and to Punish the Kidnapping of Such Persons" ostensibly was designed to protect the rights of free blacks. In reality, it made it difficult for black settlers to remain in the territory, which was filling with ambitious easterners drawn to the western wilderness by the Erie Canal. The law required all black Michiganders to carry court-signed papers attesting that they were not escaped slaves and forced them to register with local courts. New black immigrants had to post a $50 bond to ensure good behavior. The law, though, was lightly enforced and routinely ignored, and slowly the black population of Michigan—and Detroit—grew.

In 1820, before the Erie Canal opened, there were 67 black people living in Detroit. By 1834, there were 138, most of them free men and women who joined the westward flow from New England and New York to establish themselves as farmers or farm laborers. But some had slipped their chains in the South and headed north, often seeking to cross the Detroit River into British territory in Canada where, in 1833, slavery was formally banned and from which escaped slaves were unlikely to be extradited. Unfortunately, where escaped slaves sought freedom, slave hunters were never far behind.

Thornton and Rutha Blackburn, two escaped slaves from Kentucky, had arrived in Detroit in 1831 and gone to work for a local stone mason named Thomas Coquillard. Generally described as poised and full of charm, the couple quickly insinuated themselves into Detroit's small black community. Two years later, in June 1833, one of the slave owner's sons and a lawyer from Kentucky arrived in Detroit, chasing down a tip from a friend of the Blackburns' owner that he had seen Thornton Blackburn during a trip to Detroit. The slave catchers detained the Blackburns and turned them over to Sheriff John M. Wilson to hold in jail at the foot of Gratiot, near the Campus Martius public square, pending a court hearing on whether they should be returned to Kentucky. The Blackburns had no legal defense—they were, indeed, escaped slaves—and on Saturday, June 15, Judge Henry Chipman ordered them to be sent back to Kentucky. Expecting that ruling, the slave catchers had already made arrangements to take the couple aboard the steamship *Ohio* for the first leg of the trip down the Detroit River to Toledo.[2]

Detroit's free black community had suffered the outrages of slave hunters before, and the threatened spiriting away of the popular Blackburns grated deeply. The Sunday morning after Chipman ordered the Blackburns returned to Kentucky, a forceful group of protesters from Detroit and Canada descended on the commons in front of the jail. During the day, the sheriff let two of Rutha Blackburn's friends, Tabitha Lightfoot and Caroline French, spend several hours visiting with her, an emotional send-off before their friend was to be returned to bondage. While the three women talked, they also concocted a plan—Blackburn would change outer clothes with French and try to escape. "The trio remained together until near dusk, when Mrs. Lightfoot and the pseudo Mrs. French took a sorrowful departure, the tears falling like rain, and all wringing their hands in terrible anguish."[3] The guard fell for it. "So effectual was the disguise that she was not recognized by a deputy sheriff who stood near her when she passed."

The jailers didn't realize they had lost one of their prized inmates until they brought breakfast to the cells the next morning. By then, Rutha Blackburn was safely across the Detroit River. French was detained for a while but eventually released. As the Kentucky slave owner began legal actions to have French enslaved to make up for his loss, she crossed into Canada, where she stayed for a few months until the Kentuckian gave up.[4]

The morning after Rutha Blackburn's escape, some of the protesters returned to the area around the jail, armed with clubs and, in some cases, guns. The men were open in their intent: Thornton Blackburn would not be taken away. But Sheriff Wilson, emboldened by pistols and a whip with which he said he "could scare every Nigger that would be there," was determined to collect his share of the reward for returning Blackburn to his master. As four o'clock neared, the time at which Blackburn was to be ferried by cart from the jail to the riverbank, about fifteen black men hovered in front of the jail. Scores more were out of sight in nearby alleys and streets. As Wilson, flanked by the slaveholder's son and two other men—justice of the peace Lemuel Goodell and someone identified only as McArthur—emerged from the jail with Blackburn to climb aboard the cart, the protesters descended in a horde, chasing the men back inside the jailhouse. Blackburn, his hands in chains, persuaded Wilson to let him talk to the crowd in hopes of pacifying them. Blackburn and the four men returned to the top of the steps, where Blackburn and the mob turned on the sheriff—one account claims Blackburn drew a revolver, which seems unlikely. All but Wilson slipped back into the protection of the jail building. Wilson pulled out his weapons and fired eight to ten shots, wounding one man, Louis Austin, in the chest, but Wilson was quickly overwhelmed. His skull fractured, Wilson would later die of his injuries.

As a general alarm rang out, white men grabbed their weapons and began collecting in the heart of town. By then, Blackburn and some of his protectors had commandeered a horse-cart and were headed northeast along the Fort Gratiot Road, which eventually followed the Saint Clair River north to Lake Huron. A posse quickly formed and took off after the cart and caught up with it about a mile from Detroit. But Blackburn wasn't in it—he had been let off shortly after the cart entered the wilderness outside Detroit. Once the posse figured out they had been duped, they split up and ranged through the forests and along the riverbank, arresting some thirty blacks they accused of complicity in the daring rescue. In truth, the posse was just rounding up black men. Some sought arrest, serving themselves up as distractions, including one young woman who waved a handkerchief from a canoe in the Detroit River as though she were Rutha Blackburn, distracting manpower from the search.

Hiding in the woods, Blackburn's rescuers used an ax and a sword to break his chains, then traveled in a wide arc around Detroit to the west and then south. At the mouth of the River Rouge one of the rescuers bribed a boatman with a gold watch to ferry the fugitive Blackburn across the river to join his wife in freedom. The couple later was arrested at the request of Michigan authorities, but only held for a few weeks before the Canadian governor, unwilling to return the couple to slavery, let them go. The Blackburns eventually settled in Toronto.[5]

It was a solidifying affair for Detroit's small black community—but also for the white community, which feared a more broad-based uprising among blacks. A clampdown quickly ensued. Black Detroiters were barred from the streets after dark unless they carried a lit lantern.[6] Previously ignored laws requiring blacks to carry papers attesting to their free status were suddenly enforced. Two suspicious fires in July—both at the jail, one minor and the other destroying the horse stable—fanned fears, and the mayor successfully beseeched former territorial governor and present secretary of war Lewis Cass to dispatch troops to Detroit as peacekeepers. (It would not be the last time US military forces took to Detroit's streets to quell racial disturbances.) Many blacks converted their possessions to cash and left Detroit; others simply kept their heads down waiting for the backlash to pass.

The incident revealed racial fault lines that have never gone away. Five years later, efforts to free another escaped slave named Henry failed when, after a crowd of rock-throwing protesters descended on the caravan escorting the prisoner from court to jail, Henry refused to escape, preferring to return to his master. But that and other legal cases provide evidence of Detroit's growing role as a key station in the burgeoning Underground Railroad, the loose network of abolitionists who helped slaves on their northward journey. As Detroit's role grew, so did its black population, rising from 193 in 1840 to 587 a decade later. Many were free black men and women fleeing the pre–Civil War tightening of laws in Virginia and elsewhere that made life more difficult for blacks.[7]

Detroit was heavily segregated then, as it is today. The growing black community clustered on the eastern edge of downtown. It was a relatively cohesive community that began building institutions in its neighborhoods. The Second Baptist Church—the city's first black house of worship—was founded in 1836 when several members of the predominately white First Baptist Church quit because, as blacks, they were forced to spend the Sunday services in the balcony. Among the splinter group was Madison Lightfoot, whose wife was one of the two women who helped Rutha Blackburn escape the city jail. That act of courage, and of resistance, would be repeated as Detroit evolved.[8]

Movements require leaders, and several men among Detroit's black residents emerged over time as the key figures in its growing abolitionist movement. The highest profile was George De Baptiste, a flamboyant businessman and former valet to the late President William Henry Harrison. De Baptiste was born in Virginia to free black parents and trained as a barber. He was a slightly built man, just over five feet seven inches tall, light-skinned (mulatto, according to his Virginia-issued certificate of freedom), with a dark blemish in the white of his left eye. In photos of him as an older man, he's balding, with a thick beard.

In 1838, at the age of twenty-four, De Baptiste and his wife moved west to Madison, Indiana, just across the Ohio River from the slave state of Kentucky. Indiana law, much like in Michigan, required free blacks to prove they were not escaped slaves, and to post a bond guaranteeing their behavior. When De Baptiste refused to comply, he was arrested and ordered to leave the state. De Baptiste challenged the legality of the law under the Indiana constitution, and his case went to the state supreme court, which upheld the law but allowed De Baptiste to stay in Indiana because of a technical problem with his deportation order. De Baptiste eventually went to work for Harrison, then a general, and followed him to Washington after the 1840 election. But Harrison's four-year term only lasted a month; he caught a cold shortly after arriving in Washington, DC, for his March 4, 1841, inauguration, and died April 4.

De Baptiste returned to Madison and resumed his barbering—and his efforts to help slaves cross the Ohio River from Kentucky to find safe haven in the North. Five years later, threats from angry pro-slavery whites led De Baptiste to abandon Indiana for Detroit, likely because of its role as the penultimate stop for escaping slaves heading to Canada.

No records exist, but it's also likely that De Baptiste, as a conductor at the Ohio River juncture of the Underground Railroad, had already been sending escaped slaves on to Detroit, and he probably had met or knew the names of his fellow abolitionists to the North, including William Lambert, a tailor from New Jersey. They would form a powerful partnership in helping hundreds, if not thousands, of escaped slaves find freedom in Canada.[9]

Lambert was eighteen when he moved to Detroit in 1838, the same year De Baptiste arrived in Madison, Indiana. Lambert had been raised for part of his childhood by a Quaker schoolteacher who taught him to read and write, and he had sailed the Great Lakes as a cabin boy for a year or so. His move to Detroit came about five years after the Black-

Abolitionist William Lambert. COURTESY OF THE BURTON HISTORICAL COLLECTION, DETROIT PUBLIC LIBRARY

burns' rescue, which was widely reported in the eastern newspapers, and around the time the slave Henry spurned the mob's efforts to free him. There had been several other showdowns in Detroit between slave hunters and mostly black abolitionists in the meantime.

Within a few years, Lambert emerged as a key figure in his adopted city. The black community then, as now, was fragmented by the usual distinctions of class and self-image. One slice, dominated by the upwardly mobile, took on the airs of the white upper classes, propelled both by a desire to be accepted in that world and to be separated from those deemed less worthy—the poor, the uneducated, and the criminal. The most successful black businessmen, including tailors like Lambert, targeted customers from the white upper class, since that's where the money was.

But Lambert straddled the worlds of the upwardly mobile and the working class. He became instrumental to Detroit and Michigan's various social reform movements, from temperance to education to prison reform. He was one of the first elected leaders of the Colored Vigilant Committee, formed in 1842 and relaunched in 1851 as the Committee of Vigilance, which pushed the cause of voting rights for black men. He was a vocal presence at related meetings and state conventions, and it was usually his pen that wrote the calls to meeting and the petitions and proclamations that came out of them.

But ending slavery was his main issue. He was an articulate and persuasive advocate, but he also was willing to act on his beliefs, even if the acts—for a greater good—violated contemporary law. He and De Baptiste helped form the shadowy group eventually known by three names, the African-American Mysteries, the Order of the Men of Oppression, or the Order of Emigration.[10] The aim was to have a network of freed blacks in the North ready, with weapons, to help end slavery, either in practice or by helping those escaping it reach freedom in Canada. The extent of the group, and its precise makeup, remain unknown, and most of what is known is based on late-life memories of De Baptiste and Lambert in interviews.[11]

But there were other related causes and groups. The Refugee Home Society consisted of "the more humane abolitionists," and was "designed to furnish homes and succor to the starving negroes stolen from the South and run into Canada." It listed De Baptiste in its board of directors. An October 19, 1859, write-up in the *Free Press* of one of its meetings reflected the group's typical activities: making financial arrangements for blacks to buy farms and settle in their own community on two thousand acres of land in Sandwich and Maidstone Townships (present-day Windsor).[12]

Other activists, mainly people who believed black people would never be free in the United States, supported emigration to Africa. Most of these activities were conducted out in the open, and several published newspapers argued their causes. But other plans were discussed more privately. In 1858, John Brown convened a meeting in Chatham, Ontario, that became a founding convention for the free-black state that Brown, fresh from the Bloody Kansas fights, wanted to create. Lambert was among the forty-five delegates who approved the constitution for the new state, which would arise after a Brown-led insurrection in the American South. It was a secret meeting, but word eventually leaked out to Brown's financial backers in Boston and to political figures in Washington, DC, and Brown's support dried up, squelching the still-nascent revolution. But Brown, as history bore out, was not done plotting.

In a world of necessary secrecy, it can be hard to find clearly defined stories. And one wishes that someone had been around taking notes on the evening of March 12, 1859. Sometime that Saturday, John Brown had arrived by train from Chicago, the last stop in a dangerous trip from Kansas, where he had helped eleven slaves escape, then escorted them north and east to Chicago. They were to follow him on a later train that day, and once all were in Detroit, Brown used his connections to get the escapees ferried across the Detroit River to freedom in Canada. That Brown was able to move so freely, and openly, was a testament to the support he had among abolitionists. There were several price tags on his head—$250 offered by President James Buchanan, $250 by Kansas governor Samuel Medary, and $300 by Missouri governor Robert Marcellus Stewart[13]—because of his role in the Bloody Kansas violence that framed the debate in Kansas and Missouri over whether they would enter the Union as free or slave states. But no one turned him in.

That evening, Frederick Douglass, the former slave and leading abolitionist from Rochester, New York, filled a room at Detroit city hall to talk about "Equality of the Races," with an unidentified—and racist—reporter from the *Free Press* in the audience. "He was greeted by a mixed audience of whites and blacks, the woolly heads predominating. The admittance fee of fifteen cents charged probably gave him money to live on until he reaches his next 'field of labor.'" It was a brief and mocking story that made light of comments the writer attributed to Douglass: "White folks had better not throw stones at the niggers, because two thousand years ago the white race occupied the same position the blacks did, and two thousand years hence the blacks may be just as good as the whites are now. This occasioned another outburst of enthusiastic feeling, under cover of which our reporter beat a retreat, fearful of the 'power of such copious showers of truth.'"[14]

After the speech, Douglass slipped away to a house owned by William Webb, another black abolitionist, on East Congress Street near Saint Antoine, where he met with Brown, Lambert, De Baptiste, and a few others. The details of what Brown said are lost; all that is known of the meeting is that it took place, and Lambert and De Baptiste's recollections of it years later. The two men said Brown told Douglass and the rest of the men that he planned to attack the federal arsenal at Harpers Ferry, West Virginia, and use the weapons there to arm an insurrection among slaves in the area, hoping to build it into a broad rebellion. It was, Brown argued, time to use violence in the name of freedom for black people. Douglass disagreed vehemently, saying Brown's plans were foolish, destined to fail, and that resorting to insurrection would harm the abolition movement. "Brown grew wrathy, and asked Douglass if he were a coward." De Baptiste, on the other hand, urged a more direct approach. He suggested gunpowder kegs be placed at fifteen prominent white churches across the South, to be detonated in a coordinated attack on a Sunday morning. Brown rejected the idea as too deadly; his plan, he said, was to shed blood only if necessary.[15] In the end, Brown conducted his ill-fated raid; Douglass left the country for a time in the aftermath, fearful of arrest because of his close association with Brown. De Baptiste and Lambert were uninvolved in the raid itself.

Lambert's life ended with a tragic turn. Around 4 AM on April 28, 1890, Julia Lambert awoke to find Lambert, her husband, missing from their bed. It was a Monday morning, and they had spent the previous day as a typical Sunday. They had attended services in the morning at Saint Matthew's Episcopal Church at East Congress and Saint Antoine, where Lambert was a founding member, followed by a family dinner at home, only a block away, and an afternoon of rest and reflection. They walked back to the church for another service in the evening, then returned to their home at 497 East Larned Street, between Beaubien and Brush Streets, around 9 PM. Julia, sleepy, headed to bed while Lambert "sat down in his favorite rocking chair near a base-burner stove in the family sitting room, and alternately dozed and meditated," his usual end to the day. Lambert's twenty-six-year-old son, Crummell, returned about 11 PM and found his father asleep in his customary chair, and headed off to bed himself.[16]

It might have been a day of routines, but Lambert, seventy-one years old, had been struggling with health problems since January. "Soft in the brain" was the doctor's diagnosis. He had trouble concentrating, trouble remembering. He would wander aimlessly, and at times his wife had trouble getting him to understand exactly where he was. Two months earlier, he had disappeared in the middle of the night and was found the next morning sitting quietly by himself in his tailor shop, uncertain why or how he came to be there. Lambert's doctor, fearing he would get hurt in his confusion, advised Lambert not be left alone. So when Julia Lambert awoke to discover the bed, and then the rocking chair, empty, she presumed Lambert had wandered off again. She roused Crummell and another son, Benjamin, twenty-two, from their beds, to look for their father. They first checked the rest of the house again, and the yard. Benjamin peered into the woodshed and found his father hanging lifelessly from a rafter. The coroner later determined that sometime after midnight Lambert had arisen from his rocking chair and walked to the shed, where he wrapped a thin clothesline around his neck four times, climbed up on a low wall of the coal bin, tied the loose end of the rope around a metal ring in a ceiling rafter, and then stepped off into the void.

The suicide of the man the *Free Press* described as "Detroit's most prominent and distinguished colored citizen" was big news in both black and white Detroit. Accolades poured in, and in a mark of Lambert's community standing the funeral was planned not for his blacks-only Saint Matthew's church, but the nearby Christ Church, which was predominately white and founded by descendants of some of the city's early families. Thus in death Lambert was granted the kind of respect that few of Detroit's black residents received in life.

The services were led by Christ Church's Rev. Joseph H. Johnson, who told mourners that although he was relatively new to Detroit and had only known Lambert for four years, "I have discovered that the great trait of his character was zeal. I am sure you could not have conversed with him for a half hour without recognizing the intense earnestness of his nature." Fighting slavery was the propelling issue in his life, Johnson said, but "whatever cause he espoused received his best attention."[17] Johnson was assisted by his boss, Bishop Thomas Frederick Davies, who only the year before had been placed in charge of the Episcopal Diocese of Michigan, and eight other ministers, including the Reverend C. H. Thompson, Lambert's minister at Saint Matthew's. After a long cortege of carriages and walkers to Elmwood Cemetery, twelve blocks away, it was Thompson who finally committed Lambert's body to its grave.[18]

With the onset of the Civil War, Detroit—like most northern cities—became an exporter of men and material. Some sixty-five regiments were formed in Michigan, including the all-black 102nd Colored Regiment. It was organized in July 1863 after the Emancipation Proclamation and changing policies led to the lifting of the ban on black men serving in the military, and in the spring of 1864 the regiment's nearly fourteen hundred soldiers were deployed to South Carolina, Georgia, and Florida. Yet for all the abolitionist sentiment in Detroit, and the state's broad involvement with the war, Detroit and Michigan were not particularly hospitable to blacks. The prejudices that informed life elsewhere in the North were no different in the bustling river city, and as the Civil War began there was considerable backlash in Detroit. Blacks were scapegoated as the reason for the war.

In that era, the Democratic Party was the party of slavery, and it was pushing the political position that abolitionists forced the South to secede. The *Free Press* staunchly backed slavery and dismissed the war as an "abolitionist crusade."[19] The war had driven down wages, and white laborers feared that freed blacks would swarm northern cities, competing for jobs and eroding pay rates even more. But the mood was primarily based on racism rather than politics or economics. The *Free*

Press routinely reprinted stories from around the nation about the latest "negro outrage," and when several blacks beat a white man in nearby Hamtramck, the paper all but called for a lynch mob. "We are opposed to granting the same privileges to the negroes, as citizens, that we give to the whites," the paper said in a March 12, 1863, editorial.[20] The secretive Knights of the Golden Circle, a southern prewar order that sought to expand US slavery to Cuba and Mexico (as well as running its own illicit slave ships to Africa), had supporters in Detroit. "By every demagoguic [sic] act, they inflamed the passions and the prejudices of the mob against the blacks," according to a summary of the mood at the time by the *Detroit Daily Post*. "The city was then intensely Democratic. It was close to the 'refuge' of deserters, bounty-jumpers, and fugitives from the impending draft, in Canada. In some respects it was like a powder magazine, only needing a spark to produce an explosion."[21]

The spark came in the form of the arrest of Thomas Faulkner on February 26, 1863, on charges that he had raped "one Mary Brown, a large and coarse girl." Brown, who was white, was a nine-year-old orphan taken in by her widowed aunt, Rose Brown, who lived in a market area at Croghan Street near Woodward (eventually renamed Monroe Street). The report to police, which came ten days after the alleged attack, was that Brown was walking to the post office to mail a letter for her aunt when a young black girl, Ellen Hoover, approached her and suggested they go into a nearby saloon on Michigan Avenue owned by Faulkner to warm up and get something to eat. Brown went along, and once there the black girl went into a back room with Faulkner, who was of mixed race (he was described as having "but a trifle of Negro blood in his veins"). Brown told police she left out of nervousness, but that Hoover quickly followed her out to the street and tried to coax her to return, then dragged her back inside where Faulkner grabbed her and took her into the back room "and outraged her person."

Faulkner denied he had touched Brown, and said that he had twice kicked the girl out of his bar, including on the day of the alleged rape, which was also the only time he had ever seen Hoover. Hoover at first denied any of the events had happened, then supposedly confessed to a *Free Press* reporter—which was playing up the story—that she had seen the attack. By the time she got on the witness stand in Faulkner's trial, her story had shifted again and she said she had been in the saloon, but hadn't seen anything.[22]

With the *Free Press* fanning the flames—it referred to Faulkner as "the monster" or "the villain"—large crowds formed outside the jail at Clinton and Beaubien Streets, and the courthouse a few blocks away overlooking Campus Martius, for both the preliminary hearing on rape charges and for the two-day trial, which began on March 5. The court-room was packed to hear Brown's sordid descriptions of her rape.

At the end of the day, as Faulkner was being returned to jail, he was nearly lynched. "A perfect storm of hisses, curses, and threats greeted his appearance, and a general rush was made for him by the excited crowd" of more than one thousand people, the *Free Press* reported. Three police officers shielded Faulkner as they moved along close to buildings until they reached the German protestant church on Monroe. "A sudden rush was made for him, and someone directly in his rear struck him with a large paving stone," knocking him unconscious. The officers pulled their revolvers and ordered the crowd to back off. After a few moments Faulkner came to and the officers slipped him among alleys to Beaubien Street then snuck into the jail by a back entrance as yet another mob gathered at the front.[23]

The trial resumed the next day, and the emotions of the crowd were even higher. Hoover's mother testified, calling into question much of her own daughter's testimony, to catcalls and hisses from the gallery. Defense attorney A. W. Henssler sought a delay to seek out more witnesses who could testify about Brown's character and reputation, because, he said, the ones he had lined up had failed to show out of fear of the mob. The judge denied the request, sending the case to closing arguments. The jury barely got to hear Henssler's because of the boisterous crowd. The case went to the jury, which took five minutes to convict Faulkner. The judge imme-diately sentenced him to life in prison. Around 3 PM court was adjourned. "The trial, the verdict and the sentences," the *Detroit Daily Post* would conclude seven years later, "were concessions to the mob spirit."

The trial may have ended, but the passions were just beginning to rage. And a mob that big was bound to vent somehow. In this case, any black person found on the streets of Detroit was fair game. "Neither age nor sex was spared. Women, children, and old men, who happened to be black, were beaten." The mayor, at the sheriff's request, summoned soldiers from the federal provost marshal's military garrison at Fort Wayne, on the river southwest of downtown, to help protect Faulkner as he was taken back to jail. About seventy-five uniformed soldiers arrived, which may have added another layer of provocation to a crowd that was inclined to blame blacks for the war. As the phalanx, Faulkner in the middle, made its way from court to jail, a hailstorm of rocks hit them, and members of the mob armed with clubs tried to break through to get to Faulkner. Some of the soldiers fired blank cartridges as warnings; others fixed their bayonets and moved down the street, blades pointed at the mob. But the rocks kept coming. The guns were loaded with balls, and several soldiers opened fire. One man, Charles Langer, dropped dead with a bullet through the heart, and several others were wounded, four seriously. The crowd fell back. Faulkner was hustled into the jail and the soldiers moved in quick time back to their garrison before the crowd could build again.

And build it did. In quick order, as word of Langer's death swirled, the mobs intensified and began moving into the black neighborhood just east of downtown. The first target was a cooper's shop with about a dozen black employees on Beaubien Street. The men heard the horde and barricaded the door while arming themselves with a shotgun and a few revolvers. They managed to fend off the mob until one of its members climbed the roof and torched the building. "Finally the half-roasted negroes burst out, one by one, and were at once hunted down, and stoned, clubbed, shot, pounded, and jumped upon, until they were left insensible, strewn about the place." One, named Joshua Boyd, was attacked as soon as he fled the building. With his head split open and serious injuries to his arm and back, he crawled back into the burning building to get away from his attackers—in this case, two boys who were pelting him with stones. Dennis Sullivan, "an officer of this city," enlisted another man to help and followed Boyd into the building. They picked the groaning man up from the floor and took him to a saloon on nearby Fort Street, where Sullivan, revolver drawn, stood at the door to keep the mob from lynching the wounded man. Boyd died anyway. An autopsy recorded a deep cut to the back of the head with severe swelling, and burns a half-inch deep in the flesh of his right thigh. Either of those injuries could have killed him, according to the examiner, Dr. John C. Gorton. "His eyes were put out, his nose was broken, and he was beaten to a mass of jelly," Gorton said at the coroner's inquest.[24]

The violence spread building by building, house by house. Blacks fled the mob, many making for the river, hoping for safety in Canada. As they ran, whites ransacked their homes—in many cases, simple shacks or decrepit wood structures. They stole the few valuable items they could find and in some instances emptied the rest of the contents into the middle of streets and torched them. Furniture, musical instruments, clothing, all went up in bonfires. "Feather beds were ripped open and the contents scattered over the streets, and everything valuable totally destroyed."[25] In other instances, the fires were started before the pillage could begin, and black families and the elderly were forced into homelessness one by one. One whole block of Lafayette, between Beaubien and Saint Antoine, was burned to the ground as the fire brigade watched helplessly, having been threatened by the mob to only protect homes in which whites lived or see their equipment smashed.

By 9 PM five squads of soldiers arrived by train from Ypsilanti, thirty-five miles to the west, and began dispersing the mobs while protecting the fire brigade—setting a pattern for rioting and occupation by military peacekeepers that would be repeated in generations to come. In the end, more than thirty-five buildings had been burned and at least two people were dead; the death toll could well have been higher, as injured and wounded blacks left the city, their eventual fates unknown. Many fled to Canada, never to return, though conditions there weren't that much better. On March 7, the day after the Friday riot in Detroit, a white mob in Oil City, Ontario, about fifty-five miles away, marched into a black neighborhood, ordered the residents to leave, and, before they could respond, descended on them in a violent riot, beating scores of people (none were reported killed) and burning their homes.[26]

While the ruins in Detroit were still smoldering, the *Free Press* absolved itself of any blame and accused the soldiers who fired into the mob of instigating the riot even as it acknowledged "an irrepressible conflict of races" in the North. "With such a state of feeling, it only required a crime of the magnitude of the one of which Faulkner has been convicted to endanger the peace of the community."[27] Some of the broader sentiments of the white community can be found in a March 11 private letter to Samuel Douglass, a lawyer and former state judge, from his wife, Elizabeth, who was with their young children at their farm on Grosse Ile a few miles down the Detroit River. The letter was a timeless indicator of the relations between Detroit's future suburbs and the core city. "I received two papers from you last night and was glad to hear that the riot was not so serious as had been represented. Abstractly considered, the burning of those houses was something to be thankful for."[28]

Yet in the end, the case against Faulkner—and the spark that ignited the riot—was based on lies. There had been no rape. The girls, who two months after the trial were jailed on larceny charges, eventually recanted their accusations against Faulkner. He was pardoned in 1870 after serving seven years in prison for a crime that never happened.[29]

5

DETROIT TURNS
INDUSTRIAL

In the decades after the Civil War, the United States weathered an unusual mix of economic recessions followed by economic depressions. The National Bureau of Economic Research counts at least nine contractions between 1865, when the war ended, and 1900, with the longest stretching from October 1873 to March 1879, or five and a half years.

Yet it was also a period of massive economic growth, from the completion of the first railroad lines to the West Coast in 1869 to the expanding heavy industries like coal mining and steelmaking to the booming success in laying telegraph lines along the bottom of the Atlantic Ocean, cutting communication time between the Old World and the New from weeks to seconds. The nation's gross domestic product more than tripled from $23.2 billion per year after the Civil War to $77 billion at the turn of the century.

The nation grew physically, too, adding nine states—from Nebraska (1867) in the Great Plains to Washington (1899) in the Pacific Northwest—and nearly doubling its population, from 38.6 million in 1870 to 76.2 million in 1900. Detroit grew right along with it, from 45,620 residents in the 1860 decennial census (the nation's seventeenth largest city), conducted on the eve of the war, to 79,600 people in 1870, to 286,000 people in 1900 (the thirteenth largest).

While Detroit weathered the same economic cycles as the rest of the nation, it had an engine behind it that most other cities did not: the opening of Lake Superior to ship traffic. In 1855, a new set of locks was completed at Sault Sainte Marie that let ships skirt Saint Mary's Falls, the run of rapids in the narrow Saint Mary's River that drains Lake Superior into Lake Huron. There had been canals built around Saint Mary's Falls before, on the Canadian side, but they had been relatively small endeavors. For a few years, the Chippewa Portage Company operated a small tram on the American side that would haul goods from one end of the rapids to the other, in essence an automated portage. It moved three thousand tons of freight in its first year. But after the opening of the Erie Canal and the discovery of vast deposits of iron and copper ore in 1844—not to mention the massive virgin forests of hardwood trees— in the Upper Peninsula and in northern Minnesota, American interests began lobbying for a large set of canals and locks on the Michigan side of the rapids.

Eventually Congress agreed to cede 750,000 acres of federal land to the state of Michigan, and in 1853 a two-year project began to dig a canal big enough to handle ships drawing 11.5 feet of water. Now the massive deposits of iron ore, copper, and coal could be mined and smelted, the logs cut and planed, and all of it could be shipped from Lake Superior to markets in the East. Business grew so rapidly the locks had to be expanded twice in the next half century. And fortunes were made, particularly in Detroit, the pivot point for goods floating down from Lake Superior and for supplies heading upstream.[1] "The Lake Superior trade has become the life blood of the prosperity of Detroit," the Detroit Board of Trade reported in its "1860 Annual Review of the Trade, Commerce and Manufactures of Detroit." "The immense cargoes for that region, embracing almost every article that can be named, taken into the monstrous holds of our steamers, must be seen to be appreciated."[2]

By the time that report was published in 1861, the Civil War was already underway. Even though it was fought far away, it embroiled Michigan deeply. Some ninety thousand Michigan soldiers—about one of every four adult men in the state—stepped into uniforms and marched off to fight. More than fourteen thousand of them died, most from disease. But with growing metal works, sheep farms—wool was the natural replacement for cotton no longer available from southern plantations—and a doubling of agricultural output, particularly grains, Michigan's economy gained.

The machinery of war had to come from some place, and Detroit's Novelty Works, a metalworking factory, began making and supplying blades for Union lances. Other small factories, previously selling in the local markets, began producing items that shipped far beyond Detroit, including stoves, smelted copper, forged iron, railroad cars, and even bridges built by the Charles Kellogg Co. In Wyandotte, a dozen miles downriver from Detroit, a former Great Lakes shipbuilder and skipper named Eber Brock Ward—believed to be the region's first millionaire—adapted a new steelmaking process developed by Henry Bessemer in Great Britain and opened the first American Bessemer steel mill. The method revolutionized steelmaking and would be the primary process for the industry for more than a century.

There are many ways to measure the growth and development of a place from primitive frontier to established city, but one of the more telling is the exponential expansion of Detroit's water system, which in 1860 served 6,950 families through 63 miles of pipe. By 1870, the number of families served had more than doubled to 14,717, as did the system itself, nearing 130 miles of pipe. By 1883, more than 27,000 families were receiving city water through 242 miles of pipe. It was a city not only growing in population, but also modernizing at a prodigious pace.[3] Streetcars, first introduced in 1862, were making it easier for people to get around, though the city's privately owned Detroit City Railway Company was slow to update, so more than half of the routes were served by smelly horse-drawn carts instead of the new electric ones. Still, they offered the first steps toward suburbanization, allowing the carriage-less to live farther away from the commercial and manufacturing center of the city.

"Detroit is without a doubt the best-drained, the best paved, the best shaded, the cleanest, and in general the healthiest city in the west,"

Elevated view of West Fort Street, late 1800s. COURTESY OF THE BURTON HISTORICAL COLLECTION, DETROIT PUBLIC LIBRARY

boasted the *Michigan Gazetteer* of 1875. "It covers an area some six miles in length, up and down the river, by a depth of 2½ miles. Having so much ground the dwellings are not crowded together in solid blocks, but are mostly detached, with plenty of intervening space. This with the wideness of the streets, and the prevalence of shade trees, gives the place more of a village than a city air."[4]

Detroit was primed to explode economically, and in many ways the seeds were sown then for the present makeup of the city. With the advent of heavy machinery, small craftsman's shops—from cigar rollers to cobblers—were pushed aside by new factories, which turned independent craftsmen into laborers. Small craft guilds—unions of craftsmen—that had formed before the war grew until the 1873–79 depression, when most died off along with the work of their members. As the economy recovered, heavy industry began to dominate Detroit. And with it came significant wealth.

The diversity of Detroit's growing industrialization carries something of a sense of lost potential, given the later dominance of the automobile industry. By the 1890s, Detroit was home to nine drug manufacturers, including two of the largest in the nation—Parke, Davis and Co. (eventually Parke-Davis) and Frederick Stearns and Co., with more than one thousand workers combined. Parke-Davis's three-story "laboratory" at the foot of Joseph Campau Avenue, with its own dock on the river, still stands as Stroh's River Place, which includes a hotel. The Stearns complex on the west side occupied a full block at Twenty-First Street and Baker Street, before moving to East Jefferson in 1899, which by then was the heart of Detroit's heavy industry—led by the Detroit Stove Works and the Michigan Stove Co. Those two companies helped make Detroit one of the nation's largest producers of stoves, and between them employed more than twenty-five hundred workers on East Jefferson industrial sites across from the western end of Belle Isle, the city's new island park (designed by Frederick Law Olmstead, who also laid out Manhattan's Central Park). Railroad car manufacturers also set up shop on the east side, including the Detroit Car Works adjacent to the Michigan Stove Co. on Adair. Smaller factories making everything from standardized bolts to custom machinery filled in along East Jefferson to the edge of the black residential neighborhood along Hastings—the old Moran farm—which then gave way to more commercial businesses downtown, from dry goods stores to cigar-making shops. And nine out of ten of the factories were powered by steam boilers, massive energy sources that were dangerous if not properly tended.

When the boilers blew up, they exploded with a staggering amount of force. On November 6, 1895, the *Detroit Journal* newspaper building on West Larned Street was all but leveled when a boiler in the building exploded, killing thirty-seven people. A few years later, on November 26, 1901, another boiler at the Penberthy Injector Co. at Abbott and Brooklyn Streets on the west side, between Sixth and Eighth Streets, exploded, killing twenty-six people. "What had been a three-story brick structure . . . was converted into a mass of rubbish, out of which stuck tangled masses of pipes, broken beams, and shattered timbers," the *Free Press* wrote. "Fire added its horrors, and if any of the unfortunates escaped the first crash, they were either cremated, suffocated by the smoke, or drowned by the torrents of water the firemen were force to pour into the ruins for many hours."[5]

Detroit's evolution from trading center to industrial engine can be traced in the decennial census. In 1870, by far the biggest industry in the state was lumber, employing nearly nineteen thousand people, from the crews in the woods felling trees to those manning the planers in the sawmills that turned logs into boards. In fact, more people worked in the lumber industry in Michigan than in any other state. Michigan's second highest occupation was in the clothing manufacture industry, with about twenty-six hundred workers, followed by furniture making with nearly twenty-four hundred workers and the carriage and wagon trade with twenty-two hundred workers. The vast majority of the lumber jobs were outside Detroit, with Saginaw the early center of production, while Detroit held most of the carriage and wagon jobs.

Ten years later, Michigan—with Detroit leading the way—was already becoming a center of heavy industry. Nearly $3 million of the city's total $15.6 million in private capital investment was in iron, steel, foundry, and machine shops, employing some two thousand people. Pennsylvania was the undisputed king, though, with $107 million in capital investments in steel alone, employing 58,000 workers, most of them in and around Pittsburgh. But Michigan was the largest producer of iron ore in the nation, with 1,837,712 tons, edging out Pennsylvania's 1,820,561 tons. And it remained the largest producer of timber, with 24,000 people working in the forests and mills producing $53.5 million in lumber products, or 23.5 percent of the nation's lumber output.

By the turn of the century, though, the lumber industry was all but dead, the vast majority of the old-growth hardwood forests sheared off at the ground. The mines of the Upper Peninsula had become overshadowed by the even richer lodes found in Minnesota's Mesabi Range of iron ore, which was controlled by John D. Rockefeller, and then Andrew Carnegie. The riches from those deposits went elsewhere—to Manhattan and Pittsburgh. But enough wealth from Michigan's lumber and mining industries had stayed in Detroit to make it an enviably well-heeled city. "The Paris of the West" was the common description, a marketer's dream. And where there's wealth, there are ostentatious displays by its holders.

In Detroit, that money gave rise to a new neighborhood just north of downtown, on the subdivided Brush family farm. Initially the land was claimed in 1647 by Eustache Gamelin, then transferred in 1659 to Jacques Pilet. It continued to change hands—as did Detroit itself through wars and occupations—until Elijah Brush, a lawyer from Vermont, bought the 138-acre tract from his father-in-law in 1806, his deed confirmed by the US government in 1807 as Detroit was emerging from the ashes of the 1805 fire. Brush, who was the second appointed mayor of Detroit under an early charter, was also a member of the territorial army and was part of the ignominious surrender of Fort Wayne in the War of 1812, after which he was shuffled off to Toronto with other surrendered troops. He eventually won his release through the help of a British brother-in-law and rejoined the American troops in Ohio in time to march back into Detroit in October 1813. Six months later, he was dead (the cause is unknown).

Brush's oldest son, Edmund A. Brush, then a teenage student at Union College in Schenectady, New York, came home and took over the family land, and followed his late father into law. He didn't stay with it long, though, focusing instead on the nexus between public policy and private gain. Well-connected, Brush moved easily into Detroit's small but growing class of elites. In 1820 he accompanied Gov. Lewis Cass on his exploratory trip around the lower and upper peninsulas of Michigan—Cass's reports from that trip helped counteract the earlier descriptions of the state as mostly unusable swamp, and spurred a land rush northward. Brush also served as a city recorder, member of the water board, and a volunteer with the fire brigade, and he played a role in the mundane elements of devising and enacting local regulations. He was also instrumental in establishing the city's first railroad connections. There was more than civic altruism in Brush's efforts to help Detroit evolve from frontier farm town to industrial city. As the owner of what would become one of the most valuable tracts of land, Detroit's success was inextricably tied to his own.[6]

Slight of build and with an austere, intense air, Brush seemed to take little pleasure from life, and invested relatively little of his own money in it. He connived to find ways to avoid paying taxes on his land holdings.[7] "To the world at large, he appeared as a stern, unbending man," his obituary reads. "But in his home, or when associated with congenial friends, he was open, sunny, animated, and a most entertaining and instructive conversationalist." Yet his friends were few. "His friendships were not hastily made or very numerous, but they were ardent and lasting," according to an appreciation published two days after his death, which ascribed perceptions that he was "cold and hard in his ways" to Brush's fear of letting loose his "naturally somewhat impetuous and excitable" personality. Part of his hardness could well have been the normal reaction to human tragedy. Four of his five children died before he did, two of them while they were in their twenties.

Brush was a shrewd man. As he rose to local prominence, he didn't trust others to handle his affairs, down to managing the household—in that era a role usually reserved for wives or hired housekeepers. He made the first moves toward dividing up and developing the family farm during the boom that followed the opening of the Erie Canal. Brush Street, the north-south route defining one edge of the farm, was named after the family in 1828 as streets were being labeled along the borders of the old French ribbon farms. At the time, Detroit's elites had built along Jefferson, Fort, and Woodward, erecting fairly grand, mostly wooden, homes within easy distance of their offices. But after the Erie Canal opened, the city began expanding to accommodate the new residents and the new wealth. Brush registered the first subdivision of his property—the southern end, closest to the city center—in 1835, but the first serious wave of building didn't begin until the 1850s, and the new houses embraced the latest styles, including slate roofs. Brush subdivided the northern part of the family land in 1862, and the neighborhood reached its peak of construction in the 1870s, with three-story Victorian, Italianate, and other period designs going up to house the captains of industry.

The nouveau riche created for themselves ostentatious showcases near their business offices and each other. Brush helped cement the exclusiveness of his new development by requiring his customers to develop their home sites within a specified amount of time, to minimum standards and value, on lots at least fifty feet wide.[8] As he subdivided the land, Brush decided the new neighborhood would reflect the family legacy. Adelaide Street was named in 1853 for his daughter; Alfred Street in 1869, Edmund Place in 1867, and Eliot Street in 1871 for his sons. Records are vague on whether Brush ever named a street after his fifth child, his daughter Lillie, who died in early adulthood. Brush's approach to developing his land made him a rich man. Rather than selling all of the lots, he kept title to many of them and leased the ground to the owners of the homes (it's unclear when people stopped leasing and began buying the lots upon which their houses stood). By the time Brush died in 1877 at his country estate in Grosse Pointe, he had amassed a fortune.

And Detroit had its first exclusive, and well-heeled, neighborhood. The capitalists who made money from the lumber, ore, and shipping businesses—or financed those enterprises through local banks and investment portfolios—built homes with all the latest amenities. One of them was William H. Craig, a local lawyer and real estate speculator who was a founding director and eventually president, in 1860, of the Detroit Board of Trade. In 1872, three years after Alfred Street was platted, Craig was living at 1 Alfred Street, right at Woodward. Nearby he was building a beautiful three-story Gothic Revival home of red stone with high, arching doorways and windows, twenty-three rooms, and eight fireplaces. Outside, the roof was edged with a heavy stone cornice, and two workmen were apparently killed when the pulley system failed as they were trying to heave a section of it into place, sending four men freefalling thirty feet to the frozen ground. Two of the men were not expected to live; the other two faced long convalescence, according to a *Free Press* story about the accident. The paper described the men as workers, one from across the river in Canada, and three with families, but didn't bother to follow up later on whether the two men had, indeed, died, as the initial story said was expected to happen.[9]

Craig sold the house in 1875, three years after he moved in, to a local lawyer and judge named Elisha Taylor. He later left Detroit for Colorado, where he died in 1893. Taylor was born in 1817 near Saratoga, New York, studied law at Union College in Schenectady, and moved to Michigan in 1838 with a cousin. When they arrived, each bought a horse and the duo spent the next several months roaming the southeastern part of the state. One of the stops was a farm near Grand Blanc that Taylor and his siblings had inherited from their father when he died in 1836, a four-hundred-acre spread bought years earlier as an investment in the wilds of the new frontier.

The cousin eventually moved on west to Chicago, but Taylor decided to stay in Michigan and settled in Detroit. With letters of introduction from legal friends in New York, he quickly found a role in the growing network of lawyers and judges, practicing law in the winter and overseeing work on the farm in the summer. He became a city attorney, then a court commissioner, and a school board member, and served as clerk of the state supreme court from 1848 to 1849. He was appointed a federal land agent and a pension agent—a lawyer turned bureaucrat. When his son, De Witt, became a lawyer, the two set up a partnership, both in law and in managing the family holdings. The son also became a real estate developer—he developed Taylor Avenue, three miles north of Brush Park on Woodward, and other streets in Hamtramck. The Taylors, along with the city, became wealthy. The elder Taylor was generally unremarkable in appearance—five feet, ten inches tall, about 175 pounds and "well-proportioned," with blue-gray eyes. But he was also a bit of a throwback, with a penchant for wearing a dress coat whenever he went outdoors, and for cultivating a thick, flowing beard that reached his stomach.[10]

In the greater arc of Detroit's history, Taylor is a bit player. But when he decided in 1875 to abandon his longtime home on Jefferson Avenue, among Detroit's old guard elite near the river, and move into the capacious Craig home in Brush Park, it was a clear marker of the massive changes underway in Detroit. That it was becoming, in effect, a new city. And unlike most of the houses from Detroit's original grand neighborhood of wealth and privilege, Taylor's home is still standing.

DETROITERS II

MICHAEL FARRELL

A lot of neighborhoods have risen and fallen in Detroit, but none has been more emblematic than Brush Park. It is the visual center for "ruins porn," as locals refer to the unending stream of photographs of empty, crumbling buildings.

They are hard images to resist. The vast majority of Brush Park's old Victorian and Italianate homes have been torn down or are collapsing under their own weight. Urban prairies surround the crumbling walls of the few shells still standing and the fewer-still reclaimed buildings. The downtown skyline—and, if the angle is right, the new sports stadiums—lines the southern horizon, where the top of the seventy-three-story Renaissance Center serves as both accent mark and reminder of Detroit's long-running efforts to save itself. Brush Park itself hasn't collapsed so much as it has been eroded by neglect, the remaining buildings looking like mesas in a southwestern desert.

The Taylor House, as it is now known, almost went the way of its neighbors. Elisha Taylor's son, De Witt H. Taylor, lived in the house until he died in 1927. By then, Brush Park had already lost its luster as Detroit's wealthy were building even bigger mansions in the Indian Village neighborhood, about four miles to the east, and Palmer Woods, six miles north, the start of a trend that bedeviled Detroit's development through the twentieth century. Rather than staying in established neighborhoods close to the city's core, and investing to keeping them vibrant and safe, wealthy Detroiters moved ever outward, first along streetcar lines, then along boulevards, and eventually along freeways.

William Fogo, a dental supplies salesman, and his wife, Harriet, bought the Taylor House in 1929 and made it their home until 1936, when, during the depths of the Great Depression, David P. Davis and his wife, Jeanette, bought the building and turned it into a boardinghouse. By then the commercial heart of downtown had spread up Woodward, and most of the mansions that Elijah Brush had so carefully nurtured into a grand neighborhood had been carved up into flop houses. By the 1970s, the rot had gutted even the boardinghouses, and one by one they were abandoned by owners who couldn't sell and didn't want to keep paying the taxes. Once a house was boarded up, it became prey for scavengers.

But the Taylor house found a savior: Michael Farrell, a professor of art history who bought the building in 1981, making him one of the first in a small wave of urban pioneers who still struggle to resurrect Brush Park. It was a boarding house when Farrell bought it, its twenty-three rooms divided into one- and two-room flats with shared kitchen and bathroom space. A few blocks from the Cass Corridor—Detroit's skid row—the tenants were mostly jobless, either retired or unemployable, and predominately black. Farrell converted it back into a meticulously detailed single-family home where he lives with his partner, Marc Herrick.

Farrell sits on a light-colored wicker couch on the screened back porch, the yard hidden from view by green shrubs. A coffee mug sits on the table and from somewhere beyond the shrubs Farrell's two small dogs bark at every provocation, real or imagined. The occasional roar of a car can be heard from Woodward Avenue, a few hundred feet away. It's late July, and a cool morning breeze stirs the air a few hours before the humidity and the thermometer head past ninety.

Farrell was born in Birmingham, Alabama, and moved to the Detroit area in 1968 to teach at the University of Windsor. After his marriage broke up, he rented an apartment on Woodward Avenue near Six Mile Road, at the time a trendy neighborhood for those who refused to flee. It was also the repeated target of thieves. Farrell was once robbed in his own apartment while wrapping Christmas presents, an incident he says helped overcome his fear of crime. "I realized that security in Detroit, as it is everywhere, is in your mind," he says. "You can have all the locks in the world. But it's really in your mind. It's a healthy paranoia."

Farrell spent a year in Florence, Italy, while working on his PhD, an experience he says helped him understand the difference "between existing and living." He decided he wanted to live—in the grandest sense—in Detroit. "I ran into a real estate agent who said, 'I've got the house for you. . . . When I walked in the front door of this house, it was like living in Europe." He was reacting to potential; the place was a dump. "It was in deteriorated condition, but it was never abandoned, and it never had cannibals in it" to steal the copper pipes and wires, and the ornate fireplace mantels. "It was never destroyed."

But it was neglected. Plaster was falling in, exposing the 110-year-old lath work beneath. The roof was shot and there was water damage. The floors—parquet and tile—bore the scars of decades of rough shoes and light care; and the rooms themselves needed to be converted back from their boardinghouse adaptations. But the price was right: only $65,000. The trouble was, without a roof, no bank would float a mortgage for the project. "I told them I needed the mortgage so I could fix the roof," Farrell says. "The logic was so circular. Then a group of friends who had been listening to me whine founded the Friends of the Art House and loaned me the purchase money." Farrell went to work.

Now a showcase, Farrell both lives in the house and uses it as a living museum, charging for small group tours of the period designs and architecture, as well as his collection of a wide range of art. But once the visitors step back outside the thick wooden front door, the romance of the past vanishes into the hard-edged present.

"I realized, in order to save this house, I had to save the neighborhood, in a sense," Farrell says. "I had to convince other people to buy in. Slowly but surely we were able to do that, and make people aware of what's here." But there were struggles. City of Detroit planners had bundled vacant lots and tax-foreclosed buildings into large parcels, hoping to entice developers to revive large sections of the neighborhood. That policy had the unintended consequence of hastening the area's ruin. When developers didn't step forward, or those that did failed to deliver, individual properties that could have been saved by people like Farrell languished and slipped further into decay until they passed the point of reclamation.

Bob Berg, longtime spokesman for the late Mayor Coleman Young Jr., believes at the time that the city was pursuing the best policy. "Hindsight's twenty-twenty," he said. "But the vision was you do the one house, but you still have all these vacant lots on either side. You want to redevelop the whole area." And the city was also wary of letting people buy up individual lots and then sit on them as a hedge in case the city turned around. But as the big developers failed to materialize and individuals were still ignored, it became clear the policy didn't work. "In retrospect," Berg said, "you could probably argue that you should have let people proceed."[1]

There were some successes when preservationists were able to buy properties from other individuals, properties that never fell into the city's hands over unpaid taxes. A block northeast of the Taylor House, Bill Atwood, a native Detroiter, bought his seventy-four-hundred-square-foot Victorian-style home in 1992 for $12,500 from the city. It was a rare individual transaction with the bureaucracy; he had recently bought, from a private owner, another ruin a few blocks north that the city wanted to house a social agency. Atwood agreed to sell that property to the city if he could buy the house on Edmund Place, a shell of a building with the roof missing and severe water damage. The stairway was destroyed. Scavengers had made off with the fireplace front, sections of original molding, and woodwork, as well as the wiring and pipes. But Atwood saw potential in the building and hoped to turn it into apartments; he finished gutting the building and put a roof on it, renovated fifteen hundred square feet at the rear mostly by himself, and moved in in 2000. In early 2011 the remaining six thousand square feet was still empty, awaiting a second wind—and more cash. "I got burned out after a while," Atwood said. "I kinda hit a wall."

Still, flag-planting by a handful of preservation-inclined individuals hasn't been enough to save the neighborhood. On Farrell's block,
between Woodward and John R, there are only three of the original
thirteen buildings standing. In the two square blocks just to the east
of his—south across the street from Atwood's house—only five of the
original forty houses remain. The first floor of one is sealed up with
plywood, but the upper levels are windowless and open to the elements.
The other four buildings are fully boarded up and sealed off behind a
chain-link fence and a weathered sign that promises redevelopment is
coming. The home next door to Farrell's has been renovated. The one
across the street is inhabited but in rough shape, with boards on some
of the windows. And the roof of Farrell's house, for all the meticulously
detailed renovation work inside, is covered by what he calls "the blue
condom," sheets of blue plastic to keep the rain from leaking through.
It will cost about $100,000 to reroof the house, but Farrell says he can't
get a mortgage to cover it. After he paid off the initial mortgage to
the Friends of the Art House, the group disbanded in 2002 without
notifying the Wayne County Register of Deeds that the debt was paid.
The property still lists a $25,000 lien by the group against the property.
Unless he can get the lien lifted, no bank will loan him the money to fix
the roof. And the principals of the defunct Friends of the Art House are
dead. "That," Farrell says, "is why I have the blue condom on the roof."

It's been a struggle to live in the neighborhood. Farrell has been
burglarized several times. He jokes about the lack of services. There's
no handy grocery store, and no retail shopping of note. "I couldn't buy
anything," he says, "and being a compulsive shopper, that's good for me."
Behind the punch line, though, is a cold reality. "Commerce is the lifeblood of a city, and when you lose the commerce, you lose the city,"
Farrell says. "Detroit has no commerce."

But Farrell's neighborhood is convenient in other ways. He can walk
to the Detroit Opera House about eight blocks away. The University of
Windsor, where he still teaches, is just a few minutes away (depending
on backups at the immigration checkpoint through the Detroit-Wind-
sor Tunnel). And the predominant suburban regions, where Farrell often
lectures on art, history, and architecture, are easily reached by freeway.

For a time it looked like Brush Park might finally get the renaissance for which Farrell has harbored so much hope. New renovation projects were announced in 2006, and several bore fruit, including the opening of the 113-unit Brush Park Manor Presbyterian Village subsidized-housing complex for retirees, and a townhouse project on Woodward. But then the 2008 recession hit. Financing dried up. The rest of the renovation projects died. And housing values dropped by more than half. In October 2010, Farrell's home, which he bought for $65,000 nearly thirty years earlier, was valued at $110,000; Atwood's was worth $70,000—these mansions would be worth millions in other urban markets.

"I don't care," Farrell said. "I'm not going anywhere."

6

THE AUTO ERA

In 1890s Detroit, the chorus of city life—the din of horses and carriages, the occasional clattering streetcar or railroad whistle—began picking up a new and sporadic sound: the rattling and barking of gasoline-powered internal combustion engines. The machines, and earlier incarnations using steam, had been around for a while. But tinkerers were beginning to find new uses for them. The desire was to marry engine to wheel, and create a cart that would propel itself.

Similar experiments were going on in Germany and France, but the Americans were well represented. Ransom E. Olds of Lansing, Michigan, had built two steam-powered horseless carriages. William Morrison of Des Moines, Iowa, had already developed and driven an electric-powered cart through the streets of Chicago. He sent one to the 1893 Chicago World's Fair, where attendees could thrill as they rode it for short distances. At least two other electric carts were also on display, including one shipped in from London. And German mechanical engineer Karl Benz had sent along a new cart propelled by a noisy and smoky gasoline-fueled internal combustion engine.[1]

In Detroit, the lead tinkerers were Henry Ford, who had been experimenting with designing a horseless carriage while working as an engineer for the Edison Illuminating Company, a commercial electric production company, and Charles B. King, who was an engineer helping to make railroad cars for Detroit's Russel Wheel and Foundry Company. King was a half step ahead of Ford, and on March 6, 1896, he rolled his first working model out of the shop, a wooden wagon propelled by a four-cylinder engine. Ford followed three months later, using an ax to widen the door of the work shed behind his house on Bagley Avenue to get the machine out. He and an assistant, James W. Bishop, took the machine in a circuit around Detroit in the early morning darkness, Bishop leading the way on a bicycle to warn anybody else who might be out and about at that hour that a machine was chugging its way through town. The vehicle died—an errant spring was to blame—and Ford and Bishop pushed it a few blocks to the Detroit Edison shop. Ford replaced the broken spring, and then fired the car back up for the return drive to Ford's house and workshop. "It was considered something of a nuisance," Ford wrote later, "for it made a racket and it scared horses."[2]

While King had the lead in trying to devise a marketable motor vehicle, he soon ran into trouble raising investment cash. He eventually turned his design and marketing ideas to engines for boats, a booming business in the Great Lakes. Others kept at it, though, as Detroit joined what historian Alan Trachtenberg described as "the incorporation of America." The American dream shifted from one of freedom to one of riches and acquisition. The self-made millionaire became the hero, the iconic role model. Workers—from the assembly line to the sales office— became members of bureaucratic organizations.[3]

The creative and entrepreneurial vibe in Detroit was contagious, and a magnet. In 1899, Olds, seeing the future in Detroit, had moved his family down from Lansing and built a factory on East Jefferson, near Belle Isle, where he started producing one or two cars a day. David Buick, who had built a solid business making farm machinery, turned to automobiles. And the Packard brothers moved their young luxury-car company from Ohio to Detroit in 1902.

Other tinkerers and investors, emboldened by the early successes, also began playing with the new devices to see what riches they might be able to wring out of them. Some 270 miles of Detroit's mud roads were paved with cedar planks and then, increasingly, stones, helping cement Detroit's image as the cradle of the new automobile industry. Electric rail service competed with the new machines for space as they shuttled Detroiters around the growing city.

In an amazingly short amount of time, what had been a noisy oddity was taking root as both a major technological leap and a new industry, destined to make already wealthy local investors even richer. It was a precursor of sorts to Silicon Valley, where only a few generations later modern tinkerers would find risk-taking investors to finance their experiments in computer and software design, which—much like the automobile—transformed the way individuals engage the world. And it marked Detroit's maturation from its gawky adolescence as a regional economic center building railroad cars, stoves, and furniture, to its future as a full-grown global industrial center.

In 1900, the US Census reported Detroit's population at nearly 286,000 (ranked thirteenth in the country), with just over 115,000 people, age ten or older, working. Of those, some forty-five thousand, or nearly 40 percent, were in manufacturing, led by machine shops and other facilities tied to making railroad cars and stoves. A separate count in 1901 by the state Bureau of Labor tallied 1,387 factories in Detroit (the firms had been in operation for an average of thirteen years), making 405 different types of goods by 61,237 workers (the difference between the census and state labor numbers may be the result of differences in definitions).[4] By the 1910 federal census, the city had exploded in a new direction, with the population reaching 466,000 (ranked ninth), of whom 215,000 were working and more than half—122,000—laboring in manufacturing. And for the first time, the census counted a new category: exactly 5,304 people were reported working in automobile manufacturing. Ten years later, some 35,000 people were working in that sector, and by 1929, the number of wage earners in the metro Detroit's motor vehicle industry (which would include Ford's massive Rouge plant in Dearborn) had climbed to 158,000 in a city of more than 1.6 million people, trailing only New York, Chicago, and Philadelphia among the nation's largest. And the count of autoworkers didn't include those working in ancillary support industries.[5]

The key innovation was Ford's automated assembly line, which revolutionized manufacturing worldwide with his concept of placing work-

ers along a conveyor belt, where each would do the same task for the
entire shift, rather than a single crew of workers building a car start to
finish. It reflected how Ford's view of the auto market differed from his
early competitors. The others saw cars as luxury items, and created and
marketed cars that would appeal to those who could afford, in essence,
a display of cutting-edge conspicuous consumption. Ford, though, saw
the car as a machine that could revolutionize society. He envisioned the
power of the mass market and what producing for large-scale consumption could do to costs. From 1909 to 1910, Ford produced 18,664 cars
with an average retail price of $950. Over the next eight or nine years,
he doubled production each year until 1918 to 1919, when he produced
533,755 cars, which sold for an average of $525. So as his prices came
down, the growing middle class could afford cars, which expanded his
sales. Ford's riches grew.[6]

In the same era, the Wayne County Road Commission decided to
experiment in road building and laid down a one-mile stretch of concrete over the existing Woodward Avenue, north of Six Mile Road—
near Ford's Highland Park factory. Dirt roads, and streets overlaid with
timber, were rough, hard to steer on, impassable in heavy weather, and
placed a severe limitation on the speeds the new cars could achieve.

The experiment was a success. Road engineers from around the
country flocked to Detroit to assess the innovation, and returned home
as converts, setting the stage for the rapid expansion of the nation's road-
way system. In 1909, there had been 394,000 square yards of concrete
roadways nationwide—primarily, that inaugural section of Woodward
Avenue. By 1914, there were 19.2 million square yards of concrete streets,
which then began to get measured in miles. Two years later, Congress
approved the Federal Road Aid Act, which made $75 million in match-
ing federal funds available to local governments for road construction.
That gave rise to the 1921 Federal Highway Act, the first step in creating
the system that led to today's interstate freeways. Detroit, and Michigan,
not surprisingly leapt on the programs, and travel time across the sprawling state shrank appreciably over the next few years. The new roadways
also made it easier to build houses in outlying areas of Detroit, sowing
the seeds of the suburbanization and sprawl that eventually would empty

the city core.[7] And it bears noting that without government-funded road projects, the market for the new auto industry likely would have been severely curtailed. The entrepreneurs innovated, but it was government help that launched the industry.

If the new emphasis on roadways marked an advance in human connections, Ford's automated assembly line achieved the opposite. It was the first critical step in the dehumanization of manufacturing work. Skilled craftsmen lost out to unskilled laborers who performed a single task, day in and day out. Ford acknowledged the "terror of the machine," as he called it in one of his memoirs, describing repetitive labor as "a terrifying prospect to a certain kind of mind. It is terrifying to me." Yet all work ultimately is repetitive, he rationalized, and he blamed laborers for their resistance to the soul-deadening assembly line. "The average worker, I am sorry to say, wants a job in which he does not have to put forth much physical exertion—above all, he wants a job in which he does not have to think." Those with a "creative type of mind and who thoroughly abhor monotony are apt to imagine that all other minds are similarly restless and therefore to extend quite unwanted sympathy to the laboring man who day in and day out performs almost exactly the same operation."[8]

Despite Ford's dismissive view of those whose work was making him one of the world's wealthiest men, early in his career he saw the sense in paying a top wage. He reasoned that a well-paid worker would be a motivated worker, and would become a consumer, feeding the cycle of production and consumption. An iconoclast to the core, he despised bankers as parasites, thought stockholders' corporate roles ended with receiving dividends, and believed that money should not be the ultimate fruit of capitalism but one of the ingredients in making the system work for the betterment of society. Wars were a massive waste engineered by bankers and arms makers, he believed. He found himself in surprising agreement with socialists, pacifists, and others who faulted the evolving corporatization of American business. Such progressive muckraking journalists as Ida Tarbell and Lincoln Steffens sang his praises. While Ford abhorred unions, he established himself as having a deep concern for the welfare of his workers—paternalistically so, and, as it turned out, only when business was good—and believed in self-improvement.[9]

Still, the nature of the work itself was a source of abject frustration for his employees. First off, it allowed Ford to replace skilled tradesmen with workers who could be taught to perform a single, simple task, shifting the power from the worker to the hiring agent. Labor costs—and wages—dropped as the tedious nature of the work increased. So deadening was the work in the early years of the assembly line that laborers quit in droves, forcing Ford to constantly train new workers. In 1913, Ford's hiring office had to sign up fifty-two thousand men to maintain a workforce of fourteen thousand.

That disaffection provided a wedge for the Industrial Workers of the World—the Wobblies, with their dream of "one big union"—who were drawing up to three thousand people to lunchtime rallies outside Ford's Highland Park factory. Fearing unions, and the spread of labor strikes that were already rocking Patterson, New Jersey, and Lowell, Massachusetts, Highland Park police arrested one of the main Wobbly organizers, Matilda Rabinowitz. But the real showdown occurred spontaneously on the other side of town at the new Studebaker plant at West Jefferson and Clark Streets. Workers there had been getting paid every other week, a persistent cause of friction. Dale Schlosser, a tool-shop worker and one of the more vocal advocates for a weekly payday, was fired June 17, 1913, after an unexcused absence from work. His coworkers saw the dismissal as an act of retribution, and a walkout among his colleagues in the tool shop quickly spread to the whole facility, with some thirty-five hundred men dropping their tools and marching off the job. The strike didn't last long, and it was unsuccessful. But it marked the first tentative flexing of collective muscle in the auto plants and helped spur interest in the Wobbly movement among more radical sections of Detroit's fast-growing working class.

It also made an impression on Ford, one of the most virulently anti-union of Detroit's new capitalist class. Yet he was also a financial pragmatist. Tired of losing money to keep the fresh tides of workers trained for only a few weeks' worth of work—and with an eye toward removing the unionists' main rallying issue, money—Ford announced in January 1914 a new profit-sharing plan that would boost workers' pay to $5 for an eight-hour workday.[10] That was more than double the $2.25 he had been paying for a nine-hour day.

There was a very thick string attached. To qualify for the program, and the job, workers had to allow representatives from Ford's new Sociological Department to inspect their homes to ensure the workers and their families were living clean lives of frugality and sobriety. They had to meet one of three criteria: be married and living with and taking care of their family; be single and over age twenty-two with "proven thrifty habits"; or under age twenty-two but providing sole support for relatives.[11] Thousands were happy to make that trade and went to the Highland Park plant hoping to land one of the jobs. Ford, though, wound up hiring relatively few new workers—the vast majority of those already in the plant accepted the personal intrusions, and the money.

On January 12, the first day of the new wage structure, some ten thousand men still hoping for work showed up outside the Highland Park factory to join those who had been hired, each employee designated by a small but, given the size of the crowd, hard-to-see Ford-issued badge. The interlopers tried to crash the gates, leading to a massive showdown with plant security and Highland Park police, who turned fire hoses on the crowd, pinning and battering those in the front against the mass of humanity behind them. It was a brutalizing decision given the time of year—a stiff wind was blowing in from the northwest, and the temperature was hovering near zero.[12]

"For 15 minutes, while those within range of the hose fought wildly to retreat and those out of range struggled to come forward, the police poured water over everyone within reach," the Detroit Free Press reported the next morning. "Then the mass broke, like an exploding bombshell. Lunch stands, small wooden shops, 'hot dog' wagons and other light structures . . . were overturned and smashed in the wild scramble for cover. Many of those who had been soaked by the water, turned when out of range and picked up stones, bottles, and bricks, which they hurled at the hose users." Others slashed the fire hoses, tried to attack the cordon of police, and threw rocks through whatever factory windows their aim could reach. But the hoses—and the Detroit winter—did their work.

Those with badges eventually entered the plants while those soaked to the skin fled in their ice-sheathed clothes to warm safety. Still, throughout the day, small groups of angry men materialized to launch stone attacks on the plant windows in guerrilla-style raids, then disappear into neighboring streets.

But Ford's experiment in paying a livable wage worked. He later described the pay hike as the best cost-cutting move he ever made. Turnover shrank, slashing training costs, and absenteeism decreased as productivity increased—the expectation from managers was that the increased wages deserved increased speed on the line. Wall Street investors and fellow automakers initially excoriated Ford for his wage scheme, but other carmakers eventually followed suit, propelled by Ford's massive leaps in production while reducing his per-unit costs. A Model T that cost $850 in 1908, on par with cars sold by the new Cadillac company, dropped to $290 by 1920, helping make Ford one of the world's wealthiest men.

And the high wages made Detroit a magnet. Nondecennial surveys by the Census Bureau chart the impact. In 1909, Detroit had 81,000 wage earners who made $43 million working for 2,036 establishments that cranked out $253 million worth of products. In 1914, after Ford's $5 day began, the same number of establishments employed nearly 100,000 people who made $69 million while producing $400 million worth of goods. In 1919, with World War I raging and the $5 day in full force across the automotive industry, 2,176 establishments were employing 167,000 people, who made $245 million as they produced $1.2 billion worth of goods. In short, the ranks of industrial workers more than doubled, and their wages and the value of the products they made nearly quintupled. Detroit's ancillary businesses, from clothing stores to restaurants, thrived.[13]

Detroit's economic base lurched its way forward on the backs of the (mostly) men who did the labor. And that, naturally, led to frictions. Detroit's first labor strike was likely by a handful of journeymen carpenters who in 1837 took to the streets in protest over low wages on the heels of a business slump that coincided with a spike in inflation.

They carried signs hawking their demand: TEN HOURS A DAY/TWO DOL-LARS FOR PAY. In 1850, typesetters and printers joined together to form the city's first union, the Detroit Typographical Society. The explosive growth of factories during and after the Civil War led to more organizing, though they were primarily craft unions—cigar rollers, shoemakers, carpenters, and machinists banding together to try to establish a floor of pay and conditions, and to maintain an element of exclusivity by limiting guild membership. Businesses that tried to undercut the guilds would find themselves under strike or boycott.[14]

In 1873, Detroit was steamrolled by a deep and lengthy national depression that followed a severe contraction of the young and ambitious railroad industry, which had embarked on a disastrously competitive building binge in the post–Civil War years (much of it fueled by government investment and land giveaways, and marked by scams and scandals).[15] As some of the rail lines went bankrupt or were bought out, and the rest enacted severe cutbacks, the shock blasted through the economy. Thousands of businesses went under, unemployment reached 20 percent and stayed there for several months, and wages were slashed for those who managed to hold on to their jobs. Workers revolted across the nation, with pitched and violent street battles erupting from Baltimore to Chicago. In Detroit, fear of uprisings led to a clampdown by police and civic leaders, including marshaling more than three hundred volunteers to help break a strike against the Michigan Central Railroad. The nascent union movement in Detroit was all but killed.

When the economy recovered in the early 1880s, the union movement revived, including a local branch of the national Knights of Labor, which orchestrated a strike in May 1885 against Detroit's Pingree & Smith Shoe Company factory. (One of the co-owners, Hazen S. Pingree, would serve as Detroit mayor from 1890 to 1897, and as Michigan governor from 1897 to 1901.) Some two hundred shoe and boot makers walked off the job over the single issue of union recognition and a "closed" shop, cutting into production but failing to shut down what was one of the biggest shoe factories outside New England. Part of the strike strategy was to give the striking shoemakers alternative jobs and consumers an alternative source for shoes and boots. The Knights opened a

worker-owned factory and store. The boycott added pressure on Pingree
& Smith, and the owners finally agreed with the union leaders to submit
their differences to an arbitration panel. The workers won a contract and
most of the conditions for which they had struck, seemingly a loss for
the owners. But the experience had an impact on Pingree, who saw the
arbitration process as a reasonable alternative to strikes.[16]

Whatever bounce labor received from the strike disappeared, though,
with Chicago's Haymarket Affair in 1886, when eight police officers
were killed by a bomb tossed in the middle of a labor demonstration.
It was never determined who threw the device, but four union men of
doubtful guilt were hanged for their alleged involvement, another committed suicide to cheat the gallows, and three others were sent to prison.
The incident added to public perceptions that unions were hotbeds of
violent radicalism. With the advent of the debilitating 1890s economic
depression and concerted efforts by business owners and managers to
maintain "open" shops, by the end of the century unions in Detroit were
floundering badly.

Four years after the Pingree & Smith strike, Pingree's fellow Republicans persuaded him, at age forty-nine, to run for mayor—a sacrificial
lamb in Democrat-controlled Detroit. Pingree had been largely apoliti-
cal. He agreed with the Republican Party's basic tenets of reducing taxes
and supporting the business environment, but he had not been involved
in the issues of the day. So he was a bit of an unknown quantity. In accept-
ing the nomination, he promised to represent "the whole city, without
regard to class faction or party." He also showed a remarkable streak of
political ingenuity and a hard-to-stifle competitiveness. Pingree understood the potential of organizing politically disaffected new immigrants
and smartly took advantage of an unusual election law that allowed non-
citizens to vote as long as they had declared at least six months before
the election that they intended to become citizens. Opposed by all the
local papers, including the ethnic press, Pingree secretly bought one of
the German newspapers, *Sonntags Herold*, and hired a new editor who
reversed the paper's earlier course and began backing Pingree's candidacy with German-speaking voters. At the same time, Pingree made the
rounds of the ethnic saloons, the community centers of the era, and built

up a grassroots network of support among marginalized ethnic voters—mostly Poles and
Germans—who felt ignored
by the Irish-dominated Democratic political machine.[17]

On Election Day, Pingree
won by 2,338 votes, or a 10
percentage point margin. The
Republicans also took over the
city council, winning sixteen
of the thirty-two seats (two
successful independent candidates precluded a tie between
the Republicans and Demo-
crats). Pingree didn't run on
a detailed platform, and in an
election night interview with
the *Free Press* he seemed sur-

Hazen S. Pingree. LIBRARY OF CONGRESS. DETROIT PUBLISHING COMPANY
COLLECTION (LC-D4-40050)

prised by the win and couldn't offer a specific course of action other
than to try to do something about the deplorable conditions of the city
streets.

But Pingree quickly found a mission. In his first year or two in office,
he embarked on a campaign to rid the city of corruption, canceling
contracts with crooked contractors who held monopolies on the city
street paving and sewage projects, routing questionable managers, and
reducing the overall size and cost of the city patronage system. In a sense,
he brought an ethos of professional management to what had been a
political playground, and won the support of the city's civic reformers in
the process. Street paving was revamped, new machinery added, and over
the next decade Detroit developed the transportation infrastructure that
helped make it the heart of the automotive industry. Parallel success in
ousting the corrupt contractors and upgrading the sewage system helped
cement Pingree's reputation as a mayor capable of getting things done—
and part of an urban reform movement that swept other cities, as well.

Pingree also displayed an admirable flair for the dramatic. Corruption was endemic within the public schools, where the mayor ostensibly held veto power over expenses, a role that was routinely ignored by the school board. On August 15, 1894, Pingree showed up at a regular meeting of the school board and delivered an accusation of corruption in which he initially named no one specifically, but asked the offenders to identify themselves and resign to escape the embarrassment of public exposure. The board sat in stunned silence for a few moments before Pingree resumed, calling out four names and detailing their individual crimes as city police officers moved into the room bearing indictments Pingree had obtained from a secret grand jury. By then, Pingree had already made it clear he was more closely aligned with the working class than with his fellow factory owners, many of whom shunned him on the street and in the private clubs and business associations.

Pingree had been in office just over a year when a labor crisis pushed the city to the brink of violence. In April 1891, the privately owned City Railway Company trolley system fired more than a dozen workers for suspected union organizing. The rest of the workforce walked out in protest and was promptly replaced by scabs. Over the next three days, thousands of striking workers and supporters jammed the main rail lines along Woodward, Michigan, Gratiot, and Jefferson, as well as some of the lesser lines. Some of the horse-drawn trolleys were able to travel their routes under heavy police guard; others were turned back as mobs stopped the trolleys, unhitched the horses from one end, and rehitched them to the other and sent the cars back to their originating barns. In some places, protesters ripped up the rail lines by hand. Squads of police had to scramble to keep at least three trolleys from being run into the river by the mobs (some reports say that the strikers succeeded at least once). Where the trolley lines passed such manufacturing centers as the collection of stove works on East Jefferson, workers on break added their bodies to the masses on the streets aiming to shut down the trolleys.

Pingree, in a horse-drawn carriage, cruised the streets to assess the action, and fell under intense political pressure to convene a special session of the City Council to address the strike. Instead, he leaned on the owners of the City Railway Company to send their workers' grievances to arbitration, which the company eventually did—in Pingree's office. Management quickly agreed to reinstate the fired workers and to hold further discussions on working conditions and hours (the firm had threatened to cut wages if a state law enacting an eight-hour workday was passed).[18]

The episode not only showed the potential muscle of Detroit labor, but it also boosted Pingree's political standing among Detroit's growing working class while further distancing him from the old guard Republicans who first enticed him to run for mayor. But it was not a united front against Pingree: the mobs on the streets had included such notables as James Couzens—a future confidante of Henry Ford, Detroit mayor, and United States senator—who reportedly tossed a few bricks himself. Merchant J. L. Hudson, whose massive Hudson's Department Store (the Macy's of the Midwest) would dominate downtown Detroit for decades, set up a collection box for the striking workers. Other business owners followed suit, and the labor confrontation quickly morphed into a city-wide, multiclass uprising against the poorly run and nonresponsive private rail company, which had resisted expensive electric modernization of the horse-drawn system. Pingree parlayed that public frustration with the privately owned rail service into a municipal takeover of the system.

But one of Pingree's more endearing policies was his decision, during the depression of the early 1890s, to use the power of government to try to alleviate the suffering of the poor. The depression led to a series of violent showdowns between starving and jobless workers and supervisors on outdoor jobs. Roving bands of Polish immigrants arrived at job sites and threatened the men working to hand over their shovels—and the jobs—or take a beating. In April 1894, the city water board changed wage policies from hourly rates to piecework. Spontaneous protests erupted, and at one work site at Connor's Creek, a small group of sheriff's deputies was overwhelmed by a mob of Polish workers. The deputies emptied their guns as they were attacked, and eighteen men—including the deputies—were felled by either gunshots or bludgeons. Three died.[18]

The severity of the depression drained the city's small fund for helping the destitute even as the demand on the fund increased. Pingree pushed through plans that had the city borrowing money in unorthodox (and probably unconstitutional) ways, and transferred money from other city programs to augment the poor fund. He pressured city contractors to add extra work, and extra men, even if they had to borrow, spreading the social responsibility to the private sector. He threatened to open a municipal bakery if the price of bread from private business was not lowered. And in 1894 he set the precedent for one of the current plans for utilizing the empty spaces of Detroit by establishing an urban agriculture program under which those on public relief—many just a few years removed from farm life—were given access to land and tools to cultivate their own gardens. "Pingree's potato patches," they were called, and the idea soon spread to other cities. At its heart, the plan was an attempt to show that idle workers were not lazy workers, and that those relying on public assistance would, if given the opportunity and a little government help, work for their own futures. But it also was a signal moment, looking to the past to try to resolve the problems of the present. Key, as Pingree himself pointed out, is that such solutions are often stopgaps.[19]

Pingree moved on to become governor of Michigan in 1897. Facing ill health, trouble with the leadership of his own party, and a series of scandals, he decided not to seek reelection in 1900. Instead, he sailed for Africa to hunt elephants and died of intestinal cancer in London, England, on the return trip.[20] But the reforms he had pushed in Detroit had taken root, and the city's political class shifted from corrupt ethnic-based fiefdoms, and the string-pulling of invisible businessmen, to a more independent and democratic representation of the people of the city. Ultimately, he made the city more responsive and set the template for future mayors to use the power of their personalities and visions to lead.

But municipal politics was only a small sliver of what made Detroit tick. At its heart, Detroit was an entrepreneur's city, and as such the capital class maintained a healthy fear of organized workers. By 1901 the city had begun to rebound economically from the 1890s depression. Detroit's unions also began showing fresh signs of life, led by the machinists, who were the key workers in the burgeoning automotive industry. A handful of successful strikes helped propel union membership from eight thousand in 1901 to fourteen thousand three years later. The rise infuriated the plant owners, who saw the union organizers as impediments to their control of their own enterprises, and their profits. Their response was, in effect, to unionize themselves and take collective action.

In December 1902, sixteen of the city's leading manufacturers created the Employers' Association of Detroit (EAD), whose genesis seems to have been one key issue: battling the union concept of the "closed shop," which meant all workers had to be union members. Under the direction of Secretary John J. Whirl, by 1911 the EAD had grown to represent 190 employers accounting for about half of the city's jobs, all in "open shops." Circumventing the local unions, the EAD ran its own hiring hall, the Detroit Free Employment Bureau, which that year placed 17,325 workers in jobs offered by their members, more than half of the jobs the members had filled that year. (The rest of the new hires presumably applied directly to the factories.) The EAD maintained a list of one hundred thousand workers, and kept tabs as they moved from job to job. They notably excluded African Americans from their lists of vetted workers—and would continue to do so until 1949 when state law compelled them to integrate—leaving those placements to the local Urban League's employment bureau.

The EAD managers claimed they were neutral on unions and did not discriminate against union-friendly workers, but given the deep anti-union sentiment of the members, which is what brought them together in the first place, it's hard to imagine the EAD placing a known union sympathizer in a job in one of their open shops. And its asset to the hiring agents was that a worker placed through the EAD came vetted for skills, personal attributes, and union sympathies.

Unions in Detroit collapsed. By 1917, automakers in "open shop" Detroit were producing one million cars a year through the efforts of 140,000 workers (one in three Detroiters, in fact, owned a car by 1916). Unions had a significant presence in only three trades: cigars, stoves, and the production of overalls, each an industry that was already fading in significance as the auto industry became Detroit's dominant economy. Labor peace was achieved on the owners' terms.[21]

7

A GREAT MIGRATION

Detroit's massive population growth nearly a century ago was not, obviously enough, the result of a massive baby boom. With labor shortages stemming from the United States' entry into World War I, the hungry and the ambitious—particularly rural African Americans—flowed into Detroit from the Deep South. In 1900 about a third of Detroit's 286,000 residents were foreign-born, and 4,711, or 1.5 percent, were black. By 1920, the number of foreign-born had grown to 290,000 but had shrunk in relative terms to just under 30 percent of the city's nearly one million residents. Another 247,000 people were native born of foreign parents, or first-generation Americans. Combined, that amounted to 537,000 immigrant or first-generation residents in Detroit, or more than half the total population. It was truly an immigrant city, though much less so than places like Manhattan, where nearly three out of four people were immigrants or the children of immigrants. Detroit was also a magnet for native-born Americans from other states. The 1920 census found 252,000 native residents of the nearly one million total residents had been born outside Michigan, which means altogether only one in four Detroiters in 1920 had been born in Michigan.

And it was a constant influx. The number of foreign-born alone had nearly tripled in twenty years, and they were settling into Poletown, Corktown, Germantown, and other neighborhoods based on ethnicities. Poles were the largest single ethnic group, and their arrival helped the Catholic Church expand. The first ornate churches, such as Saint Albertus, had gone up in the 1880s, but the diocese went on a church-building boom as the city expanded outward. Its anchor, the Cathedral of the Most Blessed Sacrament, was built in 1913 on Woodward near the new upscale Boston-Edison neighborhood—one of several outlying residential areas that took over Brush Park's role as the neighborhood of the elite. Five more churches would go up in the next fifteen years.

Meanwhile, the number of black people in Detroit had increased tenfold, to nearly forty-one thousand (which was about a third of the black population of New York City, and less than half that of Chicago). The new arrivals squeezed primarily into segregated slums just east of downtown and spread into the nearby immigrant (and heavily Jewish) neighborhoods of Paradise Valley and Black Bottom (named for the richness of the soil from the former Savoyard River, which had been buried as a sewer as Detroit urbanized).

Black residents still only accounted for a sliver of Detroit's population, but there were enough flowing in from the South to form communities and neighborhoods with their own class distinctions. During the post–Civil War years, the black community had settled into an uneasy racial détente with white Detroit. Racially motivated attacks such as the 1863 riot had not been repeated to any great extent, though the everyday expressions of white supremacy, and segregation, were unrelenting. But the new influx strained relations—within the existing black community, as well, which looked down at what it saw as the crude manners and low work ethic of their rural brethren. Some of the wealthier established black residents began moving into white neighborhoods, which heightened tensions with the white immigrant neighborhoods.

"The fall of 1914 found Detroit suffering from an acute attack of indigestion," wrote Gregory Mason in a report for *Outlook* magazine. "The city had bitten off more immigration than it could chew." It wasn't Detroit's problem alone. All the immigrant magnets—the industrialized northern cities—faced a flood of fresh residents who couldn't speak the language of their employers. Cleveland, at the other end of Lake Erie, had an estimated one hundred thousand residents who couldn't speak English.

But Detroit's troubles were exacerbated by a down cycle in the economy. Detroit was making half of the cars produced in the nation by 1914, but still wound up cutting eighty thousand jobs that year. "Great melancholy mobs of the jobless prowled the streets," Mason reported. Adding to the problem was the lack of English-language skills of the new immigrants, which led to a protracted effort by some industrial leaders to persuade the polyglot workforce to make English the common language. The city school system, buoyed by the backing of the Board of Commerce, launched a program of evening English-language classes, which was expected to cost $87,500 for sessions in twenty-seven public schools in 1917. For those without jobs, the schools offered a one-year program of language, culture, and citizenship instruction, culminating in helping the immigrants apply for citizenship.

The Board of Commerce sent letters to every factory employing more than one hundred men extolling the need to teach the workforce English, and some companies, such as the Saxon Motor Company, made night school mandatory for non–English-speaking workers. The Solvay Process Company offered a wage hike for those who learned English. Packard adopted an "Americans first" program in which only citizens, natural or naturalized, would be eligible for promotions. That, newly appointed company president Alvan Macauley said, helped cut down on ethnic segregation within the plant, presumably as workers feared exhibiting excessive nationality would harm their prospects for promotions and raises. "German workmen would object to working with Russians, or vice versa. Men of one race could hardly tolerate a foreman of another race. But since we launched our policy of 'Americans first,' all that has disappeared." It also, he said, reduced the power of ethnic leaders in the plant—a charismatic English speaker could hold sway over non–English-speaking countrymen—making it easier for company supervisors to mediate disputes. Which, Macauley didn't mention, also made it less likely the workers would unionize.[1]

Ford, naturally, developed its own program in which tutees were told to "walk to the American blackboard, take a piece of American chalk, and explain how the American workman walks to his American home and sits down with his American family to their good

American dinner." By late 1916, train stations bore signs urging new arrivals to LEARN ENGLISH AND GET BETTER PAY. Tellingly, those efforts were aimed at white workers, and the tone of the effort seeped into Mason's report: "One plant, I was later told, which uses gang labor, has been forced to employ Negroes because of the scarcity in Detroit of white workmen who speak English."

The "scarcity" increased with the advent of World War I. With whites fighting overseas, European immigration stalled, and production demands increasing, Detroit factory owners began integrating their worksites purely to keep the production lines moving—part of the magnet that drew the Great Migration of half a million mostly poor and rural blacks to northern cities.

The influx strained Detroit's delicate détente. In 1911, well before the war began, the National Urban League was created to try to improve the lives of mostly southern black migrants moving into urban areas. In 1916 the group tried to create a chapter in Detroit, but it was rebuffed by the old guard leadership of the black community, mostly the black clergy, who feared an organization helping southern blacks settle in Detroit would upset the racial balance (which essentially was that as long as blacks remained self-segregated, there were no problems). And they also resented what they saw as outsiders telling them how to care for their own people. But the Urban League founded its Detroit chapter anyway with the help of seven young African American men who saw black-white relations differently than the community leaders. It found funding, and support, from the Associated Charities, which had heavy backing from the city's leading antiunion industries—and which had a policy of refusing services to indigent or newly arrived blacks.[2]

In 1916, the Urban League, under its Harvard- and Columbia-educated director Forrester B. Washington, surveyed Detroit employers about their black workers, and found that only thirty of the seventy-five firms that responded (or at least whose responses still exist) employed a total of 330 black workers. Most employed a few; Chalmers Motor Car Company had the largest force, with one hundred black workers out of forty-five hundred total employees. But all the black employees were janitors. Of the respondents, only three said blacks were working in their foundries.

There was little space for elaboration in the surveys, but one respondent hinted at a key management concern with hiring black men: how their white workers would respond. George A. True, president of the Northern Engineering Works crane and hoist manufacturer, said the firm had hired blacks in the past and paid them the same as whites. "We recall some years ago, we had a colored man operating a lathe and he received better wages than some of the white men which caused some dissatisfaction," he wrote. "Some of these fellows made it rather unpleasant for him finally and he left."[3]

Through the Associated Charities, the Urban League was quickly co-opted by the antiunion forces and by the white-owned and segregated businesses. The Urban League, which depended on the leading industries for its financing, initially had little success landing good jobs for newly arrived blacks. Those who did get work were subject to lectures and newsletters from the Urban League blaming them and their work habits for their own lack of upward mobility and ignoring the deeply drawn lines of residential segregation enforced by violence. If only the southern blacks would develop "industrial efficiency," Washington said in an April 1917 speech tellingly titled "What Can Be Done to Assist the Negro Immigrant?" that equated the internal migration of American citizens with the influx of the foreign-born, complete with exotic work habits. But for Washington, fitting in with the new factory culture of the North was crucial to remedying the deeper effects of segregation. "If the community in general can be made to believe the Negro will be an asset to the industry of the municipality then the solution of the problem of employment, housing, recreation etc., will be all the more easy," he said. In a subsequent speech in Detroit, he said the Urban League aimed to "develop individual industrial efficiency by calling the attention of Negro employees to the fact that they must be punctual, zealous, and ambitious in their work. We always emphasize these points when we send a Negro to a job."

Washington also helped create the Detroit Dress Well Club to persuade fellow black families to become more conservative in their dress and demeanor as a tactic to attack segregation, which was increasing "partly on account of southern whites, but chiefly on account of the loud, noisy, almost nude women in 'Mother Hubbards' [floor-length shifts] standing around on the public thoroughfares. . . . There are, of course, untidy and uncouth whites, but white people are the judges and colored people are being judged." Job prospects, he lectured, hinged on how the black applicant looked. "This does not mean that a man must be a 'dude.' Flashy clothes are as undesirable and harmful as unclean clothes."

Washington also recognized that the new arrivals needed livable housing. The existing conditions were deplorable. According to one estimate, some fifteen thousand blacks were packed into ill-kept rental housing in the sixty-block Black Bottom area east and northeast of downtown. Before it became a black ghetto, the neighborhood held about seventy-five hundred residents. To the east lay an Italian neighborhood, and the northern reaches transitioned into a Jewish neighborhood. The legendary Hastings Street, with its barrooms, pool halls, music clubs, and whorehouses, was the north-south spine. There were other smaller pockets of African Americans elsewhere, including a twelve-block area east of Woodward and north of Grand Boulevard, and a slightly larger enclave in Hamtramck. On the west side, there were three small pockets: southeast and northwest of the intersection of Warren and West Grand Boulevard, and east of McGraw and Grand River. But the heart of the black community was the near east side: Black Bottom.

A city Board of Health inspector visited 407 families living in Black Bottom at the beginning of the war, as the population was surging, and found that 63 of the families were living in single rooms. Another twenty-four families had two rooms, thirty-four were in three rooms, and thirty-five families had four rooms. The rest were in larger houses or apartments, and all but six of those families were taking in boarders to help with the rent, which averaged $5.90 per month per room. City-wide the average rent was $4.25 per room, which meant black tenants were paying premium rates for vastly substandard housing in the only neighborhoods in which they could find someone who would rent to them. Even some of the families in single rooms carved out space for a boarder or two, "a pressure against wholesome family life which is extreme," in the eyes of one chronicler. And indoor plumbing was a luxury. Fewer than half of the families in the Bureau of Health survey were confirmed to have bathrooms in their homes "in a section of the country where a house with a bathroom is the rule." Given that the survey was taken at the beginning of the war—and at the beginning of the Great Migration—conditions were about to get significantly worse.[4]

To try to alleviate some of the problems—and to improve white perceptions of black Detroit—Washington proposed a new housing bureau under the aegis of the Urban League. He found that while the Associated Charities and industrial leaders were willing to help place black workers—who offered cheaper labor than whites and were barred from many unions—in their work sites, few were interested in helping improve their daily living conditions. Still, Washington was able to persuade two companies to erect housing for the new black workers, and worked with the city police to take over the leases of closed-down whorehouses in the black neighborhoods, converting them into working-class boarding houses.[5]

By April 1917, as the United States was declaring war on Germany and preparing to send thousands of troops to Europe, another Urban League study found twenty employers had a total of 2,874 black workers, and four of the firms employed more than two hundred each. Packard by far led the way with eleven hundred black workers, more than a third of the total. Those workers—mostly men—were taking essential jobs, not just pushing brooms or tending to the factory yards. Black women, also, were finding jobs in the city's still-busy cigar-making shops (a key entry was gained when Polish women walked out on strike, leading their bosses to seek out a less-organized labor pool and further exacerbating white-black tensions). And Washington was emerging as a key power broker among black Detroiters as the city's elite effectively gave him vetting power over proposals by other black leaders or black-directed organizations to try to improve housing or address other social issues. If Washington didn't approve of a project, it didn't get the backing of the Associated Charities.[6]

Job prospects for blacks picked up with the labor shortage that followed America's entry into World War I. Suddenly race was less of a hindrance; if you could work, you could get hired. And the Urban League's employment bureau was the key conduit for Detroit's blacks. Among the major carmakers, all but Ford, who relied on black churches, turned to Washington's group when they needed men for their assembly lines, further cementing Washington's role as Detroit's most powerful black man.

As black labor kept the factories humming, Detroit's corporations made heavy profits from the war economy. But acceptance of black labor in the factory was one thing. Outside work, informal segregation was strictly enforced. On August 22, 1917, upward of fifty blacks began moving early in the morning into a four-unit apartment building on Harper Avenue, near Woodward Avenue (it's unclear how many were renters and how many were simply helping with the move). It was a white neighborhood, and both the color and the number of the new tenants quickly drew attention and a crowd. By late afternoon some two hundred people gathered, and deputized William Koenig and John Van Dusen—both former city aldermen—to tell the new tenants they had to pack up and move out. The blacks at first refused, arguing that they had rented the apartment and had a right to live there. But with an eye toward the math, the intervention of an Urban League mediator, and the police who arrived to support the white crowd, the blacks packed up their belongings in trucks supplied by some of the white protesters and, under police escort, moved to a building on Riopelle, back in Black Bottom.[7]

But in late 1920, after a postwar economic surge—and the peak of the Great Migration flow into Detroit—Detroit hit another economic crisis. Thousands of jobs were cut in Detroit as banks curtailed lending and manufacturers reduced production, fearing new tightened credit policies would burst a consumer buying bubble. Black employment was particularly hard hit. In a matter of months, the balance of power inverted. Where workers had been free to walk off a job confident they could land as good a spot the next day somewhere else, now jobs were dear and hard to find. Employers suddenly had the luxury of culling their workforces of the least-reliable, and least-productive, members. And, from a racist standpoint, the least desirable. Despite earlier surveys in which employment managers had been generally positive, if stereotypical, about their ethnically and racially diverse workers, old prejudices resurfaced.

On November 11, 1920, as a short but devastating economic depression was deepening, seventy members of the Detroit Employment Managers Club met at the Detroit Athletic Club to swap notes and experiences. On the agenda was a discussion of the nature of black workers, and the minutes and reports from the meeting reveal a deep, though not unexpected, bias from many of the hiring agents. But the true surprise could well be the number of managers who spoke positively of their black workers, even as they were firing them. In one survey, twelve of twenty-five firms responding expressed positive views of their black employees. The rest drew hard lines, including several who said they had fired their black workers, were replacing as needed with white workers, and didn't plan to return to their experiment in integration.

8

THE ROARING TWENTIES

The 1920s were, in just about every way imaginable, Detroit's salad days. As the nation morphed from the deprivations of the war economy into the full-throated embrace of consumerism, Detroit was making and selling the ultimate consumer item: the car. That brought massive wealth and massive growth, both in people and in geographic space. The city population tripled between 1910 and 1930, with more than half a million people arriving in the 1920s alone. Since the days of Judge Woodward, the city had indulged a voracious appetite for annexing surrounding farm and timber lands as city leaders decided they needed more space—or speculators could persuade the city that their new plats of planned homes should be added to the city tax base. But the 1920s represented the last spurt of physical growth as Detroit completed its final land annexations, adding the far northwest, far northeast, and far southwest neighborhoods that established Detroit's current boundaries.

The city grew upward, as well. As elsewhere in the nation, the Roaring Twenties would define the face of the modern city. Skyscrapers replaced the low and rundown office buildings in the core of the existing downtown, along Griswold between West Larned and West Fort streets, and another cluster emerged a few blocks to the northwest along Washington Boulevard. Three miles up Woodward the massive General Motors headquarters and the neighboring Fisher Building sprouted on

The modern city: Detroit, 1929, from Windsor. LIBRARY OF CONGRESS, DETROIT PUBLISHING COMPANY COLLECTION (LC-DIG-PPMSCA-15308)

opposite sides of Grand Boulevard, the aptly named avenue that curls in a jagged twelve-mile horseshoe around the heart of Detroit. But downtown was where the action was, near the ferry docks and the rail stations that connected Detroit to the world and the hotels that housed the visiting business travelers.

Simon Murphy, the old lumber baron, had begun the process of building up instead of out in 1905 when, on the corner of West Fort and Griswold, he erected his twelve-story Penobscot Building, named for the river in Maine where he first entered the business that would make him so rich. The building, at the time the grandest in the city, reflected recent advances in urban office design by housing the power plant—boilers and other heat generators—in an adjacent structure to reduce the buildup of heat in the main building (and deaths when they exploded). The Penobscot offered Murphy and others working on the top floors "practically an unobstructed view of the surrounding city." It was a "splendid, substantial structure and will probably never be built

any higher," the *Free Press* gushed. "The building will be at the top of
the hill, so that all of the offices on the south side of the structure will
have an uninterrupted view of the river, first-class light and ventilation,
advantages seldom realized in crowded downtown districts."[1]

But those unobstructed views only lasted a few years. By 1908, the
eighteen-story Ford Building opened behind the Penobscot, just down
the slope toward the river. The name notwithstanding, it had nothing to
do with Henry Ford. Rather, it was the new headquarters of the Edward
Ford Plate Glass Company of Toledo, which despite keeping its factory
in Ohio decided to cast its lot with the boomtown of Detroit. This
Ford family already had stakes in Wyandotte, the small Detroit River city
where Edward Ford's father had been among the first to mine and market the vast natural salt deposits that lay underground (making Wyandotte for a time the third-busiest shipping point in Michigan). But the
Ford family likely was watching the vast growth of the car industry in
Detroit and thought that moving its headquarters there would improve
chances of landing lucrative contracts supplying glass for the assembly
lines. Ford also was angry at the inflated prices he faced in Toledo once
local landowners discovered it was he, with his deep bank accounts, who
was interested in their land. So Ford spent $250,000 in 1906 for the land
beneath a mishmash of "low, unsightly structures" conveniently located
kitty-corner across Griswold from a property the Union Trust Company
had recently bought for $276,000, planning to build its own skyscraper
headquarters.

The Ford Building proved to be harder to build than anticipated—
and more deadly. Contractors were told to expect a dry dig to bedrock
120 feet below ground, upon which pillars undergirding the foundation would be built. Instead, water gushed into the holes on October
20, 1906, killing two workers and more than doubling the cost of the
foundation work. A few weeks later, another worker died in one of the
holes when a frayed rope gave way, dropping a heavy bucket on top of
him. That prompted a wildcat strike by his colleagues over conditions
and pay—they demanded another seven cents an hour to compensate
for the dangers. A few months later, in May 1907, a fourth worker died
when he slipped as he made an ill-advised effort to push a wheelbar-

row across a board bridging an open shaft high up in the building. (His body, according to the news reports, was barely recognizable by the time it had bounced off the walls and landed in a heap.) A fifth worker was killed in September when he fell from the third floor as he was riding a hoist. Tellingly, while the local papers were filled with laudatory stories about the wisdom and genius of the successful businessmen behind the construction boom, they offered little more than brief notices about the deaths of the men who did the actual building.[2]

The Ford Building was just the preamble to the eruption of new sky-scrapers in the 1920s. The twenty-six-story neo-Gothic Buhl Building opened in 1925 south across Congress Street from the Ford Building. Three years later, the Penobscot Building was added on to, sending it soaring forty-five stories into the air and giving the Detroit skyline the tallest building in the United States outside of New York City and Chi-cago. The spectacular Union Trust Building, later renamed the Guard-ian Building, opened the next year, its custom red-orange brickwork and inlaid tiles making it a downtown landmark. The Book brothers put their mark on nearby Washington Boulevard, expanding the narrow street into a wide avenue to mimic the best of Manhattan. They had built the thirteen-story Book Building in 1917, and in 1924 erected the thirty-three-story Book-Cadillac hotel. Two years later they added the thirty-six-story Book Tower to the original Book Building, and erected a scattering of other, smaller buildings. Farther up Woodward, the Detroit Institute of Arts (DIA) moved in 1927 from its existing home on East Jefferson Avenue at Hastings Street, into its new Beaux Arts building across the street from the six-year-old Detroit Public Library. As a group, the buildings—all still standing today—marked Detroit's emergence as a self-aware city, with its moneyed class investing massive sums in their signature properties, trying to rival Chicago as a center for urban archi-tecture and culture.

At its heart, though, it was a salesman's culture. "No doubt about it, Detroit is coming to be a city sweet to the eye and satisfying to the intel-ligence of the salesmen and mechanics who inhabit it," poet, journalist, and author Leonard Lanson Cline wrote in November 1922, part of a series of the *Nation* magazine articles by authors about different states.

Cline was a native of Bay City, on Lake Huron's Saginaw Bay, and had worked for six years at the *Detroit News*, though by the time the article appeared he had moved on to the *Baltimore Sun*. His take on Detroit was scathing: "Sublimated peddlers, 'get-it-across' advertising men, and other hundredpercenters look on their work with a smile of perfect admiration. Proper credit is also due the real-estate agent swaggering in the glory of his new title of realtor, proud of the miles of pleasant woodland he has turned into 'subdivisions' with sidewalks and lamp posts but no water, trees, or houses. Salesmanship it is that makes the prospect visualize a 'home' in this 'development' for so much down and so much a month." And the new cultural center with the library and the then hole in the ground for the new DIA "are the outward and visible signs of an inward and spiritual salesmanship. They are a gesture, like the carnation on Mother's Day in the buttonhole of the man who has not written home in twelve years." Although the last laugh might have been Detroit's. Cline later served ten months in prison for the shooting death of a friend in Connecticut during a drunken argument, and he died of a heart attack in his Greenwich Village bed in January 1929 at age thirty-five.[3]

Beyond the cultural affectations, it quickly became apparent that Detroit's roadways, workable for horse-drawn carriages and electric streetcars, would not suffice for the new wave of automobiles. That wasn't Detroit's problem alone. Across the nation, cities engaged in massive building booms, and in the Midwest there were industrial expansions, all propelled by the soaring consumer demand for and use of automobiles. As car use skyrocketed, local infrastructure demands increased, leading to substantial construction projects building or improving roadways and bridges, gasoline stations and repair shops, and motels to serve the suddenly much more mobile nation. Production of paints and lacquers, rubber and glass—and oil and gasoline refineries—transformed the physical layout and appearance of the nation's cities and small towns.[4]

In Detroit, the new consumerism threatened to choke the city. Local officials struggled with rules of the road, in 1923 designating some of the main roads as "stop through streets," requiring motorists entering from side streets to come to a full stop before entering intersections and banning right and left turns from the arterials themselves in the most congested sections of downtown. Roofed towers were erected in strategic places to oversee the worst intersections, and the police department assigned 138 officers to do nothing but tend to traffic and referee disputes between "the 80 percent of the people who ride on the cars and buses, as against the 20 percent who ride in autos but nevertheless occupy more than 80 percent of the streets."

Detroit was the nation's fourth-largest city in population but was second in traffic congestion, after Los Angeles (some things never change) and ahead of New York and Chicago. There was talk of banning street parking in downtown Detroit, relegating the new machines to off-street lots and new garages. State and local government officials began spending heavily on new road construction and on covering existing dirt roads with concrete. Major streets were being widened to handle the noisy, clattering load—Woodward Avenue, the main north-south artery, was widened from end to end, a ten-mile-long project beginning at Jefferson Avenue, near the Detroit River. And using surplus war machinery and convict labor, Grand River Avenue was paved from Detroit to the state capital in Lansing, seventy-five miles away. Planners laid out the first proposed network of "super-highways," more than two hundred feet wide, with one lane in each direction for "rapid transit surface lines" and another for local traffic, and with bridges carrying the rapid transit lanes over intersecting local streets. What had been farmlands just a few miles from downtown quickly became suburban, and almost exclusively white, subdivisions. It was Detroit's first brush with the concept of freeways that would come to define the city forty years later—and help lead to its collapse.[5]

The work that created all that wealth, that made it possible in 1923 for there to be 250,000 automobiles scurrying around metro Detroit, and that gave rise to the distinctive modern skyscrapers, was happening far from downtown. The Packard brothers had built the first modern auto factory in 1903 in northeast Detroit, spreading ten buildings over thirty-five acres. Fisher Body opened its new six-story Fisher Body 21 plant in 1919 near Hamtramck, at the edge of the Poletown immigrant community. Through the 1920s, other carmakers similarly opened or expanded factories to handle the consumer demand, even as General Motors began expanding worldwide by opening factories in Denmark (1923), France and Germany (1925), Argentina and Brazil (1925), India (1928), and China (1929).

But Henry Ford trumped them all with his River Rouge plant in Dearborn, southwest of downtown Detroit. The Rouge plant was and is an incomprehensibly large factory complex with, at its peak, ninety-three buildings covering more than fifteen million square feet on a lot that measures one-and-a-half miles wide and one mile long. The complex held one hundred miles of rail lines, and put into play Ford's concept of a factory that would take in the raw materials for steel, rubber tires, and other auto components at one end and churn out completed cars at the other. It was an effort to refine the assembly line to its most efficient point. But it also fit in with the other 1920s construction in Detroit, and as a group the new industrial plants and skyscrapers were monuments to, and the tools of, capitalism and power, and helped establish Detroit as the nation's new industrial heart.

The growth of the factories also fueled the passions of socialists and others for the plight of the working class. Several unions launched and tried to gain footholds. In 1891 a spin-off of the Knights of Labor came together as the International Union of Carriage and Wagon Workers, aiming, obviously, to organize workers in those industries. With the advent of the car-making plants, they sought to expand their strength by adding automobile factories to their portfolio—a shift that led to direct confrontations with small craft unions already claiming jurisdiction in the car plants (with limited success). The American Federation of Labor suspended the carriage workers union after it refused to drop "Automobile" from its name and from its efforts. The union morphed into the Auto Workers Union and, in the days after World War I, grew rapidly to forty-five thousand members across thirty-five local units, about a tenth of the auto industry, before collapsing.[6]

The rise in labor strength coincided with—or perhaps grew out of—a national rise in political radicalism, including a series of bombings by anarchists and others. One bomb went off outside the Washington, DC, home of US Attorney General A. Mitchell Palmer, which led to a predictable reaction. Palmer ordered a nationwide roundup of foreign radicals. It was a crippling blow for Detroit's nascent labor movement as 827 people were arrested in and around the city, and 234 eventually deported, decimating the ranks of union organizers and activists. At the same time, the Employers' Association of Detroit renewed its "open shop" drive, cutting deals with conservative unions. In 1922, the AWU had fewer than one thousand members even as hiring in the auto shops increased. Adding to the organizing hurdles was the spread of something akin to corporate paternalism, providing workers access to limited benefits such as profit sharing and savings plans, factory clinics, and other benefits aimed at pacifying them and reducing the frustrations that could lead them to organize.[7]

But those benefits from the employers did little to alleviate the suffering among Detroit's poor. Smoke-belching factories, car-clogged streets, and sparkling new skyscrapers may have defined the city in the go-go 1920s, but overcrowding and disease defined the poorer, overstuffed, working-class neighborhoods that were unable to handle the flood of newcomers. In April 1920, the city health department reported 138 cases of smallpox. Forty-three of those patients, or nearly one-third, were single black men, most of whom had been in Detroit for less than a year—fresh migrants who had never been immunized and who were living in densely packed rooming houses. "The absence of cases among colored women and children indicates that disease is not present among the settled colored men with families," the May 1920 report said.[8]

The growth of the factories, the workers' neighborhoods around them, and the onset of the automobile all had another unhealthy effect on Detroit: air pollution. By the end of the decade, Detroit was third in the nation in measurable dust particles in the air, trailing Saint Louis and then Pittsburgh.[9]

Throughout the 1800s, the American temperance movement had slowly gained support for its key point of advocacy, the legal prohibition of alcohol. In 1830, Michigan territorial governor Lewis Cass capitulated to demands from political supporters in the city of Jackson, the heart of Michigan's early temperance movement, and delivered an abstinence speech in Detroit. It was likely the first such message to the masses from a Michigan politico, though there's no indication that Cass found much sympathy in a city where small local breweries were part of the immigrant culture.[10] But the temperance movement and the Anti-Saloon League grew in strength nationally and gained crucial political traction just after the turn of the century, leading local and state governments to curtail, and in some cases outlaw, the manufacture and sale of alcohol.

By 1907, half of the states had some sort of ban in place, including Michigan with its "local option," under which municipalities and counties could decide whether to ban alcohol in their jurisdictions. The temperance movement came with a racial overlay. Going dry gave local authorities in the southern states another weapon with which to combat "the degeneracy and criminality of the drunken negro," as the *Free Press* so indelicately described it in a 1907 article lauding prohibition.[11]

In an era of deep faith in science and the betterment of man, the temperance movement managed to corral enough political support to amend the US Constitution. On January 16, 1920, the Eighteenth Amendment went into effect, barring the manufacture and sale of alcohol in the United States. One can only imagine the hoarding and weeks of bacchanalia—a New Year's Eve party that wouldn't stop—that preceded the shutting off of the tap.

But in reality, the rest of the nation was simply following the lead of Michigan and a few other states that had already adopted prohibition laws. Michigan voters amended their state constitution in 1916 to ban booze effective May 1, 1918, in a vote that found wide and deep support in rural Michigan, but that lost in Wayne County, with Detroit as its seat. Other states, such as Maine, had already found prohibition was much easier to enact than to enforce, and Detroiters for the most part decided to treat the ban as little more than a nuisance.[12] By November 1918, six months after the ban went into effect, enforcement was so ineffective in Detroit that Claude L. Bennett, the private detective from Saginaw hired specifically to lead the enforcement team, was fired. Bennett and his men were adept at finding and confiscating illicit pre-prohibition stockpiles, but were completely ineffective against imports. "We know that liquor has been pouring into Wayne County and has been on sale here under conditions that would allow arrest and prosecutions without much trouble," state food and drug commissioner Frederick L. Woodworth said when he announced he was firing the man he had personally appointed. "Liquor has been sold openly, in dozens of places and by many persons who could be run down easily."[13]

So by the time prohibition went into effect nationally, Detroit's drinkers already had two years' experience finding ways around the liquor ban and its enforcers. And providentially, it must have seemed, wartime prohibition laws across the river in Canada ended on January 1, 1920, a little more than two weeks before the American booze spigot was officially shut off.

The new laws created an odd situation. The province of Ontario decided to continue its ban on the sale of liquor, but its distilleries could make booze for export to wet Quebec or to foreign nations. Thus Detroit, within a rowboat's distance from Windsor and its boom economy of new distilleries, breweries, and loading docks, was uniquely poised to become one of the nation's key pipelines of illicit booze. Eight months after Michigan's ban went into effect, Woodworth, whose office was in charge of enforcing prohibition, lamented that enforcement was difficult and that the bulk of the whisky runners were, in effect, underworld businessmen who saw arrests and fines as just part of the cost of a lucrative trade.[14]

Much has been written about the rise of organized crime with the advent of Prohibition and the wealth amassed by the likes of Al Capone in Chicago, who oversaw the lion's share of smuggling through Detroit. In Detroit, rum-running became a way of life, though it also had its dangers—from poaching by rival gangs to shoot-outs with woefully overmatched police and federal agents. Collusion by local officials reached comical proportions. On the evening of November 14, 1921, just over a week before Thanksgiving Day, Detroit police confiscated a pretty good party's worth of booze from John Sarvis of 55 River Front. Under the lead of Joseph Buehler of the liquor squad, the authorities grabbed 19 quarts of champagne, 1,219 pints of beer, 201 quarts of wine, 135 quarts of whiskey, 119 half pints of whisky, and 15 quarts of gin. The reports didn't specify, but it seems like Sarvis was operating a blind pig, a regional term for an illegal bar. Sarvis contested the seizures, arguing that while the liquor squad arrived with a search warrant in hand, the warrant did not say that police had the authority to enter the premises at night. Detroit recorder's court judge John Faust agreed, ruling the search warrant was invalid after sunset. He ordered future warrants include the time they would be served, and ordered the confiscated booze be returned to Sarvis even though it was still contraband. After the ruling, police often arrived at blind pigs only to discover empty rooms.[15]

And booze could be bought everywhere. By 1923, police estimated there were ten thousand blind pigs in the city. In Grosse Pointe Park, the well-to-do lakeside suburb adjoining Detroit's eastern border, police vetted their rumrunners. "We let certain ones use the shore, but certain others who had reputations, we kept out," former sergeant Tim Mead told a local magazine years afterward. "We didn't want the violent types."[16]

Other police were more aggressive. In Ecorse, a small downriver city that became a vortex of smuggling, a patrolman noticed an unusual amount of foot traffic at a machine shop in April 1919. After arranging to buy a few bottles, a squad of police raided the shop. Inside they found bottles of booze "corded up like wood" in a block five feet high and ten feet long. They confiscated two thousand bottles and arrested three men.[17] The smuggling business was so good that Canadian farmers gave up spring planting in favor of rum-running, letting fields on the south side of the river lie fallow as they moved booze across the river in small launches.[18]

The inventiveness of the smugglers was admirable. There were rumors of electric-run fifty-gallon torpedoes cruising from one side of the river to the other and of a pipeline of liquor (or beer, depending on the teller) laid across the river bottom. Those were "bootlegger canards," according to Roy A. Haynes, a US prohibition commissioner in 1923. But the truth, he said, was bizarre enough. "It is wits against wits in this business and perhaps nowhere along the Canadian border is the contest more keen than about Detroit. Right over the busy river there is Windsor, and standing on American soil you can see the liquor boats loading there. You see them back away from the docks, and you know beyond a doubt that they are starting for the Michigan side with a load of liquor. Yet until the line is crossed there is no transgression."

After the first few months of prohibition, the rumrunners skipped Detroit proper for other landing spots along the thirty miles of the Detroit River, vastly expanding the geographic enforcement terrain to be covered and overmatching federal, state, and local authorities with superior—and faster—boats. Winter in some ways made it easier. Once Lake Saint Clair froze over, booze-laden iceboats scooted across the ice with impunity, propelled by the winter wind. Old Model Ts were put into their last service as rumrunners. If they cracked through the ice, they were simply abandoned.[19]

Under the Canadian liquor laws, all an exporter needed to get an export permit was to swear that the liquor was destined for a non-prohibition country—often Cuba or Mexico. So each afternoon scores of rumrunners in small craft, or major exporters with access to railroad cars, would buy hundreds of cases of liquor and beer ostensibly for the long journey down the Saint Lawrence Seaway to the Atlantic and then Cuba, or by sealed rail car for the Mexican border. In reality, the cargo disappeared into the illicit American booze underground. From the Canadian government's standpoint, once the cargo left Canada it became some other government's problem. James C. Young, a reporter for the *New York Times*, spent an evening on the Windsor docks to witness the dance of duplicity. His story focused on a man named Red Bannion, "rumrunner extraordinaire," who, when asked by a Canadian customs clerk where his booze was headed, said: "Oh, Cuba will do, I suppose. Yeh, make it Cuba. I ain't been there in a long time." Other claimed destinations: Pernambuco in Brazil, Mombasa in Kenya, and Tahiti. "One of the jokes of the river trade is thinking up ports that send the Canadian customs agents looking for dictionaries and atlases."[20]

But there was a deadly underside as different gangs fought for turf. With markups as high as ten times the wholesale price, there were millions of dollars to be made. By 1923, what had started as a disparate and grassroots effort to find ways to get booze had become an underworld business, with various gangs and mob families waging wars. Scores of police, US Coast Guard, and US Customs agents were convicted of taking bribes or being directly involved in smuggling themselves, adding to the porous border. The mayor of Hamtramck and sixteen other city officials were jailed for liquor violations. Occasional gun battles broke out between the rumrunners and the police.[21]

A *Detroit News* series in 1923 recorded ninety-seven killings known to have been directly tied to the bootlegging underworld since the onset of Prohibition.[22] The bodies mounted up in the morgue, pulled from the river, from alleys, and from ditches along lonely stretches of rural roads. In some respects, Detroit's flagrant disregard for prohibition presaged the illegal economy that would arise in the 1970s (heroin) and the 1980s (cocaine and crack), and the overwhelming levels of violence that accompanied the fights for turf, and revenge.

The hundreds of thousands of African Americans who left southern farms and small towns to head north weren't just chasing a dream of steady work and better wages. In many cases, they were running for their lives. Between 1915 and 1922, at least 490 African Americans were lynched, primarily in the Deep South, where everyday life for black Americans was marked by oppression, deep poverty, and the belief that powerful forces of history and racism precluded improvement in the foreseeable future.[23]

As blacks moved north, some of the old hatreds followed, and new ones arose among the established immigrant communities in Detroit and elsewhere, where Europeans, particularly the Polish and German working class, freighted existing white-black racism with fears that adding poor rural blacks to the urban labor pool would drive down wages and job opportunities.

Jews, also, were the targets of prejudice—particularly by Henry Ford, who was becoming increasingly erratic. In May 1920, Ford's *Dearborn Independent* newspaper began a nearly two-year propaganda campaign against Jews in one of America's most remarkable mainstream outpourings of anti-Semitism. Included in the extended diatribe was the publication of the "Protocols of the Elders of Zion," a forgery purportedly detailing plans by a secret cabal of Jews to run the world. (The document is generally believed to have been created by secret police in Tsarist Russia in the late nineteenth century.) This wasn't the disillusioned rant of a politically and economically marginalized man trying to resurrect a genteel past that, in fact, never existed. It was a statement of intolerance and hatred by a man largely revered as the epitome of the American Dream, the son of an immigrant farmer who (in the broadest view of the legend) had risen by his own wits and drive to become one of the leading lights of the industrial world. That made him a folk hero to many Detroiters, in particular. Add in the political rise of nativist anti-immigrant feelings, a sputtering economy, the onset of Prohibition-related crime and the resulting sense of lawlessness, and the times were fertile for a political and social backlash. Or exploitation.

Both occurred, propelled by a trio of southerners who, mixing white supremacy and the fad of fraternal organizations, brought the Ku Klux Klan back to life. The resurrection was spawned by the 1915 release of D. W. Griffith's *Birth of the Nation*, a film version of a series of novels by Thomas Dixon that held Klansmen up as gallant defenders of the Old South.[24] The film galvanized racist elements in broader American society, which William J. Simmons, a failed minister and salesman, tapped (with the aid of Edward Young Clarke and Elizabeth Tyler, lovers and business partners in the fledgling Southern Publicity Association) with staggering success.

By 1921, the Klan had more than one hundred thousand dues-paying members around the country, with its biggest support coming from the Midwest. At ten dollars a head, Simmons and his partners grew rich. They licensed production of Klan paraphernalia, including the robes, to Gate City Manufacturing Company of Atlanta, and controlled their publications through the Searchlight Publishing Company. The Klan even had its own real estate arm, overseen by Clarke.

Despite a spike in racial violence and exposés in newspapers about the dark side of the new Klan, it grew to more than three million members while morphing into a political movement that backed Prohibition and opposed unions and just about anything else that smacked of foreign agitators. Using a law-and-order platform, the Klan elected a governor of Indiana, influenced elections in other states such as Kentucky, and took control of the city of Anaheim, California. In the city that thirty years later would give birth to Disneyland, Klansmen hired as police officers patrolled city streets in their robes. Several states began enacting laws aimed at forcing the secretive Klan into sunlight, adopting laws requiring Klan membership lists to be filed with the state and banning the wearing of masks in public except for such events as masked balls and Halloween.[25]

The Klan in Michigan was a late bloomer, reaching its peak of about eighty thousand members in the mid-1920s. Its strength, not surprisingly, was in the rural areas of the state (it helped elect a mayor in Flint), but it had its adherents in Detroit as well—mostly Protestant whites uncomfortable with the polyglot, increasingly Catholic, and multiracial composition of the city. The state had enacted its own mask ban in 1923, but enforcement relied on the whims of local police and prosecutors. In 1924, Klan-backed candidate Charles Bowles came in third in the 1924 primary election for Detroit mayor but continued a write-in campaign that, had it not been for the disallowance of some fifteen thousand ballots, might have succeeded. His target was incumbent Republican—and German Roman Catholic—John W. Smith, generally described as a veteran ward heeler of the old school who had worked his way up through the party's patronage system. An elementary school dropout and steamfitter by trade, Smith ran his political campaigns from a corner table in a saloon, despite Prohibition. Bowles pursued an antivice platform, but Smith turned the election into a referendum on the Klan itself. Three Klan-backed candidates managed to win council seats in the same election, possibly a voter response to Detroit's standing as among the most violent and crime-ridden cities in the country.

The crime wasn't all part of the Prohibition black market. There were as many as thirty thousand "gangsters" in the city by 1930, and a 1926 report by the American Social Hygiene Association found, using undercover operatives, 570 whorehouses operating openly within one mile of city hall, and another 141 brothels operating surreptitiously (presumably they were trying to avoid paying police bribes). In a six-month period beginning December 1, 1925, some 3,213 women appeared in court on prostitution-related charges. Given the level of corruption, it's hard to imagine what those women had to have done to get themselves arrested, but that's a pace of about seventeen arrests a day.[26]

Amid the ferment, a slightly built African American doctor named Ossian Sweet, born and raised on a Florida farm, and his wife, Gladys, returned to Detroit from a year of medical study in Europe. Sweet had opened a practice in Black Bottom in 1921, then won affiliation with Dunbar Hospital. Upon his return to Detroit from his European sojourn, Sweet wanted to move his wife and infant daughter into a quieter, safer neighborhood than Black Bottom.

There was precedent in Detroit. A few black families had been able to buy homes in white neighborhoods over the years—if they were willing to pay a premium and could get the financing. And black community leaders became inventive in how they addressed those needs. Michigan's first black-owned corporation was formed in 1925 by funeral director Charles Diggs by tapping fellow successful black businessmen as investors in Detroit Memorial Park, a sixty-acre block of land in Warren, just northeast of Detroit. They created an African American cemetery to give their relatives more dignity in death than they received from the established and segregated cemeteries in Detroit. It was highly successful, and within a few years, Detroit Memorial Park began granting home loans to members of the city's black upper class—loans the white-owned banks had refused to extend.[27]

The welcomes these new, and few, black home owners received were mixed. In fact, Sweet's wife's family was living in a white neighborhood, and in the first years of their marriage Sweet and his wife had lived there without notable problems. Other black residents weren't so lucky. Since the early 1920s, new homes built in Detroit invariably came with deed restrictions, assigned by real estate developers, that barred the sale or resale of the property to black families.[28] Older homes didn't have the formal restriction, but many blacks who sought to move in to those white neighborhoods were terrorized into fleeing, often by members of Klan-organized, or Klan-backed, neighborhood "protection associations." So Sweet knew he was rolling the dice when he and his wife decided to buy a two-story bungalow on Garland Avenue in the middle of a mostly Polish American neighborhood. In early September, they moved in, Sweet arranging to keep some friends and his brother with them for the first few days to ensure peace.

It didn't work. On September 10, a mob of more than one thousand whites—under the watchful eyes of Detroit police—began pelting the Sweets' home with rocks and bottles. Gunshots rang out from the second floor, and two white men fell, one fatally wounded.[29]

Sweet, his brother Henry, and several supporters were arrested and charged with murder in a case that riveted the nation. For white supremacists, the shootings were the ultimate expression of all they feared—a violent response by blacks who didn't know their place. For African Americans, and particularly the young National Association for the Advancement of Colored People, the Sweet case was a line in the sand. If a black man couldn't protect his home and family from a white mob in a northern city, then there was no safety anywhere. The case was assigned to a young liberal judge, Frank Murphy, and with funds from the NAACP, Clarence Darrow was hired to lead the defense team, which included Julian W. Perry, a black Detroit lawyer and friend of Sweet's. The first trial ended with a hung jury. In the second trial, focusing solely on Henry Sweet as the gunman, an all-white jury voted for acquittal after a lengthy and impassioned summation from Darrow detailing what it was like to be a black man in America. The charges against Ossian Sweet and the rest of the black defendants were dropped.

The trials didn't change race relations in Detroit—housing remained as segregated as ever, and the practice solidified with the growing use of restrictive deeds and violent "welcome wagons." Within a year of the end of the second trial, Perry, one of Sweet's Detroit lawyers, bought a home in an all-white neighborhood on Detroit's east side, on Marlborough Street near the Grosse Pointe Park border and just a couple of blocks from the riverfront. The house was firebombed, but Perry forged ahead, and by 1930 he and his wife, a schoolteacher, were part of the neighborhood. Like all of their neighbors, they owned a radio, a key consumer luxury of the day, but they were the only black family on their block. And the estimated value of their house, $6,000, was about half that of most of their neighbors' homes.[30]

9

GREAT DEPRESSION

The Roaring Twenties party in Detroit—and elsewhere—ended less abruptly than we think. In retrospect, most look at the stock market meltdown of late October 1929 as the economic collapse that sank into the Great Depression.[1] In truth, signs of the bursting bubble began emerging well before then. (This is a bit of a historical minefield, with debates still ongoing over what really happened to spur the worldwide depression.) In February 1929, concerned over the vast amounts of money the nation's private banks were lending to speculators investing in the stock market, the Federal Reserve asked member banks to "restrain the use, either directly or indirectly, of Federal Reserve credit facilities in aid of the growth of speculative credit." It didn't do much good. Broad consumer faith in the economic boom began to falter, and then turned into a financial panic with the Wall Street sell-off, likely sparked by a mix of scandals and feared regulation of public utilities, and criticism at home and abroad of the "speculative orgy" on Wall Street.

News stories detailed the first hemorrhages, which helped fuel the panic. In rapid order, several million people lost their jobs, their life savings, and their homes. Banks failed across the nation, and personal fortunes large and small evaporated. Small businesses withered and died; home owners were evicted; farmers were booted off land they could no longer afford to tend. In an era of unregulated banking, thousands of

small banks shut their doors, never to reopen, the deposits of their customers gone. By the end of 1931, the Great Depression was on. Billions
of dollars in equity evaporated as the nation's publicly traded companies lost 73 percent of their value through 1932. Ultimately the market
would lose 90 percent of its value.[2]

Every city suffered, but few sank as deeply as Detroit. At the turn
of the century, Detroit had been home to a diverse and vibrant mix
of industries, from stove making to shipbuilding to the manufacturing
of railroad cars, pharmaceuticals, cigars, and clothing. But by the early
1920s, Detroit had effectively become a one-industry town, its massive
growth dependent on the explosively successful—but recession-prone—
auto factories. Even in good times auto companies oversaw inconsistent
production schedules, with entire factories shutting down for weeks at
a time as assembly lines were adjusted for new models. Auto workers'
sporadic unemployment became chronic with the onset of the Great
Depression. The automotive industry was one of the key girders of the
American economy, and when the economy collapsed, Detroit fell with
it, attaining a level of economic paralysis worse than most of the rest
of the nation—establishing a trend that continues into the twenty-first
century.[3]

At the time, the vast majority of American cars were being manufac-
tured in or around Detroit, so a look at the drop in national production
can be seen as Detroit's loss as much as the nation's. In 1920, American
auto companies produced nearly 2.3 million cars and trucks, and the
total number of vehicles registered with state motor vehicle departments
reached 9.2 million (look at it as "cars in circulation"). In 1929, the year
of the stock market crash, nearly 5.5 million vehicles were produced, and
26.5 million were registered to operate on the nation's roadways. But
in 1932, as the Depression hit its worst stretch, Detroit produced fewer
than 1.4 million vehicles, and the total number of registered vehicles had
dropped to 24.1 million. In a span of three years, auto production withered to one-quarter of what it had been. By July 1930, nine months after
the stock market collapse, a third of Detroit's auto jobs had disappeared,
leaving more than 150,000 men idle and without incomes, and more job
cuts were on the horizon. Absent a meaningful safety net, foreclosures

skyrocketed, cars were repossessed, and homelessness grew. And banks that had once been thought secure began teetering.[4]

Back at the turn of the century, Detroit banks had been relatively minor and local institutions. It was a city of significant wealth, reaped from the forests and mines of the north, but when it came time to bankroll the construction of the auto industry's massive factories, the commercial banking was done from afar—New York City and Chicago, primarily. By the mid-1920s, Detroit's industrialists, seeing Detroit as one of the nation's now-premier centers of industry, thought they should have their own Detroit-based commercial banking services. In 1927, a group of local bankers, with auto executives tagged for seats on the board of directors, formed the Guardian Detroit Bank, which consisted of a traditional bank, an investment branch, and a trust company. Edsel Ford, Henry Ford's only child, was a key player despite his father's misgivings about banks, and it grew quickly, developing a reputation as the auto companies' bank. Guardian merged with or swallowed up twenty-three other banks or trust companies. To stay competitive, in 1930 rival bankers formed the Detroit Bankers Company around the existing First National Bank of Detroit, despite the deepening economic crisis. It quickly grew to encompass forty smaller banks, in effect giving Detroit two behemoths.

Detroit's new and mighty industrial banks proved to be as vulnerable as the small farm-based banks in the Great Plains. By February 1933, the Guardian bank was insolvent and turned in desperation to the federal Reconstruction Finance Corporation (RFC) for loans to bail it out. The RFC required that there be sufficient assets to cover the loans, and Guardian didn't have them. To keep Guardian alive, Alfred P. Sloan Jr., who ran General Motors, and Walter P. Chrysler agreed to keep one million dollars of their companies' deposits in the bank. But Ford—a banking skeptic—refused to pledge to keep his $7.5 million in assets in the bank. After several days of complicated negotiations, and direct pleas from President Herbert Hoover to Ford, the automaker still refused unless there were guarantees that his money would be safe. He further warned that he would also withdraw $20 million in deposits from the First National Bank, part of the rival Detroit Bankers Company, forcing both of Detroit's giant banking institutions into insolvency. Part of Ford's impetus was his belief that the bad banks needed to fail, on philosophical grounds, regardless of the effect on their hundreds of thousands of depositors—many of them his current and former workers.

To avoid the failure, newly inaugurated Governor William Comstock was persuaded to declare a bank holiday to give the banks time to regain their footing. On February 14, 1933, he ordered all state and federally chartered banks in Michigan to close until February 21, shuttering 550 banks holding $1.5 billion in assets owned by some 900,000 people. Detroit, with a population of nearly 1.6 million, was out of cash.

The effect spread. If the Detroit banks, filled with the fortunes of people like Henry Ford, could be forced to the brink of extinction, no bank was safe in the eyes of the nation's depositors, and the fatal bank run began. By the time Roosevelt was sworn in as president on March 4, 1933, nearly every bank in the country was on "holiday," or operating under restrictions over how much money depositors could withdraw. Once he was in the Oval Office, Roosevelt declared a national banking holiday.

"We had a bad banking situation," Roosevelt said in a national radio address announcing the suspensions. "Some of our bankers had shown themselves either incompetent or dishonest in their handling of the people's funds. They had used the money entrusted to them in speculations and unwise loans. This was of course not true in the vast majority of our banks but it was true in enough of them to shock the people for a time into a sense of insecurity and to put them into a frame of mind where they did not differentiate, but seemed to assume that the acts of a comparative few had tainted them all. It was the government's job to straighten out this situation and do it as quickly as possible."

It was a remarkable step, shutting down the nation's banking system. But it created breathing room and spawned significant structural reforms that set the foundation for the modern American banking system.

Economics and politics are inextricably linked, and the political implications of the Great Depression in Detroit were significant. In November

1929, as the stock market was reeling, Bowles, the former Klan-backed mayoral candidate, finally won the office, still campaigning on an anti-crime platform. It turned out he was anticrime in voice only, as evidenced by a chain of events that cost him critical political support. His ascension to the mayor's office was followed by a spike in gangland slayings that the police seemed unable to address, in part because Bowles had fired several top-level career police officials. In May, Bowles went to Louisville to attend the Kentucky Derby. While he was gone, his newly appointed police commissioner ordered a series of effective raids on illegal gambling dens that had been the subject of newspaper exposes. When Bowles returned, he fired the commissioner, furthering rumors that he was tied to Detroit's gangsters. And then came the gangland hit on Gerald E. "Jerry" Buckley, a radio broadcaster who had been critical of Bowles's administration.

The timing of Buckley's murder was significant. Bowles won the mayor's race the previous November, but his political support was not very deep or loyal. After the scandal surrounding the firing of the police commissioner, recall petitions were circulated that forced a public vote in July on whether a new election should be held. Buckley was a loud and persistent voice in the recall campaign, part of a populist persona he had established two years earlier when he began his radio career after working as an investigator for Henry Ford. He had gained a loyal following among Detroiters who liked his on-air tirades against the city's pervasive gambling rackets and gangland violence, his lobbying for financial aid to elderly unemployed workers, and his advocacy for government jobs programs to mitigate the effects of the Depression. His support for the recall, which he regularly repeated in speeches before different civic groups, made him one of the most visible of Detroit's unelected political players. But he was a controversial figure, too, with purported links to some of Detroit's underworld figures and, despite being a married father of one, was rumored to be an undiscriminating womanizer.[5]

The vote on whether to hold a recall was held July 22, 1930. Buckley had spent the evening reporting the results on radio station WMBC, whose studios were in the Hotel LaSalle, one of the city's largest hotels, at the corner of Woodward and Adelaide near the ghetto area of Brush

Park. Bowles lost; the recall was approved by voters, to be held in September in an election in which Bowles automatically would stand as a candidate.

Just after the station went off the air at midnight, Buckley fielded a phone call from a woman and was overheard agreeing to meet her "in about an hour." Buckley, who lived at 4031 Pasadena Avenue, near Livernois and Davison, about six miles from downtown, finished his work and walked his secretary down to the hotel lobby door after 1 AM, where he helped her into a cab. He reentered the hotel and took a seat in a stuffed curved-back armchair, where he began reading an extra edition of one of the Detroit papers with reports on the recall vote results. A colleague, radio operator Jack Klein, sat a few feet away. Buckley was paged in the lobby around 1:30 AM for a call from his secretary reporting that she had reached home safely and was back in the chair before 1:40 AM, paper in front of him. In front of several witnesses in the lobby, three men walked in from outside, surrounded Buckley in a semicircle from the back, and opened fire, shredding the newsman with eleven bullets, six of them striking a four-inch-square at the back of the head. Klein fled, and the other witnesses ducked for cover, none reporting later that they had seen the shots being fired. Buckley was pronounced dead at the hospital but had likely perished instantly.

The murder galvanized Michigan law enforcement, in part because of Buckley's celebrity, and in part because his was the eleventh gangland slaying in nineteen days. Buckley himself had witnessed two mobsters being gunned down in a doorway of the LaSalle just a few days earlier.

Governor Fred Green, in western Michigan at the time, flew into Detroit on a National Guard plane and ordered the head of the state police and other top state officials to meet him as soon as they could. By the morning after the killing, Green had announced that the state police would conduct their own investigation, implying that the Detroit police were too tainted by mob connections to be trusted. And he warned that he was contemplating dispatching the National Guard to Detroit to quell the violence. That same morning, the Detroit City Council met to announce a $5,000 reward and demanded Mayor Bowles reappoint the deposed police officials to help out with the investigation (they later relented). Bowles publicly lamented Buckley's death but was generally believed to have been involved. He was trounced in the ensuing special recall election by Frank Murphy, who had been the presiding judge in the Ossian Sweet trials and would later serve on the US Supreme Court.

Buckley's popularity, and the pressing issue of organized crime, preordained that his killing would carry political overtones. Some twenty thousand people showed up at his house two days after the killing to pay their respects, forming a line up to six abreast stretching for several blocks. Some forty police officers were dispatched to keep order, but the crowd was quiet, as though drained of energy.

Eventually seven people were indicted in the killing. The three alleged gunmen—all with mob ties—were the first to go on trial. Eyewitnesses told police and the grand jury that they had seen the men enter the building, but fear of reprisals led one to refuse to testify at trial (he was held in contempt) and legal maneuverings kept the testimony of the others from the jury. After more than thirty hours of occasionally boisterous deliberations—the shouts could be heard outside the jury room—the gunmen were acquitted on April 21, 1931. The prosecutions ended, the case officially unsolved, though the accused gunmen were later convicted of other murders and robberies.

Buckley's murder, and the subsequent acquittal of what most likely were his assassins, further established Detroit's reputation as a dark gangland paradise, without the folk hero overlay of Chicago (Al Capone) or New York (Lucky Luciano and Frank Costello, among others). Detroit had its own mob families, including the Zerrilis, the Toccos, and the Licavolis, but its underworld was more defined publicly by the Purple Gang, a loose-knit group of Jewish thugs who got rich hijacking trucks, targeting both legitimate cargo and illicit booze. It was a murderous gang, and the local media became infatuated with its exploits until, in the early 1930s, the gang was decimated by a series of arrests and convictions.

The stories of gangland feuds and killings were diversions from the deeper agony that spread across Detroit in the early 1930s. Unemployment was high and deep poverty endemic. Detroit tax revenues topped $143 million in 1929; by 1934, it had dropped to under $112 million as demands for services—especially by the jobless—skyrocketed. The

city Department of Welfare reported that in December 1930, before the
worst of the Depression had occurred, it had spent more than $1.6 mil-
lion supporting 39,000 destitute families. In January 1931, it was receiving some five hundred fresh applications for help each day, a seemingly peakless crescendo of hunger and hopelessness. At the same time,
another department was finding beds for five thousand homeless single
men each night and providing meals for twelve thousand people a day.
One of Mayor Murphy's first steps after assuming office in early 1931
was to form an Emergency Committee to try to devise new ways of
dealing with the rising tide. It organized clothing drives, distributing
items to ninety-two thousand people through January 31. It matched
the unemployed with jobs: in the first three months it placed 2,000
men in permanent jobs, 8,000 in temporary city jobs, 665 in Christmas-
season post office jobs, and set up another 700 as street vendors selling apples. Another 2,544 women were placed in unspecified jobs, as
well. But those successes were slight in the face of the spiraling need. In
the week of January 21, the committee was housing and feeding 5,876
destitute men and providing just meals to another 6,336. Both figures
were several hundred clients higher than the previous week's report. And
desperation grew along with the hunger. In 1931, Detroit recorded 568
suicides; in 1927, there had been 113.[6]

Private efforts were overwhelmed, as well. On Detroit's east side,
across Mount Elliott Street from the Elmwood Cemetery, the last resting
spot for most of Detroit's historically significant citizens, the Capuchin
Brothers' monastery found a steady stream of the hungry showing up
at its doors, hoping for help from the Franciscan friars. The brothers
began collecting excess food from restaurants and grocery stores, including perishables on the verge of rot, and opened a daily soup kitchen as
a stopgap measure to help until the hungry could feed themselves. In
a mark of the pervasiveness of need in Detroit, and the persistence of
unemployment in the industrial economy, the soup kitchen has never
closed. Today it remains one of the backbones of efforts to help feed the
homeless, including a growing movement to convert empty space in
Detroit into sustainable local gardens.

The City of Detroit's efforts to help were compounded by an anom-
aly of place and of attitude by Henry Ford and some of the other auto

barons. Ford, once the darling of Detroit, had by now become a popular target for protest, a function of his draconian factory policies, the violent invasiveness of his antiunion forces (including a secret security unit within the factories), his raging anti–Semitism, and the wealth he had amassed. For many Detroiters, Ford personified the coldhearted corporation and the soul–deadening assembly line. With the onset of the Depression, Ford had laid off tens of thousands of his workers, further feeding class resentment. The relatively few people who still worked for Ford labored under an intense "speed up" campaign in which workers were expected to radically increase their output to offset some of the labor lost by layoffs. In some places, a single worker was tasked with operating two dangerous drill presses at once.[7]

In January 1931, Ford announced he would hire back 107,000 workers, mostly men. The news was trumpeted in Detroit as a possible turning point in the Depression at large, and in Detroit's misfortune in particular. But the announcement was smoke and mirrors. By then the Ford Motor Company had become an international presence, and many of the jobs for which Ford was rehiring were not in Detroit. And most of the Detroit hires were actually men Ford had laid off just a few weeks before, in mid–December, in an effort to avoid building up a surplus of inventory. So the 107,000 "new" hires had virtually no effect on Detroit's staggering long–term unemployment problem. The "good news" was revealed as an obvious public relations manipulation, adding to cynicism about the auto giant.

Additionally, Ford's major local factories were outside the city limits, in Highland Park and in Dearborn, which meant that the City of Detroit—where the vast majority of unemployed Ford workers lived— was receiving no tax revenues from Ford. City officials approached Ford, asking him for cash donations to help with the relief programs supporting his former workers. Two out of five city welfare recipients had worked at factories outside the city boundaries, and half of those had been Ford workers. But Ford had a standing corporate policy to not donate to local relief groups such as the Community Fund, an unusually coldhearted stance even in good times.

By March 1932, the city welfare office was helping support twenty-seven thousand families and announced that it had to turn away another twenty thousand applications from desperate parents.[8] The city's budget crunch was so severe it rolled back teacher salaries 10 percent and reduced the length of the school year by one month. The hungry made nocturnal raids on small garden patches and stole the milk from porches in well-to-do neighborhoods. Ford could have helped alleviate some of that suffering, but chose not to.[9]

The frustration, hunger, and anger at Ford boiled over on March 7, 1932. Communist organizers had been active in Detroit, seeing in its collapse the fodder for revolution. The previous day, William Z. Foster, the head of the American Communist Party, delivered a speech at Detroit's Danceland Arena, on Woodward Avenue near Forest. He was joined by such notable Detroit communist activists as John Schmies, who had recently mounted an irrelevant primary campaign for mayor. (The election was won by Murphy, the incumbent.) Together they delivered a scathing indictment of what they saw as the evils of the capitalist system, using the broad joblessness and hunger of Detroit as prima facie evidence that American capitalist leaders had become rich at the expense of the working class. And they urged the crowd—a liberal estimate put it at four thousand—to join a march planned for the next day organized by the Detroit Unemployed Council and the struggling Auto, Aircraft, and Vehicles Workers of America union.

The plan was for a "hunger march" on the employment office at Ford's River Rouge complex, a display of bodies meant to pressure Ford to both hire back some of his workers and to spend some of his own money alleviating the needs of the others. The organizers had a full roster of fourteen demands, including rehiring all laid-off Ford workers, a seven-hour day with no wage reduction from eight hours, no discrimination against blacks, rations of coke or coal for home furnaces, a fifty-dollar "winter relief" bonus, and a recognition of the right to organize a union. None of those were likely to gain Ford's approval under any circumstances, but the men planned to march anyway. At the very least, it would give them a chance to vent their frustrations.[10]

The men began gathering around 12:30 PM on a street corner in southwest Detroit, a bitterly cold day whipped by a winter wind from the river. Some five thousand people, mostly men, turned out, bundled against the cold and carrying signs: GIVE US WORK, WE WANT BREAD, NOT CRUMBS, and TAX THE RICH AND FEED THE POOR. Some seventy Detroit police officers were on hand; organizers had alerted the city that they had planned the march. The crowd grew quickly, many leaping off trolley cars without paying the fare (the system was pay-as-you-leave).

The organizers had parked a flatbed truck near the intersection of Fort Street and Miller Road, and Albert Goetz, one of the two prime organizers, warned that Dearborn police and Ford's private security forces were already in place at the city line, and that the march would likely meet strong resistance. "We don't want any violence," he yelled over the crowd, the frigid wind whipping his words away. "Remember, all we are going to do is to walk to the Ford employment office. No trouble, no fighting. Stay in line. Be orderly. I understand the Dearborn police are planning to stop us. Well, we will try to get through somehow. But remember, no trouble."[11]

Lined up eight abreast, the marchers made their way down Miller Road toward the Dearborn line, where they met the blockade of some fifty Dearborn police officers and Ford security men. The marchers refused to stop and the police launched tear gas canisters into the middle of the throng. As the police began moving forward swinging batons, the crowd dispersed, but didn't retreat. Instead, they spread out over a wide area, including the high ground of a railroad trestle. The marchers began fighting back by throwing rocks and other debris. The stiff winter wind quickly whisked away the tear gas, making it relatively ineffective.

Vastly outnumbered, the police began to retreat. The marchers pushed forward about a half-mile until they hit a second line of defense: two fire trucks whose crews were desperately trying to connect hoses to hydrants, but who failed before the mob reached them. The firefighters joined the police and security forces in a fast retreat to Gate No. 3 at the Rouge plant, near a pedestrian bridge from the parking lot across Miller Road from the factory. More firefighters with hoses lined the bridge. A phalanx of Dearborn police and Ford security guards augmented by Detroit city police and Michigan state troopers, whose presence would be the subject of later inquiries, was arrayed directly below. As the marchers neared, the hoses were turned on and more tear gas was vaulted into the crowd. Armed with stones from nearby fields, the marchers responded with a bruising hailstorm. The police, still vastly outnumbered, opened fire.

At least twenty-two of the marchers were hit, three of whom were killed. The rest fell back, stunned and battered. The organizers feared more bloodshed and hastily called off the demonstration, urging their marchers to leave. As one of the leaders was shouting directions, a car roared out of Gate No. 3. A window opened and a man inside—Harry Bennett, Ford's notorious security chief—opened fire with a handgun. The crowd again fell away as another fusillade of rocks was aimed at the car. Bennett stepped out and was demanding a second gun from one of the security detail with him when a rock struck him in the head, sending him crumpling to the ground. The police and guards opened fire again, including one man who used a tommy gun to sweep Miller Road. Several more of the marchers were hit, and another one was killed. The remaining marchers scrambled to get outside of easy gun range, leaving Miller Road littered with rocks, the dead, and the wounded.[12]

In all, four people were killed and a fifth, Curtis Williams, died three months later of his wounds.[13] At least twenty-nine other people were seriously injured, and nearly fifty people in all suffered some sort of wound or injury.

Within hours of the confrontation, Dearborn and Detroit police began raiding the homes of march participants and known union sympathizers and communists. They also arrested those under medical care; several were handcuffed to their hospital beds. The police initially blamed the marchers for the violence, and the communists in particular. Early news accounts reported such phantom details as a communist in a car opening fire to start the gun battle between the police and the protesters, but no evidence ever surfaced that any of the demonstrators had a gun, let alone fired one.

District attorney Harry S. Toy announced that he wanted to round up communist activists, including Foster, the national leader, for a grand jury investigation. But within days the public sentiment shifted. Maurice Sugar, a Detroit attorney with radical inclinations (he was sentenced to prison for refusing to register for the World War I draft), was hired to defend the arrested demonstrators. As part of his investigation, he arranged to have an independent medical doctor monitor the autopsies of the four dead marchers, but that permission was rescinded at the last minute. The autopsies were conducted in private, and the bullets recovered from the bodies were given to the Dearborn police department, returning the evidence to some of the men who fired the fatal shots.[14] A grand jury later refused to indict anyone in the killings—and blamed outside agitators for riling up the marchers.

But the agitators were not from the outside. The roots of Detroit's working-class confrontations with Ford and other factory owners were local. Among those sought for arrest was William Reynolds, a former candidate for mayor of Lincoln Park (a small downriver city near the Rouge plant) and a leader of the local Unemployed Council. Reynolds was already free on bail as he appealed a ninety-day jail sentence for disorderly conduct stemming from a demonstration the previous October in Lincoln Park, in which police accused him and fellow leftists of rushing the jail to try to free a comrade. All that history was duly reported on the front pages of the *Detroit Free Press* and the *Detroit News* the day after the Ford Rouge killings, including an odd reference that described Reynolds as a recent "victim of the lashings administered to Communistic sympathizers by hooded men at Dearborn." There were no more details on the beating or who might have been beneath those hoods.

It turns out they were early members of a secretive and fast-growing organization of protofascists who called themselves the Black Legion, and who over the next several years would be responsible for a series of beatings, kidnappings, and murders, all in the name of a white, noncommunist, WASPish America.[15]

10

THE BLACK LEGION

The Black Legion began in 1925 as a self-proclaimed elite unit of the Ku Klux Klan in Bellaire, Ohio, a small coal-country town just down the Ohio River from Wheeling, West Virginia. The founder was a local Klansman and medical doctor, William Jacob Shepard, who sought to add yet another layer of mystery and pageantry to the Klan's rituals. He also had a soft spot for romanticized visions of chivalry in the Deep South, and a penchant for vigilante justice. They were to become a potent combination.

Shepard's Black Legion debuted at an August 1925 meeting of the Ohio Klan at Buckeye Lake in central Ohio. It was a massive gathering, drawing up to one hundred thousand Klansmen, who heard political speeches, watched some skits and even witnessed a few Klan weddings. Shepard's unit showed up wearing black robes with red trim, the inverse of the traditional white Klan robes. They appointed themselves guards of the barrels into which the Klan conventioneers deposited contributions, a highly visible role and a bit of shrewd marketing.

In time, the Ohio Klan leaders bounced Shepard and his black-robed followers from the Klan, fearing Shepard might have ambitions on their leadership positions—and the cash that came with the members' ten-dollar dues. "They thought I was trying to organize something that would replace the Klan, but I wasn't," Shepard said later. "I was a good Klansman and I never denied it. I liked the work."

The idea of an even more secretive order of the Klan was infectious, though, and the Black Legion grew. Its mission wasn't the race-based fundraising fraternalism of the second rising of the Klan. Its mission was vigilantism, and its core practices were secret meetings and night rides to enforce "community sexual and racial standards by intermittent violence."[1]

In 1932, after the second rising of the Klan had largely collapsed under the weight of public exposure and some sex scandals (though vestiges remained, particularly in the Deep South), Shepard lost control of his organization in part scam, part bloodless internal coup, to Virgil H. "Bert" Effinger, described by historian Peter H. Amman as "a burly, pot-bellied electrician from Lima, Ohio."

Effinger took over as the world, at least as his generation of Americans had known it, was disintegrating. The nation was jobless, banks were bankrupt, homes were lost—and people like Effinger saw the invisible hands of Jews behind it all. Fueled by racism and fear, Effinger's new Black Legion grew explosively across Ohio, Indiana, Illinois, and Michigan, its secret membership rolls nearing one hundred thousand. Many were conscripted. Men would be invited to a sports event or card game, only to be forcibly recruited to the Black Legion, complete with taking an oath of secrecy weighted by ominous warnings of death. In some cases, the forced recruits were inducted in the same ceremony in which a renegade would be "hanged"—a staged event in which the victim wore a harness and pretended to die. But the message was effective.

Amazingly for a group that size, the Black Legion attracted little publicity as it grew, even though its members included politicians, high-ranking policemen (favored because of their comfort within a para-military organization), and other high-profile figures. Some joined seemingly unaware of the violent underside of the organization, much like one would join the Elks Club. In Lima, Ohio, the Black Legion members included nearly all the caseworkers for the federal Emergency Relief Administration, who subsequently denied help to blacks, Jews,

Catholics, and others while giving aid to fellow Legionnaires. Meetings were cloaked by front organizations, such as Michigan's Malteka Club and the Wolverine Republican Club—a mainstream political organization—and secrecy was maintained through intimidation and violence.

But the group's focus was external: blacks, Jews, and Catholics, as well as union organizers and political radicals. An unknown number of people like Reynolds, the Lincoln Park communist, were beaten, many hospitalized, and several were killed. But police, either through complicity or through lack of investigative imagination (that the victims were black or union organizers didn't help), failed to link up victims' reports that they had been beaten by hooded men.

In December 1933, the Black Legion committed what is believed to be its first murder—a single gunshot to the head of UAW organizer George Marchuk in Lincoln Park, a few miles downriver from Detroit. His death was considered a suicide until the Black Legion was exposed three years later.[2] Another organizer, John L. Bielak, was found dead near Monroe, Michigan, in March 1934 with five bullets in his body. Labor camps were bombed, too, though without fatalities.[3] Several blacks were targeted for violence, including one man Legionnaire Dayton Dean and his comrades tried to track down but couldn't find. So they shot black steelworker Edward Armour, simply because their paths crossed. Another black man, Silas Coleman, was lured by Dean's compatriot, Harvey Davis, to a lake cottage in Pinckney, northwest of Ann Arbor, where he was shot because Davis wanted to experience "what it felt like to kill a nigger." The body was dumped in a swamp.

Black Legion members murdered their own as well. Roy Pitcock, of Wyandotte, Michigan, another downriver city, was found hanged, his outer clothes missing, on Fighting Island—on the Canadian side of the Detroit River—after he refused a Legion order to leave his Catholic wife, who, it had been discovered, had lived with another man before the marriage. There were plots to murder Catholic politicians in Highland Park and Ecorse. The leftist lawyer Maurice Sugar, who represented the victims in the Ford Hunger March, was also on the group's death list. (Sugar would later conduct his own investigation, and his files are in the Walter Reuther Library in Detroit.)

As the violent campaign played out, the legion began talking about a new order in America, an America-first government that would be led by Effinger, even if it had to come from the barrels of their guns. They explored using typhoid to infect their "enemies." Effinger hatched a plan to kill one million Jews by installing secret timer-triggered devices in synagogues that would simultaneously release mustard gas during Yom Kippur services; he had one of the machines on display in his office in Lima, Ohio.

Ironically, the Black Legion, manifestly anti-Catholic, was gaining traction at the same time Father Charles Coughlin, a Roman Catholic priest assigned to suburban Detroit's National Shrine of the Little Flower parish, had become one of the nation's most popular radio broadcasters by pounding on overlapping America-first themes. His program had begun in 1926 as a fundraising mechanism to retire the $101,000 debt from the construction of the church and grew to be one of the most influential in the nation. After CBS dropped him in 1931 because he refused to provide advance scripts for his increasingly controversial and racist broadcasts, Coughlin built his own radio network in a precursor of the modern televangelism movement. Initially a backer of FDR and his New Deal, Coughlin had turned increasingly antigovernment—and anti-Semitic—during the depths of the Depression. From Louisiana, Huey Long was also reaching a national audience through sporadic radio broadcasts and his Share Our Wealth Society.

Though their messages were disparate, the Black Legion, Coughlin, and Long touched interconnected nerves of fear in a desperate nation. For masses of people looking to affix blame somewhere, the Black Legion, Coughlin, and Long gave them structure. "Long and Coughlin were . . . outsiders, speaking for outsiders, in a society increasingly dominated by an educated middle class closely allied to the national corporate institutions of industrial America," according to historian Alan Brinkley. "Long and Coughlin were, second, both imbued with the ideological currents of populism, broadly defined."[4] Similar conditions had helped give rise to fascism in Germany and Italy. While fascism never flowered into a broad movement in the United States, it had its moments in Detroit.

The Black Legion incarnation of the invisible empire came crumbling down in 1936 with the discovery of the body of Charles A. Poole along a deserted road west of Dearborn. Poole was a thirty-two-year-old jobless autoworker, scraping by on a Works Progress Administration project, a Catholic married to a Protestant woman who was expecting their second child any day. One of her relatives, who was a Legion member, passed on a rumor that Poole had been beating her (one account says that was a lie, told because he was upset she had married a Catholic). Dean and a half-dozen others were dispatched to teach Poole a lesson with a beating, the irony seemingly beyond their grasp. Poole was approached in a bar by some of the Legion members and lured away under a ruse of going to get fitted for a uniform so he could join a factory baseball team. He was beaten, then shot five times and left dead in a ditch. A week later one of the men who had been drinking with Poole pointed out Davis, a "colonel" in the Black Legion and the killer of Silas Coleman, as the man who had talked Poole into leaving the bar. Police quickly rounded up more than a dozen of Davis's colleagues, including Dean, the triggerman, who proved to be surprisingly loquacious once he learned he had killed a man based on a bad rumor. He readily admitted his guilt and named the others involved.[5]

Dean's revelations brought the dark secrets of the Black Legion into the spotlight. He detailed killings and beatings in which he had been involved. People he named in turn named others, and the oath of secrecy was whisked away by their confessions and finger-pointing. Sixteen people were indicted in the Poole killing, and prosecutions in some of the other cases followed, though they proved to be hard cases to win since the key evidence was testimony by Dean—by then a convicted felon and admitted murderer. Still, high-level Legionnaires, including Wayne County prosecutor Duncan McCrea, tripped over themselves in their rush to disavow any connections with the violence. In fact, McCrea's prosecutions would send eleven of his former Legion brothers to prison for the rest of their lives in a trial that riveted Detroit and spawned nationwide headlines. With rumors that some of the Legion's targets were selected by antiunion thugs, leftist labor organizers viewed the Black Legion as an affirmation of the lengths industrial leaders would go to fight them.

But the Black Legion's violence had been disturbingly infectious. On June 5, 1936, three people—Raymond Buccellatti, Armando Serali, and Joseph Angelo—had taken captive two others—Albert Valenti and Joseph Ignono. When police arrived (it's unclear who summoned them) at a barn on Detroit's east side, they found Valenti and Ignono tied up. The three kidnappers had tied one end of a separate rope to a beam in a loft and a noose on the other end was around Valenti's neck; they were about to push him over the edge of the loft. Valenti was eleven; the oldest of his captors and would-be executioners was fourteen. "We didn't want these guys to go to school," Buccellatti told police. "Their marks are too good, so we were going to do like the Black Legion does."[6]

State police estimated as many as fifty killings could be attributed to the Legion, but most went unconfirmed, primarily due to lack of evidence and problems with the reliability of the witnesses within the Legion. But the organization's fascist undertone was taken up by Hollywood with the 1936 Warner Bros. film, *Black Legion*. Despite a disclaimer at the start of the movie, which was Humphrey Bogart's first starring role, the plot line of disaffected white worker Frank Taylor joining the Legion to "save America" was clearly drawn by the shape of the Poole killing. Part of Taylor's impetus is listening to a radio broadcast reminiscent of Father Coughlin, blaming foreigners for the predicaments of white Americans.[7]

For Detroit's growing African American population, the existence of the racist Black Legion, and the black men it had murdered, were chilling reminders that even though they were now in the North, old hatreds transcended place. Racism still plays a formative role in the differing ways in which black Detroiters view local police and political authorities and the ways in which whites view them. A history of lynching and summary executions, of police brutality, of marginalization of blacks as crime victims, of overt and covert racism when it came to getting jobs, getting housing, getting the basic respect due a citizen of a community, they all came into play as Detroit progressed through the 1950s, 1960s, and 1970s. Whether the robes were white or black, and no matter what the vigilantes called themselves, black Detroiters saw the movement for what it was—the Klan, and a mortal threat with deep political and law-enforcement connections.

11

HOUSING AND THE
RACIAL DIVIDE

Working and living conditions in Detroit didn't improve much through the 1930s, though there were some efforts to help those who were the worst off. On September 9, 1935, First Lady Eleanor Roosevelt traveled to Detroit for the symbolic start of slum clearance in Black Bottom, part of a $6.6 million federal program to replace dilapidated shacks with new public housing called the Brewster Homes.[1] It was a moment of grand pageantry, with the First Lady's comments broadcast live by WJR 760 radio. But the ceremony began with a visual display. Just after 3:30 PM, Roosevelt waved a handkerchief in the air as a signal and a truck roared to life. It was at one end of a cable; the other was attached to a house at 651 Benton Street. As the truck slowly moved forward the house shook and creaked, then crashed to the ground in a flurry of splintering timber and falling bricks that sent a cloud of dust wafting across the crowd of some twenty thousand onlookers.

The First Lady then told the audience that the neighborhood was a slumlord's paradise, with 92 percent of the tax payments delinquent (most of the homes were rentals), a crime rate six times the city average, and "juvenile delinquency" ten times the average. Tuberculosis was rampant, more than seven times the city average. All of that affected the public weal. "You must all rejoice today that this great work has begun," she said, her tight, wavering voice carrying through the public address system, the dust still hanging in the late-summer air. "It means much to those directly affected, but it also means much to Detroit as a whole. . . . It is lack of social consciousness which permits such conditions to develop, but we may thank the Depression for focusing attention on these sore spots in our social life."[2]

Yet the housing program didn't help the people whose homes were razed. Months later, the new development still had not broken ground. More than one hundred families had been evicted with no other place to go. All were black, and despite purported policies aimed at helping the families relocate, few received any help. Most wound up living in housing just as bad, or worse, than the housing from which they had been evicted.

Karen Dash, a social-agency official, described homes of abject squalor in an article on the program for the *Nation* magazine. One house held thirteen people—four adults and nine children. The sole breadwinner had been out of steady work for four years, when his job with the city garbage department had been cut. "Things are so bad," one of the adult women told her, "they just couldn't be any worse." Families that were getting by on twelve dollars a month, and paying rents of three to ten dollars a month, had trouble finding new rentals they could afford. Dash found the going rate in nearby neighborhoods was between ten and twenty dollars a month. One wood-frame house on Alfred Street in Brush Park, the one-time neighborhood of Detroit's nouveau riche, had been divided into four apartments. The front steps had rotted away. Inside, rainwater seeped through walls and the roof, and wallpaper hung in dissolved ribbons over sodden floors. "There was no stove to heat the flat, no gas, no electric lights," Dash wrote. "In many places the plaster had fallen away, exposing the bare laths. . . . There were no faucets in the rusty old sink, no covering on the floor, no cook stove, no icebox. In the bathroom, a bathtub stood in one corner. Three of its legs were gone, and it was not connected with the water pipes. The toilet had obviously been out of order for months." The rent: twelve dollars a month.[3]

The breadth of poverty in the city, and the desperation of the working class, set the foundation for a radical transformation in the relationship between the bulk of the city's working class and the industrialists for whom they worked. After FDR took office, the federal government became more supportive of workers' rights to organize, including passage of the Wagner Act, which gave enforcement power to the new National Labor Relations Board (NLRB). Emboldened union supporters—many of them communists or socialists—began tapping into the frustrations of idle workers, achieving what had once seemed impossible in capitalist-friendly, "open shop" Detroit: the growth of unions.

Typical slum home of black Detroiters seeking to move into Sojourner Truth homes, 1942. ARTHUR S. SIEGEL, LIBRARY OF CONGRESS, FSA/OWI COLLECTION (LC-USW3-016679-E)

Given the dominance of the auto industry—it accounted for some 60 percent of Detroit's jobs—the new United Auto Workers similarly became the dominant union in Detroit.[4] It also became an integral part of the new Congress of Industrial Organizations (CIO), a rival to the American Federation of Labor (AFL), which focused on skilled trades. (Samuel Gompers, the AFL's legendary founding president, had been a cigar maker.)

The UAW was born in fits and spurts, finally achieving success with a series of sit-down strikes in 1935 and 1936. It was an ingenious solution used successfully in strikes against Goodyear in Akron, Ohio, and Bendix Products in South Bend, Indiana, to resolve the inherent problem of going on strike. If workers laid down their tools and set up picket lines, the car companies would simply hire a fresh crew of workers from the tens of thousands of desperately jobless men, and use court injunctions backed by strike-breaking thugs to ensure the new hires were able to clear picket lines and man the assembly lines. But with the sit-down strikes, the auto workers refused to leave the factories, barricading themselves inside and using jury-rigged weapons—door hinges heaved from a roof were surprisingly effective—to keep security guards and police from physically ousting them. A factory besieged by a sit-down strike meant an idle assembly line, with the union supporters literally control-ling the means of production. And community support, even by local small businesses, began to line up behind the union movement as shop owners recognized that better-paid autoworkers meant better sales. In early 1937, General Motors was the first of the Big Three automakers to capitulate, signing a one-page agreement recognizing the UAW as the bargaining agent for its workers. The other manufacturers, as well as parts suppliers, slowly followed.

Ford, not surprisingly, was the last of the major auto companies to recognize the UAW. And it was a brutal organizing fight that had racial undertones. For years, Ford had been by far the most open of the Big Three to hire black workers, whom Ford's employment office selected based on recommendations from black church leaders vouching for the job candidates' "good moral character." That led to an informal system of preachers being hiring agents for Ford, and they rewarded him by only sending along potential workers who would be loyal to the man—and the company—that would hire them when others would not. It was an understandable point of view given the wide gap in quality of life for blacks with jobs and those without. Exacerbating the organizing prob-lem were Ford's internal spying apparatus and whites in the workforce—and in the UAW—who balked at uniting or working with blacks.[5]

Ford fought the union with a religious fervor. Suspected union sym-pathizers were summarily fired, and organizers often suffered beatings by members of Ford's security team, under the direction of Harry Bennett. Ford flouted the new laws of the National Labor Relations Act, which led to a series of complaints and trials.

But organizing campaigns are won in the streets and on the fac-tory floors. On March 23, 1937, young organizer Walter Reuther and three other union officials, including Richard Frankensteen, were pos-ing for a picture at the request of a *Detroit News* photographer on the Miller Road overpass from a parking lot to the Ford Rouge factory, near the site of the Hunger March killings. A throng of Ford security men entered the overpass and jumped the union men, severely beating them (one suffered a broken back). The photographer, Scotty Kilpatrick, kept taking pictures. He slipped back to his car, but as he left the security guards confronted him, demanding he turn over his glass-plate negatives.

Kilpatrick had already hidden them beneath a car seat and instead gave the security guards a stack of unexposed plates, then sped back to the *Detroit News* offices.

The photos were dramatic and compelling, including one of the profusely bleeding Frankensteen. Bennett had issued a statement that no Ford security men were involved in the beating, and that it had been staged by the UAW as a publicity stunt to gain sympathy because the union had failed to organize the plant. But when the photos were published and transmitted around the world, the stock of the UAW rose in the public eye, and Ford's reputation fell. "The principal Fordism of Ford Motor Company," the outraged UAW president Homer Martin said, "is fascism."[6]

Ford continued to fight the organizing efforts, including firing some four thousand suspected union supporters after the Battle of the Overpass, as it became known to unionists. But with the United States being drawn into the world war and the NLRB issuing orders—backed by the US Supreme Court—that Ford comply with federal labor law, the UAW began to gain the upper hand. In April 1941, Bennett summarily fired a grievance committee that had been established at the massive Rouge complex. Some fifty thousand workers walked out in protest, a workforce too big to replace with scabs. Ford finally gave in and recognized the UAW.[7]

The rise of the unions in Detroit is a compelling, complex, and ultimately inspiring story that has become the stuff of labor lore, and that supports its own cottage industry of historic inquiry.[8] But the move to unionism in Detroit followed a growing tide of labor militancy across the nation, from the West Coast dockworkers led by Harry Bridges, who effectively shut down Seattle and San Francisco with general strikes in 1934, to the successful socialist-led Teamsters' strike in Minneapolis, to the Auto-Lite strike in Toledo, just down the Detroit River. All of those showdowns were bloody, with at least twenty-one deaths, most at the hands of police or company security men.

In Detroit, the broad-based support for the UAW by workers and their families, particularly under the passionate postwar leadership of Walter Reuther, was crucial to what the city of Detroit would eventually become. It marked a power shift. The Henry Fords and Walter Chryslers formerly could do whatever they wanted to their employees with impunity; now autoworkers were able to enforce wage scales, safety precautions, and a measure of job security for themselves. The automakers still set the size of the workforce and production schedules, but workers overcame their daily fear of losing a job at the whim of a foreman or the suspicion of a company spy ferreting out union sympathizers.

Over the next three decades, the power of the UAW would grow significantly, and with it came the explosive growth and political power of the American middle class. Historian Kevin Boyle argues compellingly that the UAW's push for federal social welfare programs was eventually trumped by political expediency. In the 1940s, when it could have put significant power behind, say, the 1948 presidential Progressive Party candidacy of Henry Wallace, it opted instead to work within the Democratic Party. While the union helped pull the party to the left, the party pulled the union to the right, and it began compromising on many of its more liberal dreams. In the anticommunist fervor of the postwar years, Reuther led the UAW through a purge of those with socialist and communist connections, real or suspected. At the same time, the union found itself taken for granted politically by the Democratic Party. By the 1960s, the UAW had strong lobbying influence in Washington but was in reality just one of many competing interests. Its political influence slowly waned.[9]

But in Detroit, a solid middle class arose due to the union's negotiated wage and benefits packages, and across southeast Michigan workers who had once been economically marginalized became the cream of the nation's working class. A high school degree and a little work ethic could net a solid middle-class lifestyle, setting the standard for the rest of the nation's blue-collar workers. The UAW's power came from its ability to shut down a car company if negotiations broke down. Given the sizes of the firms, and the specialized nature of the line workers—plus the difficulty in finding a large pool of scab labor in union-strong Detroit—the advantage in negotiations often landed on the union side of the table. With the auto companies dominating the industry worldwide and making massive profits, the union demands were simply rolled into the cost of doing business—and the retail price of cars for consumers. It was the template for an economic disaster that began materializing in the 1970s.

12

THE WAR YEARS

The nation's economy—and Detroit's—was already recovering from the worst of the Great Depression by the time Japanese planes attacked the American Sixth Fleet at Pearl Harbor on December 7, 1941, propelling the United States into World War II. The auto industry, still centered in Detroit, had cranked out 4.8 million vehicles in 1941, less than the peak of 5.4 million in 1929 but more than triple the Depression low of 1.4 million in 1932.

Even before the Pearl Harbor attack, FDR had sought to shift the United States to war footing to help Great Britain stave off the Nazis. In a speech in December 1940, FDR referred to the nation as the "arsenal of democracy," a phrase Detroit quickly adopted as its own as the advent of war shifted Detroit's recovery into overdrive. By mid-1941 Chrysler (with US funding) was building a tank factory in Warren, just northeast of Detroit, and other existing facilities were being converted from making cars to making war machines: trucks, engines for boats and submarines, and machine guns and antiaircraft weapons. It was a massive undertaking that required a nearly complete transformation of Detroit's industries. Only 12 percent of the machine tools used to makes cars could be used to make tanks, planes, and other war machines. So the tool-and-die industry was remade, too, with its skilled tradesmen and assembly workers retrained for the new purpose.

Parts manufacturers found themselves facing surprising conversions, as well. In late 1940, a bomber was dissected and laid out, part by part, in an empty Graham-Paige auto factory near midtown Detroit. Manufacturers were invited in to see the components and determine which ones they could make. A metal snow-shovel manufacturer converted his machines to make discs for brakes. A vacuum-cleaner maker signed up to turn out specialized aluminum parts. A pesticide squirt-gun maker retooled to crank out hydraulic systems for doors. Just west of Detroit, in the rural town of Willow Run, Henry Ford built a massive new airplane factory using the concept of an automobile assembly line. By August 1944, it was producing a new B-24 bomber every hour.[1]

The increased production meant more workers were needed. More than half a million Michigan men marched off to war, and as they traded factory overalls for uniforms their absence increased the demand for labor. Nearby cities like Cleveland and Chicago began reemploying their pools of jobless workers, too, so once again the Deep South and Appalachia became a wellspring. From June 1940 to June 1943, near the midpoint of the US involvement in the war, some five hundred thousand people—primarily African Americans and women—migrated to Detroit, some drawn by industrial recruiters scouring the farm towns and small cities, others hearing rumors of work and moving on their own.[2]

The city, just a few years removed from devastating and abject poverty, was once again teeming. "This mammoth mass-production machine has a wholly new tempo, a grim, new purpose," author and journalist Hal Borland wrote in March 1941, nine months before the attack on Pearl Harbor, as Detroit's new military role took root. "Smoke rises from a thousand stacks. Buses and trolley cars are jammed. Parking yards around factories and back-alley machine shops are packed with workers' cars. Builders' trucks rumble through the streets. Out on the fringes of towns and cities the bright lumber and gleaming paints of new houses, built and building, catch the eye. Detroit is busier than it has been for years, and the wheels are speeding up."[3]

Borland was overstating the new home construction. Some was taking place, but it was woefully inadequate to absorb the demand. As had happened during Detroit's previous boom years, the city faced an immediate and desperate housing crunch. Some new arrivals were driven to take out classified ads in newspapers offering bounties if someone could find or rent them a house or apartment—a reversal of today's "first month free" teaser for apartment complexes. But segregation continued to limit options for black workers. In the Depression years, some fifteen hundred public housing units designated by the federal government for poor blacks had been built near Black Bottom—the Brewster Homes that Eleanor Roosevelt had helped launch by symbolically starting the demolition of the slum. Another project for whites had been built near auto factories in northeast Detroit, close to Hamtramck. The new units numbered in the low thousands, while the demand was exponentially higher.

The already overcrowded Black Bottom area, and the surrounding neighborhoods on the near east side, took in even more bodies. City parks filled with squatters, often entire families that had moved from the South hoping to find work. Some lived in empty storefronts while others moved into unused factories. The overtaxed welfare department began handing out train tickets to send the homeless back where they had come from. In August 1942, war restrictions on building supplies effectively froze new housing construction in Detroit (and elsewhere) at a time when the city estimated it needed thousands of new units. "There just isn't such a thing as a place to rent in Detroit," said Charles F. Edgecomb, Detroit's director-secretary of the Detroit Housing Commission. "Money and price simply have no meaning."

Some homes were available for sale, but they were mostly out of the price range of newly arriving workers. "While they may be financially self-sufficient and could make down payments, [they] lack the credit rating to buy these homes," he said. What to do with all those new arrivals became one of Detroit's biggest and most persistent social problems. It exacerbated the always-simmering racial tensions and played out in Detroit's politics.[4]

The 1939 campaign for mayor of Detroit was a showdown between the incumbent, Richard Reading, and Edward Jeffries, a city councilman. Reading was routed, primarily because he was embroiled in scandals over bribes to protect Detroit's illegal rackets (he eventually went to prison for it), and when Jeffries took office in January 1940, he turned to a UAW activist, George Edwards Jr., to serve as his housing commissioner. City elections were technically nonpartisan, but Jeffries was a moderate Republican and Edwards was a Democrat, and about as liberal as they come—part of the socialist wing that helped create the UAW. He would become a forgotten, yet critical, figure in Detroit's modern evolution.

Edwards, who was white, was born in Dallas, Texas, on August 16, 1914. His father was a socialist and a lawyer, one of the few who would defend union organizers and sympathizers, and who would take on the Klan. His mother, Octavia Nichols Edwards, was a teacher. Precociously bright, Edwards earned a bachelor's degree from Southern Methodist University in 1933 before age nineteen, and a master's degree in sociology from Harvard University the next year. He then signed on as a researcher in the socialist-led Student League for Industrial Democracy and spent two years under Norman Thomas's tutelage, traveling the country and speaking on behalf of socialist causes.

In 1936, Edwards decided to move to Detroit—the heart of the industrial union movement—where he later said he had planned to write novels. In reality, he was tired of the vagabond existence and wanted a "sane, well-rounded existence" that would enable him to keep working in the radical movement. He could have gone anywhere, but he was drawn to Detroit because of its robust industrial heart and the growing union movement, including the Reuther brothers, whom he knew. When he arrived in Detroit, he roomed in Brush Park for the first six months with an old friend, Frank Winn, who was editing a UAW newsletter.[5]

Walter Reuther had recently maneuvered the merger of three westside UAW locals into one, Local 174. After a successful eight-day strike at Detroit's Midland Steel plant, the UAW turned its sights on the Kelsey-Hayes Wheel Company, on the west side, which made brakes and brake shoes for the Ford Rouge plant and was embarking on a small hiring spree. The UAW had few members in the plant, so Walter Reuther directed supporters, including Edwards, to obtain jobs there. Edwards wound up in the paint department. Landing a job was no small feat in those Depression years, and it's unclear why the hiring agents would take on a Harvard-educated sociologist with a recent history in socialist agitation—odds are Edwards didn't volunteer many of those details. Victor Reuther also landed a job there as a punch-press operator.

Working with Edwards and a handful of others, Victor Reuther surreptitiously enlisted a number of workers to join the UAW. In December, just a month after FDR's reelection, the union men concocted a ruse, arranging for a woman sympathizer to "faint" at her machine. In the ensuing confusion, Edwards and others moved through the factory pulling switches to stop the assembly line, and Victor Reuther clambered to a high spot where he began lobbying his fellow workers to strike until they won higher wages, union recognition for the UAW, and other concessions.[6]

In a story that has become part of the legend of the UAW, Victor Reuther told management the only way they would quit the strike was if Walter Reuther, the young firebrand organizer for the UAW, intervened. Reuther was sent for and joined his brother inside the plant. But instead of telling the men to end the strike, he urged more workers to join in. When the managers accused him of breaking his promise to get the workers to return to their jobs, Reuther explained, "I can't tell them to do anything until I get them organized."

After two weeks of tough negotiations—Edwards was on the bargaining committee—and on-off work stoppages that culminated with the workers occupying the plant, the union won the strike, though not, at first, recognition for the UAW. But the success brought home the point that targeting factories that were crucial cogs in the overall production process would make the strikes more effective. Ironically, Henry Ford had as much to do with ending the strike as the UAW. Ford's agents told the Kelsey-Hayes managers that if they didn't quickly resolve the labor problem and resume Ford's supply of wheels and brakes, Ford would find a new supplier. Ford even threatened to send over some of Henry Bennett's "service men"—the company goons involved in the 1932 Hunger March killings—to seize the wheel and brake dies to pass along to a new supplier.

Emboldened by the victory at Kelsey-Hayes and a handful of other sites, the UAW exported the sit-down strike campaign directly to one of the Big Three auto companies: General Motors in Flint, which was one of only two factories that made the dies from which GM auto bodies were pressed. The courage and drive of those organizers is hard to understand from the modern era, but they faced incredible risks, not just to their careers and ability to earn a living, but to their lives. In Flint, GM was, in effect, the city government. GM executives held six of the nine city commissioner seats, and the mayor had worked as a GM controller. GM directed the police force and developed a network of spies to rival anything the Cold War produced, including placing fifty-three Pinkerton detectives as antiunion moles in its plants. Over a two-year period, GM paid a reported $836,000 trying to keep union organizers and supporters out of their factories, relying on summary dismissals of sympathizers and the occasional beatings of organizers. An unknown number of organizers were killed outright.[7]

Still, they fought. On December 28, 1936, workers at a Fisher Body plant in Cleveland, owned by GM, sat down on their jobs and refused to work and refused to leave. On December 30, workers at the Fisher Body plant in Flint did the same. It was a time of high-drama, and stress, as the GM-controlled police tried to storm the building, only to be pelted with car-door hinges and other heavy metal objects, many propelled by industrial-scale jury-rigged slingshots. Governor Frank Murphy, the former Detroit mayor and judge in the Ossian Sweet trials, rebuffed GM's demands that he deploy the National Guard to storm the plant. The stalemate was on.

Six weeks after the workers sat down, and with Murphy acting as a shuttle diplomat between GM and the UAW, the union won. (Murphy's pro-labor role would come back to haunt him; he lost his reelection bid under a red-baiting assault by Republicans.[8]) Success bred success, and over the next year the union grew exponentially. The men who helped propel it rose in influence. By February, the UAW had hired Edwards— laid off from Kelsey-Hayes because of a business falloff from the GM Flint strike—as an organizer. Within the year, Edwards, who had been studying law at night, was director of the UAW's welfare department, though some saw the appointment as a maneuver by the politically astute and manipulative Reuther to marginalize a potential rival. Two years later, newly elected Mayor Jeffries appointed Edwards director of Detroit's housing commission.

Edwards was something of a working-class hero in UAW-heavy Detroit. He was a strong advocate for public housing, and plans gelled under his administration of the housing commission for the showcase S. James Herman Gardens complex: 2,150 units covering 156 acres in northwest Detroit. The largest such complex in the Midwest at the time, the project was born amid scandal (corruption often seemed to be Detroit's second-largest industry). Two city council members and three Chicago contractors eventually went to prison on bribery convictions over cement contracts, and two other men implicated in the scandal committed suicide, both making unwitnessed leaps from buildings in Chicago. The project survived, though, setting the stage for decades of showdowns over racism and segregation. As projects were conceived and discussed, antiblack neighborhood associations came together to oppose them.

Most of that happened after Edwards had moved on, winning the first of four two-year terms on the common council in November 1941 in a race left wide open because of the Herman Gardens bribery scandal. But two years were served in absentia, as Edwards joined the US Army and eventually was shipped to the Philippines, where at war's end he was appointed to an investigator's spot on the War Crimes Division of the Armed Services of the Pacific, preparing cases against Axis war criminals before returning to Detroit in 1946.[9]

It was a different Detroit that welcomed Edwards, one that had gone through massive growth, upheavals, and the violence of explosive race relations. For in the summer of 1943, Detroit once again burned.

13

THE 1943 RIOT

While riots tend to erupt unplanned, and without warning, they also occur in the midst of predictive conditions, and the buildup to the riot of 1943 was, in hindsight, easy to see.

"Riots are . . . the end products of thousands of little irritants in an atmosphere of growing tension," Detroit sociologists Alfred McClung Lee and Norman Daymond Humphrey wrote in the months after the 1943 violence.[1] The main irritant was the exclusion of blacks from jobs and housing—the mainstream of Detroit life. A preriot survey found 83 percent of black people in Detroit felt they were not being given a full opportunity to help win the war, compared with 72 percent in Chicago and a surprising 54 percent in three southern cities. That bears contemplating. Blacks in the South, where Jim Crow laws were still controlling basic life, felt more engaged with the predominant social and political issue of the era than did their counterparts in "desegregated" Detroit.

City officials and visiting journalists had been talking about the growing tensions in the city, with overcrowding leading to racial frictions on the streets and in factories, where black workers were struggling for equal access to jobs. The federal government had barred discriminatory hiring practices in plants with defense contracts, but enforcement was spotty. When whites balked at working with blacks or objected to blacks filling what they considered "white jobs," white factory managers usu-

ally sided with the white workers. And newly arrived southern whites'
expectations of subservience by blacks ran head-on into northern blacks'
growing assertiveness regarding the equal access to jobs and housing that
they were entitled to. It was a split that also would plague the UAW.

"The atmosphere was tense, and the tension was increasing," journalist Earl Brown wrote of a visit to Detroit in July 1942. "There were
sudden gusts of strikes for unimportant reasons—a strike occurred at the
Chrysler Tank Arsenal because the men were not allowed to smoke during work. But racial feeling was most alarming of all. Groups of Negro
zoot-suiters were brawling with gangs of young white toughs; the determination of Negroes to hold the war jobs they had won was matched by
the determination of numerous white groups to oust them. There were
many signs of trouble." In the aftermath of the riots, Mayor Jeffries said
he had "been conscious of the seriousness of the race problem here for
more than a year." The Wayne County prosecutor, whose jurisdiction
included the City of Detroit, said he had "felt the riot coming. . . . Race
tensions have been growing here for three years."[2]

In February 1940, before the "arsenal of democracy" was born, several skirmishes took place between white and black students at Northwestern High School. Of some four thousand students in the school,
seven hundred were black, drawn primarily from an African American
neighborhood southwest of the school. White realtors perceived that the
black population was growing and would begin moving into white areas;
black leaders believed that the white students were effectively doing the
bidding of the white realtors to intimidate black students to scare families away from the white neighborhoods. Ultimately, the only people
arrested were protesters distributing pamphlets outside the school calling for peace, whom police feared were members of the Young Communist League. The police were happy to act against the "reds," but not
against racial violence.

Five months later, tensions boiled over again, this time on Belle Isle.
An argument over a canoe led to the arrest and then police beating of
a black man. A woman named Jane Bartley led a throng of angry pic-
nickers to the police station on the island, where Bartley apparently was
struck by one of the officers. The incensed crowd attacked the station,

leading to the arrests of several of the protesters. But the more telling response was the outrage from the white Detroiters quoted in the *Detroit News* and the *Free Press* as being offended by the presence of blacks in the public park.

The trouble spread. In April 1941, a strike at the Ford Rouge plant took on racial overtones as job-desperate blacks were recruited as strikebreakers, with Bennett's Service Department men warning them that the white union men on the picket line would beat them if they tried to sneak out of the plant. At one point a brawl broke out as a crowd of strikebreakers, on order from Bennett's men, moved out of the plant to try to break the picket line, using heavy bolts and nuts as missiles. (Future US representative John Conyers Jr.'s father, a UAW organizer, was severely injured.)

The use of blacks as strikebreakers was a cynical ploy by Ford to try to turn the labor dispute into a racial confrontation that would force state officials to intercede. The effort failed, but the incident again revealed the precarious racial fault lines in Detroit, where the Homes Registration Office—charged with helping defense workers find housing—reported 332 units available for about three hundred white applicants, and none for the eighty-one black applicants. Roving bands of young white males spent most of July 1941 attacking the homes of blacks who had moved out of the segregated zones and into white neighborhoods. There was no police response or protection for the targeted homes. And at the start of the new school year, a student was stabbed in another racial incident at the troubled Northwestern High School.[3]

An even more ominous harbinger of housing showdowns that would define the future shape of the city came in 1942. The previous year the city Housing Commission under George Edwards and the US Housing Authority (USHA) had announced plans to build two hundred units of public housing for blacks off Seven Mile Road in northeast Detroit, a project to be named for the black abolitionist Sojourner Truth. The decision came despite heavy political lobbying by Detroit's powerful real estate interests, which had both a financial incentive—they wanted any new housing developments to be done by them—and philosophical. They saw housing as the realm of the private sector, not government, and viewed public housing projects as a move toward socialism. But they were also motivated by racism: these were the same interests that enforced Detroit's de facto housing segregation.[4]

The government policy—both local and federal—was that new public housing should not affect the racial balances of neighborhoods, a de facto embrace of segregation.[5] Since the Sojourner Truth site was near an existing black neighborhood, Conant Gardens, officials expected little political backlash. They were wrong. Nearby white residents, mostly Polish immigrants and their descendants, formed the Seven Mile-Fenelon Improvement Association (Fenelon Street crosses Seven Mile) and mounted an aggressive political fight. They picketed city hall, swarmed city council meetings and housing commission meetings— Edwards often left with an armed escort—and harangued their congressional representatives. The federal designation of Sojourner Truth for black residents was quickly changed to whites-only. Then, under pressure from leftists and black leaders, the feds reversed themselves again and changed the designation back to black. At the same time, the USHA announced that it would stop insuring new mortgages for homes in the surrounding area, angering whites who believed they not only would have to accept blacks as neighbors but their housing values would likely decline because they couldn't get loans to make improvements.[6]

The first families were scheduled to move in under police guard on February 28, 1942. They were met by two groups, one white and one black, who shouted and screamed at one another until the anger broke into a vicious melee. By the time the violence ended, some forty people had been injured, though no one was killed. Police aligned with the white mob, refusing to disperse throngs of whites while turning away any arriving blacks, even those who had rented apartments in Sojourner Truth and were simply trying to get in. Blacks were searched for weapons; whites were not. And cementing expectations on both sides, all but 3 of the 109 rioters held for trial were black. The prosecutions affirmed white prejudices that blacks were prone to violence, and affirmed blacks' belief that the nearly all-white police department was the enforcement arm of a white-dominated culture seeking to keep them from good jobs and adequate housing. A few weeks later, under the guard of

some two thousand police and National
Guardsmen, black families finally moved
en masse into Sojourner Truth, the
show of force muting the neighborhood
opposition.

Protest sign near Sojourner Truth
homes, 1942. ARTHUR S. SIEGEL, LIBRARY OF CONGRESS.
FSA/OWI COLLECTION (LC-USW3- 016549-C [P&P] LOT 661)

But being forced to accept black
neighbors at gunpoint didn't change
white minds, nor did it do much to
undercut black perceptions that, the
momentary protection notwithstanding,
political and legal interventions in segregation fights would fall on the
white side of the color line. Blacks began agitating for a more equitable
share of Detroit, both from the public and private sectors.

On April 11, some ten thousand people crowded into the downtown Cadillac Square, near city hall, for an "equal opportunity" rally
organized by the UAW and the NAACP. A few weeks later an NAACP
Emergency War Conference drew delegates from twenty states who
railed against official and unofficial discrimination within the federal
workforce and the military. The public and organized agitation by blacks
exacerbated white fears.

It didn't help that Detroit was home to three religious-inspired dem-
agogues who couched their racism in terms of faith: Father Coughlin;
Gerald L. K. Smith, a member of the Silver Legion (an American version
of Hitler's Brown Shirts); and the Reverend J. Frank Norris, an early
"megachurch" minister who preached a mixture of racial segregation
and biblical fundamentalism and who shuttled by train between pulpits
at First Baptist Church in Fort Worth, Texas, and Detroit's Temple Baptist Church, which didn't integrate until the 1980s.

By 1943, Coughlin's influence had dissipated after key members of
the extremist Christian Front organization he had been championing
were charged with conspiring to overthrow the US government. All
those arrested were eventually acquitted or had the charges dropped,
but Coughlin's association with the group helped knock him off the air.
Further, in an act of dubious constitutionality, Coughlin was barred from
using the US mail to distribute his anti-Semitic and inflammatory *Social*

Justice newspaper after the US attorney general deemed it seditious. His Catholic overseer, Archbishop Edward Mooney, finally muzzled Coughlin completely by ordering him not to speak publicly on political or social issues at risk of being defrocked, though Coughlin remained pastor of the Shrine of the Little Flower until he retired in 1966.

Coughlin and his peculiar strains of racism might have been silenced, but his words still echoed in the hearts of those who agreed with him. And Smith and Norris continued to deliver their noxious stew of racism and anti-Semitism, finding scapegoats for the economic crisis in Jewish bankers, communists, immigrants, and blacks.[7]

The schisms cropped up even within the war machine. In June 1942, only seven months after the attack on Pearl Harbor and despite a "no strike" pledge by the UAW, three serious wildcat strikes broke out in Detroit factories, each sparked by management decisions to place black workers in jobs previously held by whites. The resistance crossed gender lines. At Hudson, 350 white women walked off their clerical jobs after their bosses hired a handful of black women to join them. With the UAW's acquiescence, Hudson fired four white men whom they considered the main protagonists of the hate strikes, but the work stoppages continued to crop up across the defense factories. In June 1943, three black workers received promotions at the Packard plant, which was making engines for PT boats and bombers. Their white coworkers, urged on by several Klansmen in the factory, promptly walked off the job. Several top Packard officials quietly supported the walkout, telling their white workers they did not have to work with blacks. "The racial hatred created, released and crystallized by the Packard strike played a considerable role in the race riot that was soon to follow," the NAACP's Walter White wrote in an analysis of the events in Detroit that summer. "It was also the culmination of a long and bitter fight to prevent the unemployment of Negroes in wartime industry." Similar short-lived walkouts hit other defense factories as well.[8]

The spark that lit the 1943 riot began, ironically, at an amusement park. Two young black men apparently were accosted and roughed up by a group of whites at the Eastwood Amusement Park just outside the Detroit city line, at Gratiot Avenue and Eight Mile Road, on Satur-

day night, June 19, 1943. The next afternoon the young men reportedly were on Belle Isle, where they were involved in another fight with
whites, seeking revenge for the humiliation of the night before.[9] That
sparked a series of sporadic fistfights lasting into the evening, until they
mushroomed around 10:30 PM into a full-scale melee among several
hundred whites—many of them sailors—and blacks.

The fighting spread to Gabriel Richard Park, on the mainland end of
the Belle Isle Bridge. Rumors ricocheted around the central part of the
city that a white mob had thrown a black woman and her baby into the
Detroit River, where they drowned, and, separately, that a black mob had
been sexually accosting white women. Neither was true.

White mobs prowled Woodward Avenue beating and maiming black
residents as they emerged from movie theaters and other public ven-
ues. On Hastings Street, black mobs attacked white people patronizing
bars, nightclubs, and whorehouses. More rumors of atrocities whipped
through the frenzied crowd, spawning more violence. By 3 AM the first
looting began, and by daybreak it was clear that years of latent racism
and persistent frictions had left Detroit at the edge of a cliff. And then
it fell over.[10]

Over a three-day period, 34 people were killed, 433 others were
injured, and $2 million in damage was done to houses, stores, and small
factories before the US Army was summoned to squash the violence.
One million work hours were estimated lost from war production as the
city effectively shut down in the face of the rioting.

While urban riots tend to be viewed from within a narrow modern
prism—impoverished residents rising up and, for the most part, destroying their own neighborhoods—the 1943 riot was a full-scale racial
bloodletting, with blacks bearing the brunt of the violence. And significantly, most of the killing was done by city police. When confronting
white mobs, the police routinely—if they interfered at all—just urged
the crowd to disperse and go home. When confronting black mobs, they
turned immediately to truncheons and guns. Of the thirty-four people
killed, twenty-five were black, and of those, seventeen were killed by
police, many of them shot in the back as, according to the police, they
were caught looting. (One suspects many of those were pretexts for

cold-blooded murder.) Yet whites caught beating blacks with pipes and bricks were not even detained, let alone arrested—or shot, as were blacks ostensibly committing crimes against property. In fact, none of the white deaths were at the hands of police. And 85 percent of those arrested were black. In one telling incident, on the evening of June 21 a police officer was shot (he apparently survived) in a vacant lot next to an apartment building at 290 East Vernor Highway, and his assailant was immediately shot and killed by another officer. The police, reinforced, then attacked the apartment building, fully occupied by blacks, though with no apparent involvement in the assault on the officer. They set up a bank of lights and then strafed the building with machine guns, rifles, and handguns. Tear gas was eventually used to flush out the cowering residents, who were searched and held at gunpoint while officers broke down locked doors and ransacked belongings. Residents later reported money, jewelry, and booze were missing. None of the police were ever investigated or charged.[11]

Condemnations of the conditions that led to the riot, and the behavior by the police, came in quickly. Postriot analyses by Detroit and Michigan commissions blamed the violence on rowdy black youths and new southern migrants. Once again, "outside forces" were to blame. The reports were based on interviews with, and the case files of, rioters who had been arrested on felony charges. But because police were targeting blacks for arrest, the pool was skewed, which meant most state and city officials didn't investigate the nature of white rioters. The reports delivered results that fit the "common knowledge" of the time, and that did not challenge, or reveal, the underlying conditions in Detroit.

Not all the reports were so shallow and slanted, though. The Michigan Bureau of Child Welfare conducted its own assessment of 340 black rioters, all men, and found them to be primarily working, married adults, most with children and long histories in Detroit. A later study based on historical records concluded that the rioters were, black and white, average Detroit working-class people. And their behaviors within the riot itself were significantly different. The arrested blacks tended to have been detained while looting primarily white-owned stores or carrying weapons within their own neighborhoods (intent wasn't measured but surely self-defense came into play, rather than exclusively bearing weapons of aggression). The whites—especially young males—tended to have been arrested after traveling in groups from their own neighborhoods to black neighborhoods along Woodward, bent on violence rather than looting. Obviously a sampling of those arrested is not an accurate reflection of all those out on the streets during the riot, but the broad inferences can be drawn—especially given the high number of blacks gunned down by police. Where the whites acted out of a desire to maintain the Jim Crow–like status quo, the blacks acted out of a frustrated drive to break down barriers. "In broad, sweeping terms, rioters of both races sought to protect and improve their positions in wartime Detroit and, in individual socioeconomic and political terms, protested their relationships with one another," one analyst wrote years later. "The main difference was that the blacks acted out of hope and the whites acted out of fear."[12]

As the social-service agencies had warned would happen, other riots broke out around the nation that summer, all with racial or ethnic overtones, from the "zoot suit riots" targeting Latinos in Los Angeles, to the race riots among white and black servicemen in Beaumont, Texas, to the rioting and looting that followed the shooting of a black serviceman by a white cop in Harlem. But the Detroit riot far exceeded the others both in bloodshed and in property damage. It was the worst race riot in modern American history, an unenviable record that lasted nearly a quarter century until fundamentally unchanged living conditions led to a similar uprising in the summer of 1967, when Detroit topped its own vicious record.

The underlying racial, economic, and housing tensions in Detroit continued even after the war ended in August 1945. Deed covenants— legally binding additions to real estate deeds barring the property's sale to members of specific minority groups—had been a fact of American life since the late 1800s. They were designed around 1890 by Los Angeles developers who sought to keep Asians out of white neighborhoods. From there, the covenants, encouraged by the segregation-seeking

National Association of Real Estate Boards, spread throughout the country. They found a particularly warm welcome in the northern and midwestern cities bulging from the high inflow of southern blacks. The US Supreme Court upheld the restrictions as legal private contractual agreements in the 1926 *Corrigan v. Buckley* decision, and the covenants were included in most new homes built in Detroit in the 1920s and, in a particularly significant era, during the post–World War II building boom that began filling the open spaces outside the horseshoe formed by Grand Boulevard.[13] The covenants not only preserved segregation, they bore a significant responsibility for the rising population density in the black slums.[14]

The biggest responsibility for the slums lay, for the most part, in the hands of whites who stymied efforts to build new housing for blacks. During the Depression years, black housing and neighborhood activists had managed to thwart city and federal housing authority efforts to remove a small settlement of black families in a then mostly undeveloped area around Wyoming Avenue just south of Eight Mile Road in northwest Detroit. Ultimately, proposals to condemn the land and turn it over to private developers were replaced by a compromise to build six hundred temporary public housing units for black war workers and the extension of Federal Housing Authority–backed loans for single-family homes.

It was a rare victory for proponents of new housing for blacks. Other projects were floated and shot down, often with overt racist tones. One proposal for public housing in Dearborn drew sharp opposition from Mayor Orville Hubbard, who referred to housing shortages for black workers at Dearborn's Ford Rouge as "Detroit's problem." Federal officials pushing the project were "God-damn nigger-lover guys," the mayor said. In one public hearing, Hubbard chastised the city of Detroit, saying, "When you remove garbage from your backyard, you don't dump it in your neighbor's." In the end, Hubbard won, and the housing project was squelched. A related proposal in the adjoining suburb of Ecorse was similarly thwarted, as was yet another proposal for the Oakwood section of southwest Detroit. And a suggestion that Sojourner Truth be expanded to accommodate a few hundred more black war workers was rejected by Detroit officials who feared yet another violent showdown with white neighbors. Politically, the racist antihousing mob had won.[15]

Detroit did make some progress, though progress is a relative term. During the 1930s the city wrestled with different approaches to curb urban blight, particularly in black-heavy neighborhoods like Black Bottom, Paradise Valley, and Hastings Street on the near east side. In 1933, the Public Works Administration's Federal Emergency Housing Corporation announced a $3.2 million grant to Detroit for slum clearance and low-income public housing projects, which led the city to create its Detroit Housing Commission. By 1938, $25 million in federal money was made available to Detroit, and it sparked the development of a half-dozen projects over the next four years: the Brewster-Douglass, Parkside, Charles Terrace, Herman Gardens, John W. Smith, and Jeffries homes.[16]

As part of the public housing programs, the city housing commission had proposed a ten-year plan of slum clearance within the arc of Grand Boulevard. Lack of money and the onset of the war derailed those plans, and only 5,071 housing units were built. A series of subsequent proposals were floated but none ever gained official cachet until after the war ended. In November 1946, Mayor Jeffries announced his Detroit Plan. The idea was to bulldoze one hundred blighted acres northeast of downtown, just south of Gratiot Avenue, and prepare the land for redevelopment before selling it to private builders for new residential housing. Public housing was rejected as an option because such projects wouldn't generate property taxes, and the low incomes of the families would depress the adjoining downtown retail businesses. It was in the city's best interest, it was decided, to replace the impoverished neighborhood with a middle-class one. The city's cost would, after the resale of the land to the private developers, be about $2 million, which Jeffries argued would be offset by property taxes of $134,200 a year. Within fifteen years, the project would pay for itself.

While Jeffries announced the plan, it had many fingerprints on it, including those of city treasurer Albert E. Cobo, a Republican with close ties to Detroit's real estate and private industries. Representatives from the banking, investment, retail, and real estate businesses all had a voice. Notably absent from the planning: the impoverished black people who lived in the neighborhood.[17]

By the time the project began, its scope had grown to 129 acres, framed by Gratiot Avenue on the north, Dequindre Road on the east, Lafayette Avenue on the south, and Hastings Street on the west. Condemnation began in 1947, and after a series of legal challenges over the city's right to condemn private property for sale to other private investors—the state supreme court upheld it—the demolition began in 1950.

But, as with the land clearance for the Brewster project that began with Eleanor Roosevelt's visit and speech, that was effectively where the planning ended. The bulldozed land sat vacant for some five years before private developers finally emerged to build on it. And the city's housing office failed to relocate most of the seven thousand displaced poor black families, whose lack of financial flexibility in an already tight housing market meant the overcrowding simply moved to adjoining neighborhoods, which in turn led better-off residents of those neighborhoods to move elsewhere in the city. Rather than ending blight, the Gratiot redevelopment project simply redistributed it.

14

THE POSTWAR BOOM

Detroit's social stresses worsened in the postwar years, which began with another economic boom. Auto manufacturing had been severely curtailed by government fiat during the war—no cars were built in 1943 and 1944—and with those restrictions lifted, pent-up consumer demand mushroomed. The nation's auto industry produced 749,000 motor vehicles in 1944, all trucks. In 1948, it produced 5.3 million motor vehicles—nearly 4 million were cars—which was near the record high of 5.4 million produced in 1929. The next year, production increased further to 6.6 million, and it passed the 8 million mark in 1950. The economy, and jobs, wobbled a bit during that growth, but Detroit's economic underpinnings were solid. Between 1945 and 1950, the auto industry reported nearly $1.1 billion in posttax profits on sales of more than $12 billion.

How the automakers made all that money is significant. During the war years, the car and truck plants had made a fast, and legendary, conversion from producing motor vehicles to producing war machines—tanks, airplanes, and trucks. As the war neared its end, the Big Three's leaders looked ahead and figured they could produce and likely sell as many cars as their assembly lines could churn out. So they raced to convert their plants back into automotive factories. That was a critical moment in Detroit's evolution. From around 1910 until the advent of World War II, Detroit had become a one-industry town, and it was an industry that was unusually susceptible to the ups and downs of the economy. When things were going well, people tended to buy cars. When things were going poorly, they tended to milk another year or two out of the car they already had. As sales seesawed, production did also, with factory employment levels fluctuating to match. They might have been good-paying jobs, but they were prone to sporadic and sometimes lengthy layoffs and occasional strikes.

But the war had changed the world, and the American economy with it, as the military-industrial complex took shape and American industry dominated the world. "The United States emerged from the Second World War with the only major functioning army, with more than half of the usable production capacity in the world, and as the banker and creditor to both former allies and former enemies," analysts Barry Bluestone and Bennett Harrison wrote in *The Deindustrialization of America: Plant Closings, Community Abandonment, and the Dismantling of Basic Industry.* "Such overwhelming economic and military superiority had not been seen in the world since the turn of the century when British pre-eminence had begun to wither under the challenge from the newer industrial countries."[1]

American corporations were not shy about using their strength. Under the 1944 Bretton Woods agreement, the US dollar became the anchor for international exchange rates, which allowed US corporations to effectively use excess cash from war-torn countries to finance the takeover of key industries. That spawned a massive wave of globalization efforts by US corporations, including Detroit's auto companies. Also at war's end, the two-year-old Pentagon complex outside Washington, DC, became a permanent and powerful economic engine as it planned for more wars, warily eyeing the Soviet Union. It had a lot of money to spend, a lot of jobs to create. Detroit's industrial leaders could have changed the underpinnings of the local economy by working to retain their role as defense contractors instead of reverting to what they knew first and best—making cars. It's always problematic to speculate about the road not taken, but it's hard to imagine Detroit would be in its current condition if the postwar economy had diversified significantly beyond auto making. Detroit's industrial leaders were there, but they turned back.[2]

The decision wasn't the automakers' alone, of course. Other contractors could have set up—or kept—factories in Detroit. But the Pentagon preferred a policy of decentralization, having learned from Pearl Harbor that ships moored side by side made easy targets. Better to spread critical factories and development sites out across the country, improving the chances that the means of war production would survive an air or missile attack. It also helped maintain political support in Congress to sprinkle defense contracts across as many congressional districts as possible.

Detroit, the "arsenal of democracy," was largely left out as the Sun Belt reaped the benefits, setting the stage for decades of development and industrial innovation in places other than Detroit. High-tech aircraft plants, computer engineering firms, electronics manufacturers—they all cropped up elsewhere. Detroit might have been integral to the war victory, but it was barely a second thought when it came to peacetime. Even when Detroit received defense contracts, they usually went to projects far outside the city limits. Given the suburban segregation and the travel distance from the city—not to mention the difficulties black people had getting through the hiring offices—few of those new jobs went to African Americans, who were becoming a larger and more significant part of the ethnic makeup of Detroit and its workforce.

The automakers did guess right on the market for their cars. They sold in record numbers in the first few years of postwar production, and with that consumer demand came yet new demands for labor, heaping fresh stresses on the already overloaded city. In each of the first two full years after the war ended, eight thousand houses were built in Detroit, roughly one-quarter of the total new home construction in the metropolitan area. So while Detroit was the region's population base, the majority of the new housing was being built outside the city limits. The new neighborhoods were going up in western Wayne County and north of Eight Mile Road in Oakland and Macomb Counties, which were also where the new factories were being built. Detroit had become a victim of its own success. The core city was overstuffed, and the factories themselves were becoming outdated. Empty land in the rural areas was cheaper than prime land in Detroit and didn't have the added cost of renovating or razing existing buildings.

And the slums just got worse. A Detroit Housing Commission report dated May 27, 1949, counted 252 fire deaths in Detroit in the previous five years, 182 of them occurring in homes. More than half of the residential fires occurred inside the horseshoe framed by Grand Boulevard, the old densely populated areas surrounding downtown. Seventy-six children were killed, 51 percent of them within that Grand Boulevard zone, which held less than 20 percent of the city's youth population. More than two-thirds of the fires caused by "bad conditions" were inside the boulevard. Another report found that nearly one-third of the city's residential fires occurred within three miles of downtown, a zone that held only 12 percent of the city's population but most of its black slums.

The danger wasn't just from fire. Because many homes in Black Bottom and other long-standing slums evolved from 1870s shanties, sanitary conditions were poor. The shear number of residents meant much more garbage piled up in alleys than could be cleared by the weekly pickups, and rats and mice roamed freely. From 1951 to 1952, some 206 rat bites were recorded. In Black Bottom, from the river north to Gratiot Avenue, and in Paradise Valley, which stretched northward along Hastings Street from Gratiot to Grand Boulevard, rents were lower than elsewhere in the city, but exorbitant given the quality of the apartments—they were often just a room, carved out of an old hotel, without a bathroom or kitchen. Some had no heat. There were other slum zones, such as Corktown just west of downtown, which was predominately white, as well as smaller black enclaves elsewhere. But the core zone for the slums was made up of Black Bottom and Paradise Valley, the center of Detroit's black culture—jazz and blues greats made it a regular stop—and the heart of Detroit's black poverty.[3]

A common theme among present-day whites is that blacks have achieved equality (a questionable assertion in and of itself) so the sins of the past should be left in the past. But when formative dinner-table conversations tell of family histories through such times, events, and conditions, the past invariably infuses the present. Suspicions and distrust are instilled and passed down—in white families, as well as black. It's telling that many of the same whites who suggest modern blacks forget the past also easily talk about their own families' histories in Detroit in terms of dislocation and perceptions of forced change—past familial experiences that remain open sores. The past lives, and breathes, for all.

If Detroit's industrial leaders erred in their decision to get out of the war business and get back to car making, the people of Detroit similarly made a critical postwar error. The 1949 mayoral election both cemented the hard racial attitudes of the past and set the tone for the racial frictions that persist to the present. And that had a significant impact on the quality of life for Detroit's black residents and the continuing deterioration of the city's housing stock.

Amid the postwar political convulsions, the moderate Mayor Jeffries was unseated in 1947 by Eugene Van Antwerp, described by one historian as "an avuncular and eccentric long-time city councilman . . . [who] loved parading in his World War I uniform down Woodward Avenue, and his administration was only somewhat unfairly described as one which declared war on squirrels, communists, speed traps, and taxi dancehalls."[4]

Van Antwerp didn't last long. In the summer of 1949, Edwards, the former UAW organizer and Jeffries's one-time city housing director, decided to try to move up from his city council seat to the mayor's office. Edwards was an astute politician and his council victories evidenced his electability, but he badly misread what would become the key issue of the election: housing. His radical history as a socialist union organizer and his embrace of equal rights scared the Republican-based real estate industry, which—presuming Van Antwerp couldn't win—persuaded longtime city treasurer Albert E. Cobo to run.

Cobo was a popular figure in Detroit. An accountant by training, during the depths of the Depression he had been loaned by the Burroughs Adding Machine Company to the city for six months to help it unravel massive fiscal problems. Cobo never went back to the private sector. He was appointed to the vacant city treasurer post in 1935, then won the next general election. Among his challenges was replacing the "scrip" system the near-bankrupt city was using to pay its workers. And he endeared himself to city home owners by instituting a seven-year

George Edwards Jr. (right) with Walter Reuther (center) and Franklin Roosevelt Jr., at the 1949 UAW convention in Milwaukee. COURTESY OF WALTER P. REUTHER LIBRARY OF LABOR AND URBAN AFFAIRS, WAYNE STATE UNIVERSITY

payment plan that helped thousands of the luckless avoid losing their homes for back taxes. A fiscal conservative, he was closely aligned with the city's real estate interests, and part of Detroit's corporate culture. But he was also an old-ward-style politician, maintaining close personal ties with leaders of ethnic clubs and service organizations—the lifeblood of Detroit's Democratic-heavy politics.

The UAW, with Walter Reuther now in charge, had made it clear at its 1948 national convention in San Francisco that it hoped to use its growing clout to elect labor-sympathetic candidates to Detroit offices, as well as statewide offices and the University of Michigan board of regents. (The growing strength of the UAW carried risks. In 1948 and 1949, Walter and Victor Reuther were the targets of assassination attempts, each shotgunned in his home through a window. No one was ever arrested. In another attempt, someone placed thirty-nine sticks of dynamite outside the back door of the UAW headquarters while Walter Reuther was inside; rain kept the lit fuse from detonating the bomb.)[5] The UAW leadership didn't have specific candidates in mind at that point, though Edwards's name was bandied about as a possible contender.

By summer, Edwards was committed and was the favored candidate of the progressive wing of the Democratic Party, the UAW, and the Americans for Democratic Action. In all, seven candidates filed to run for mayor, but from the start it was seen as a three-person race among Cobo, Edwards, and, to a lesser extent, Van Antwerp. Richard J. Frankensteen, a former UAW vice president who left the union after losing an internal power struggle with Reuther, also ran, though he received little attention. Frankensteen had run against Jeffries four years earlier, with broad labor support, and almost won. By now, Frankensteen was running his own tool-and-die shop, and this time labor's support was behind Edwards. The city council president had positioned himself as something of a populist reformer pushing a twelve-step platform that promised cleaner streets, more playgrounds in crowded neighborhoods, modernization of Detroit Receiving Hospital, more aggressive attention paid to development of freeways and an international airport, and modern public housing to replace slums.[6]

Early in the campaign, Edwards pledged to fire Detroit police commissioner Harry Toy, a controversial and strident anticommunist. As Wayne County district attorney, Toy had overseen the roundups of political leftists after the 1932 Ford Hunger March. No police or Ford security men had ever been held accountable for killing five demonstrators, and targeting Toy was a strategic as well as a personal move. Edwards distrusted Toy as a tool of the automakers and Detroit's capitalist class. Black Detroiters resented Toy as the personification of a police department that they saw more as an occupying force than a dispassionate law enforcement agency, and Edwards's pledge resonated widely.

Edwards also was an adamant supporter of public housing, which he had championed as the city council president, another issue that earned him broad support among Detroit's growing black population. And with his formative role in the UAW, which had underpinned his city council election victories, he was expected to receive support from the driving force of Detroit elections, the working-class vote. In fact, the UAW

loaned key staffers to help his campaign, including future UAW president Douglas Fraser and groundbreaking black UAW activist Horace
Sheffield.

To no one's surprise, Van Antwerp ran an ineffectual campaign. He
argued that his challengers misunderstood and misrepresented his track
record as mayor. He said small businesses and home owners had gained
by a tax cut he engineered even as he tried to close a $7 million bud-
get deficit he had inherited. He accused Edwards's "long-haired socialist friends" of trying to intimidate his supporters. Toy, Van Antwerp's
appointee, took to the airwaves to defend his police department, telling
radio interviewers that morale was high and crime was down. But Van
Antwerp's budget-oriented themes fell flat.

Cobo, whose campaign was managed by the same man who had
steered Van Antwerp's successful 1947 campaign, argued that as a former corporate finance man and as the city's treasurer, he had the best
grounding for both fixing the city budget problems and managing the
city government. The key, he said, was to clear Detroit's slums without
laying the cost on taxpayers. Instead, the cleared land would be sold to
developers for private projects. And he pledged to clean up streets and
alleys and resolve nagging sewer problems that had led to flooded base-
ments in different parts of the city. "The people who pay taxes want better services for their money," Cobo said in a radio interview. "If I wasn't
convinced that a more businesslike handling of the multimillion dollar corporation of which they are shareholders wouldn't produce such
results, I wouldn't be running." The key phrase was "people who pay
taxes." Those were primarily property-owning whites; most blacks were
renters. Cobo's word choice was a subtle reinforcement of racial codes.

Despite the full field of candidates, turnout for the September 13
primary was expected to be light. And Edwards was expected to win. An
"informal poll" cited but not identified by the Detroit Free Press gave him
60 percent of the vote, with Van Antwerp and Cobo fighting for second
place and the chance for a runoff general election against Edwards in
November. But defying expectations, turnout on the cool and rainy primary day set a record—and Cobo was the runaway winner with nearly
170,000 votes to Edwards's 113,000 votes. Van Antwerp was ousted with

52,000 votes and Frankensteen barely registered with fewer than 17,000 votes.

The contemporary general assessment was that Edwards's supporters had been complacent and thus didn't turn out, a reading that rings flat given the record number of voters. Cobo had the endorsement of the more conservative AFL, which gave him a veneer of working-class acceptability. And in a campaign that split along both class and racial divides, Cobo was the candidate of the wealthy, and of the white.

With the general election less than two months away, Edwards immediately went after Cobo as a front for wealthy suburbanites and tied to real estate developers. (Cobo's family had a real estate investment company.) City elections were, by charter, supposed to be nonpartisan, which meant that candidates did not run on political party lines or receive formal party nominations. Edwards sought to break that mold, running openly as a Democrat and painting Cobo as a Republican, hoping the distinctions would help in a city that overwhelming supported Democratic candidates in state and national elections. "Mr. Cobo was selected to run for mayor during the annual cruise this summer of the Board of Commerce," Edwards said in one postprimary radio interview. "He is the Board of Commerce candidate. I am confident the voters in November will not permit the Board of Commerce to take over city government."

In a misreading of the mood of the city, Edwards played up his work as Mayor Jeffries's housing director and hyped his role in developing the Brewster and other public housing projects as evidence that he was on the side of the people, not the business elite. Cobo's "evil" slum-clearance plan, he said, was simply a gift to real estate interests. It made no effort to accommodate the poor people who would lose their homes and used tax money to subsidize private investments. "Thousands of Detroiters deserve a chance to have clean low-rent housing" but would lose that opportunity because Cobo intended to turn down federal housing redevelopment money, Edwards said.[7]

Cobo couched the housing issue in philosophical terms, objecting to government ownership of "slum sites which should be developed to produce additional tax revenue. We need the added revenue from the new, privately built and owned construction to maintain schools, equip parks and playgrounds, and expand and improve all city services, so that there will be no need for raising the present high property tax rate." Cobo said he could foresee a theoretical need for public housing "in some area in order to take care of low-income families" but that slum clearance should be aimed at profitable development. "After a slum clearance site has been selected and condemned, the next step should be to decide on what part new apartments shall be located, what part single homes, commercial buildings, light industries, schools, and playgrounds. We should then offer the land for sale to private individuals for redevelopment. The apartments should be developed first, so that there will be homes for persons displaced by the redevelopment program."[8]

Lurking behind the philosophical difference was race, since the Detroit residents most likely to live in the clearance zones, and to need low-rent public housing, were black. Edwards actively sought black political support and distributed pamphlets quoting endorsements from black ministers and other community leaders. "He has always believed in and worked for public housing," one read, quoting Dr. James J. McClendon, president of the Detroit chapter of the NAACP. "One of the greatest needs of Detroit today is the construction of low-cost housing. Everybody in Detroit knows that. When we elect George Edwards Mayor, he will see to it that these houses are built."

McClendon also said Edwards would appoint a police commissioner who would not "give orders to shoot first, investigate later. The relationship between the police department and the citizens of Detroit is getting worse daily. This is due entirely to the attitude of our present police commissioner. There are many innocent individuals being shot by policemen. There are too many illegal searches and seizures. Whether we have a continuation of this or a change is up to you."[9]

Unfortunately for Edwards, black support did not mean political success in 1949. Even moderate Democrats abandoned Edwards, conspicuously aligning themselves with Cobo against a Democrat they saw as too close to the radical left at a time when the national anticommunist mood was verging on hysteria. In fact, Detroiter Carl Winter, the head of the Michigan Communist Party, had been convicted that October in

New York City of violating the federal 1940 Smith Act in the first of a wave of criminal trials of communist leaders that gutted the party and helped propel the McCarthy era.[10]

The final vote in the general election was just as lopsided as the primary had been. The pro-business "Republican tax collector," as Edwards derisively called Cobo, overwhelmed the labor activist by 309,000 votes to 204,000, winning every precinct except those in black neighborhoods. Even Edwards's neighbors turned against him: he lost his home precinct.

Detroit's independent weekly black newspaper, the *Michigan Chronicle*, saw the vote as a plebiscite on white acceptance of black citizenry. It described the election as "one of the most vicious campaigns of race baiting and playing upon the prejudices of all segments of the Detroit population." While Edwards had the backing of the UAW and the Democratic Party, the rank-and-file members abandoned him for Cobo, "a victory of conservative stand-pat forces against the liberal and progressive elements of the city." And it took special note of racist anti-Edwards pamphlets that had been distributed through white neighborhoods, and a "whisper" campaign that an Edwards win would mean more integration "in a city known for its race prejudice."[11]

In the days after the election, political organizers for the UAW met in debriefing sessions to figure out where the campaign fell apart. Part of the problem had been that Cobo had more experience in city elections, and he maintained and reforged his close associations with ethnic clubs. But the key issue had been housing, which trumped the loyalty of Detroit's organized working class to its unions. "Another thing that worked against us was this housing thing, the percentage of home owners and buyers in the city of Detroit who are definitely afraid of changing the complexion of the neighborhood," one of the campaign workers said. Another mentioned anonymous leaflets that had been handed out in working-class white neighborhoods warning of black residential encroachments if Edwards were to be elected. And union loyalty was frailer than the UAW realized.

"I had a meeting of forty-five stewards and last Saturday, before we went into the stewards meeting, I asked a lot of questions," a campaign organizer named Lee said. He had earlier found UAW stewards handing out Cobo leaflets in the plants, even though Edwards was the UAW's candidate. "They told me that the union is OK in the shop but when they buy a home, they forget about it. You can tell them anything you want to, but as long as they think their property is going down, it is different."[12]

Edwards's shellacking at the polls was only a temporary setback in his political career. Edwards was appointed to a Wayne County judgeship in 1954 (the incumbent had died) and stood unopposed for election in 1955. The next November, he became the highest vote getter in Michigan history when he won election as a state supreme court justice. So the issue in 1949 clearly wasn't Edwards's electability. It was housing and race.[13]

The election, and the factors that influenced white voters, was a watershed moment in the evolution of modern Detroit. The city effectively held a referendum on what its future would be, and white fears won the day, an electoral decision that still resonates more than sixty years later.

15

RACE IN THE FIFTIES

When Albert Cobo took over Detroit's city hall on January 3, 1950, one of his first acts was to drive a spike through the city's existing public housing plans. He vetoed a series of proposals already in the works, and when the head of the Detroit Housing Commission resigned in protest, Cobo appointed a real estate developer, Harry J. Durbin, to replace him. The new mayor then stacked the commission with people who were part of the private development industry—contractors and developers as well as leaders of building-trades unions who supported private development over public housing (most likely because of the racial overtones; by then public housing had become shorthand for black housing).

The city's policy focus immediately shifted to urban renewal projects that would eradicate existing slums without building new public housing for the displaced and impoverished residents, most of whom were black. It was the ultimate political victory for the segregationist, anti-public-housing mobs that had stymied neighborhood projects in the 1940s. Under Cobo, Detroit refused most of the new federal funds made available in the 1950s for public housing, ranking the city, which was fifth in population, eighteenth on the list of major cities taking advantage of the 1949 Federal Housing Act. Boston, Newark, Saint Louis, New Orleans, and even Norfolk, Virginia, which ranked forty-eighth in population in 1950, built more public housing during the decade than did Detroit.[1]

As Thomas J. Sugrue pointed out in his landmark study, *The Origins of the Urban Crisis: Race and Inequality in Postwar Detroit*, the 1950s cemented Detroit's racial segregation. Detroit's few public housing complexes remained strictly segregated as a matter of federal and local government policy, which reinforced private-sector segregation. The NAACP finally forced the city, through legal challenges, to drop its formal policy in 1956, but it was years before the change had a significant effect. Even then, it had more to do with the changing demographics of the city—whites began to leave—than with moral stances against segregation. And it was longer still before the private-sector segregation began to crumble.

Detroiters' attitudes toward their city, and each other, were captured in a snapshot in the summer of 1951. A team of researchers from Wayne State University, working under a grant from the Detroit Board of Commerce, spread out over Detroit armed with lists of questions and names and addresses of people—black and white—randomly selected to be surveyed about their attitudes toward their own city. The survey takers, under the direction of sociologist Arthur Kornhauser, went to great lengths to draw out honest expressions of sentiments on everything from the physical appearance of the city to job satisfaction to perceptions of race relations. The interviewers lied about the survey's sponsors to avoid tying it to the Board of Commerce or Wayne State, saying instead that they represented something called the Detroit Public Opinion Survey Company. To try to draw out more honest answers, white questioners interviewed white respondents; black questioners interviewed black respondents. Some 593 men and women, most of them living in Detroit, the rest in adjacent ring suburbs and downriver, took part in the hour-long sessions, which plumbed deeply into their emotions and perceptions.[2]

The results offer a detailed look at the underlying attitudes of Detroiters when the city was at its peak population, with some 1.85 million people, and as it began the first steps in what became a calamitous decline. At the time of the survey, the nation was fully engaged in the Korean War, and fears of communists and other leftist radicals informed the politics of the era. The civil rights movement had yet to gel, and memories of the deadly 1943 riots were still fresh. Housing in Detroit was expensive and hard to find as both new residents from the South and returning war veterans sought places to live and to raise their families. It was cheaper for many people—especially those qualifying for GI loans—to buy new houses in the outlying areas of northeast and northwest Detroit, where new neighborhoods were springing up. And with developers eyeing the easy cash that comes with sprawl, the suburbs began to take their modern shape.

So what did Detroiters think of Detroit? Most looked favorably on the city, though the wealthy and upper middle class had a lower opinion. In an open-ended question about what their attitudes were toward Detroit, 54 percent listed favorable attributes, and 46 percent listed unfavorable attributes, which Kornhauser concluded meant Detroiters were, for the most part, satisfied with the place, though with a large undercurrent of dissatisfaction. Ability to find work, the physical condition of the city, their homes and families, the caliber of the city schools, and recreational opportunities were the most-cited positive elements.

Topping the list of unfavorable elements was race relations, particularly among white respondents. "The comments are largely about the number of Negroes, their moving into white neighborhoods, their having too many rights, their intermingling with whites and similar expressions of anti-Negro feelings," Kornhauser wrote, adding that there was a slight counter tide against segregation and the plight of blacks. "Only a few respondents offered favorable views on the race situation here—principally Negroes who referred to Detroit as preferable to the South."

The survey confirmed the deep seams of intolerance that had determined the 1949 mayoral election. In one direct question, 54 percent of the white respondents said they had unfavorable feelings about the "acceptance of Negroes," and another 28 percent expressed ambivalence. Only 18 percent, fewer than one in five whites, said they favored full acceptance of blacks as their social equals. Significantly, Kornhauser concluded that southern whites were no more strident in their racism than homegrown Detroiters or those who moved in from other parts of the country, though immigrants tended to have a more relaxed view. The better-educated and higher-income whites had more favorable views toward equality for blacks; the less-educated and poorer whites exhibited the highest levels of racism, suggesting Detroit was split not just by race, but by class as well—fault lines that would yawn widely in the next thirty years.

In another open-ended question, 68 percent of the whites who said they did not accept blacks as their social equals named continued segregation as the best course of action. And some of the comments were telling. "Negroes have too much freedom," one told the interviewer. "By the time you get a home paid off, Negroes have moved in and you have got to start all over again in [a] new part of town."

And that's exactly what white Detroiters began doing. In 1950, the city of Detroit's population was just under 1.85 million people, of whom about 16 percent, or 301,000, were black. The metropolitan area, including Detroit and the nascent suburban counties of Macomb and Oakland—with Pontiac as its county seat—held just over 3 million people, which meant Detroit accounted for more than 60 percent of the metropolitan population.

Over the next ten years, that balance shifted. By 1960, the metro area's population increased 25 percent, to just under 3.8 million people, while Detroit's population dropped 10 percent to 1.67 million. The city now accounted for only 44 percent of the metropolitan population as people left the city for suburbia. New arrivals skipped the city entirely and went directly to the suburbs. And the shift was racial. In the 1950s, the city of Detroit lost 363,000 white residents while it gained 182,000 black residents. The suburbs, while gaining 926,000 residents overall, picked up only 19,000 black residents, or just 2 percent. Looked at another way, in 1950, just over half of Metro Detroit's white population lived in the city of Detroit. Ten years later, only 37 percent of the overall white population lived in the city, accounting for just over 70 percent of the city's population, down from 84 percent a decade earlier. The segregation that once defined Detroit's neighborhoods was now beginning to spread out and define the metropolitan area's growing suburban cities.

Still, for blacks in the South, the racism and segregation of the North was better than the Jim Crow society they had left behind. For all of its shortcomings, Detroit was still a promised land.

White flight wasn't the only force emptying Detroit. During the 1950s, the Big Three automakers and other leading industrial concerns embarked on massive decentralization plans to build factories closer to regional customer bases around the country, but also to try to reduce one of the main pressures on profit margins: the cost of labor.

In some ways, Detroit's economic success set the stage for its eventual collapse. The UAW, under firebrand leader Walter Reuther, had made Detroit's autoworkers some of the best-paid laborers, unskilled and skilled, in the country. The automakers' factories may have been the source of that income, but it was the UAW's hard-fought contracts that ensured that the people who physically built American cars and trucks shared in the success. In one regard, the UAW picked up where the early Henry Ford and his five-dollar day had left off. Ford wanted to create a consuming class that could afford to buy his mass-market cars. The UAW similarly sought to improve the standard of living of its members, from the ability to buy the cars they made, to accessing good healthcare and housing, to providing a foundation for strong families. It is a separate history from this one, but the UAW—following Reuther's vision of a broad uplifting of the working class—was one of the key movers behind federal social programs that flowered under the Johnson administration in the 1960s.[3] Yet the UAW, with its ability to shut down production to win its demands, was also seen by the automakers as one of the worst parts of doing business in Detroit.

So in the 1950s, the Big Three—led by General Motors—embarked on a strategy of both business integration (making their own parts rather than buying them from local suppliers) and decentralization that helped set the course for Detroit's economic collapse. In the decade following the end of World War II, GM built new plants in Atlanta, Georgia; Framingham, Massachusetts; Kansas City, Missouri; Linden, New Jersey; South Gate, Los Angeles, and San Francisco, California; Wilmington, Delaware;

and Parma, Ohio. Its new or expanded Michigan facilities were outside of Detroit, including the new Tech Center in Warren.

In 1951, fifty cents of every GM sales dollar was attributed to material bought from suppliers; by 1961 that had dropped to forty-seven cents of every dollar, evidencing GM's decision—the others were following a similar course—to reduce costs by expanding the number of items it made for itself. "There's a kind of chain reaction effect here," one business manager told survey-takers in 1961. "The suppliers of the auto industry are especially vulnerable. They've certainly been hurt during the last decade. There are fewer of them and the auto industry has been integrating, that is, it has been increasingly producing commodities, which it used to buy from suppliers. Many auto manufacturers now produce their own electrical equipment, their own glass, their own bodies, when this was not previously true."[4]

It wasn't that the business managers—in the auto industry and outside of it—disliked the caliber of labor in the Detroit area. In fact, they cited that as one of the benefits of operating factories in Michigan. They balked at the cost, and also complained about tax rates (an evergreen complaint by business owners). Half said they would be interested in moving to another state, and one-third (a plurality) of those actively planning to relocate cited labor costs (notably, not taxes or government red tape) as the primary reason. Of those considering expanding to another state while retaining a Michigan presence, the most-cited reason was labor costs (one-quarter of total respondents).

These were not decisions made lightly. Executives at half of the factories that had opened in the state of Michigan since 1940 said the plants were "located in Michigan by historical accident—because the founder lived there, liked it there, or had valuable business connections there." Other prime factors included proximity to customers, or the chance to buy an existing business. Implicit in those findings is that the older the company and the farther the distance from the original decision to locate in Michigan, the better the chance contemporary managers without those roots would choose to expand or build elsewhere—especially as customers for supply businesses decentralized across the country.[5]

In a sense, the move to decentralization was the first crumbling of Detroit's economic foundation. At the beginning of the century, Detroit was a diversified regional manufacturing and retail hub, exporting stoves, carriages, railroad cars and equipment, drugs, and boots to customers far outside the region. By the late 1920s, Detroit had essentially become a one-industry town. Going into the 1950s, roughly half of all automobile industry jobs in the country were in Michigan, predominately in Detroit and the near suburbs, and another quarter were in Ohio and Indiana. By 1960, the erosion was in full swing, with states like California in the West, Texas in the South, Kansas in the Great Plains, and Massachusetts in the Northeast gaining auto manufacturing jobs at the expense of the old hub zone in the Midwest. Only one-third of all new motor vehicles were being built in Michigan. The state still held a dominant chunk of the auto jobs, but they slowly began slipping away, too—primarily those for the working-class, blue-collar laborers. White-collar jobs—engineering, design, marketing—remained strong, but those were mostly in the suburbs. For Detroit, whose neighborhoods were built around manual and skilled labor, the effect would be profound.[6]

The UAW referred to the shifting of jobs out of Detroit and the industrial heartland as GM's "southern strategy." The union tried to follow, but it found local cultures indifferent to unions, and to "radicals" from the North coming down and telling them how they should work. UAW Local 600, one of the union's most radical and largest locals, filed a lawsuit against Ford to try to keep it from moving some of the work done at the Rouge plant out of the region. Lawyer Ernest Goodman described Ford's decision as a deliberate fraud by Ford to get out of its contractual obligations with workers at the Rouge plant, and predicted that "unless restrained by the timely intervention of this court" the Rouge plant would become "a mere shell of its former capacity."[7]

But the challenge was dead from the start. The UAW leadership, under Reuther, was trying to rid the union of communists and "fellow traveler" political progressives, and Local 600 was rife with them. Reuther refused to sign on to the legal challenge, forcing the local to go it alone—and the lack of support from the UAW leadership was read as a lack of support for the local and its argument.

At the same time the lawsuit was being argued in a downtown Detroit courtroom, the House Un-American Activities Committee (HUAC) was in town badgering political progressives. Representative Donald L. Jackson, a Republican from Santa Monica, California, urged unions to "take some of these Communists by the seat of their pants and throw them out." Reuther was doing just that, and speculation ran rampant that he had cut a deal with HUAC that they could have Local 600 if the committee left the top UAW leadership alone. (The Reuther brothers had had significant socialist ties during the Depression years.) In the end, the court sided with Ford and tossed out Local 600's challenge to the decentralization plan. The union, which had sixty thousand members when the lawsuit ended in 1953, dwindled to forty-two thousand seven years later.

At the same time, some of Detroit's old guard auto companies were losing ground to the growing power of the Big Three. Both Hudson and Packard went out of business during the decade, Hudson getting folded into the new American Motors and Packard getting gobbled up by Studebaker. Combined with the decentralization strategies of the Big Three, that meant a significant job loss in Detroit, both in the city and the metropolitan area. As auto jobs left the region, the amount of work done by local supporting industries, from the people who made windshield wipers to those who made prototypes for car seats, was reduced. The effect on Detroit employment was profound. In 1940, the city of Detroit had 625,456 residents working for pay, a number that climbed to 757,772 a decade later, according to census data. But during the next decade, total employment in the city dropped to below the prewar levels, reaching 612,295 in 1960. It was a trend, not a fluctuation, with employment continuing to drop during the 1960s to 561,184 by 1970, down 26 percent over the decade. Similarly, production workers alone shifted from 181,935 in 1939, before the war production fired up, to 281,515 in 1947, but then dropped to 232,348 in 1954 and eroded further to 145,177—lower than the late-Depression, prewar levels—by 1958.[8]

And, obviously enough, with the jobs went the income. Black Detroiters suffered the most because they were primarily relegated to the lowest-paying and most tenuous positions. The median family income for white

Detroiters in 1959 was $7,050, while the median for black families was $4,370. While the median white family income increased 71 percent during the decade, the median for black families increased only 40 percent. The vast majority of black households—73 percent—lived on less than $6,000. For white families, that number was only 41 percent. So as whites left Detroit, the growing number of black households were living on a median income less than two-thirds of what the white families had been making, with a corresponding drop in the economic vitality of neighborhood shops and downtown stores. In 1959, nearly 18.5 percent of black men had no income at all, compared with 8.5 percent of white men. The gap would only increase in the coming years. By 1969, the median family income in Detroit was $10,045, but for black families, who then accounted for just under half the population, the median was $8,645. Detroit was two cities defined by one boundary.[9]

While Detroit's population was shrinking, the rest of the nation was undergoing a massive expansion propelled, ironically, by the revived auto industry. Cities were being affected by rapid suburbanization, eased by a new system of local and interstate freeways that allowed commuters to live farther from where they worked. It wasn't long before the jobs began following the workers, as local governments used tax breaks and other incentives to compete with each other to entice companies to build in their outlying areas.

Metropolitan Detroit, which had no significant regional planning system in place, began spreading like a stain. While Detroit's suburbs boomed, new housing construction in the city stagnated. The city added 13,565 new housing units in 1950 as it was still struggling to meet the postwar demand. In 1958, it added only 2,242 as the demand ebbed and the city began running out of space. Detroit wasn't the only major urban core to shrink during these years, but none shrank as much or as fast—or have had as much trouble finding a way to stanch the bleeding.

The suburban boom and the decentralization patterns continued through the 1960s, as did the shrinkage of Detroit's economic base and its population. For the period between 1957 and 1961, some 14 percent of plant and equipment investment by US companies was done overseas. A decade later, it had doubled to 28 percent. And the automobile industry went with them. In the early 1970s, about one out of every three dollars invested by the Big Three was going to offshore sites. And a significant portion of the rest was going to the South and Midwest, particularly to states with Right to Work laws that limited the organizing ability of the UAW. The Big Three were, in effect, running away from home.[10]

DETROITERS III

HENRY RUSSELL JR.

On a Monday morning in June 1953, Henry Russell Jr. joined the rest of the recent graduates of the segregated and all-black R. B. Hudson High School of Selma, Alabama, in a ritual that, for many of those involved, would define their futures. On the previous Friday, the graduating seniors had finished their last classes and final exams and then spent the weekend celebrating—barbecues and parties, family gatherings, and, for many, Sunday church services. There was a sense of finality to the get-togethers, a mix of joy and pride for having completed high school but also a sense of leave-taking. Because come Monday, many of those celebrating graduates would stop at the high school to pick up their final report cards and diplomas and then board buses and trains that would take them off to become an American diaspora.

Like many small cities in the South, there weren't enough jobs in Selma to absorb the rising generation of workers. And given the entrenched segregation, there were even fewer opportunities for young black workers. Russell graduated a year before the Reverend Martin Luther King Jr. was appointed pastor of the Dexter Avenue Baptist Church in Montgomery, and two years before Rosa Parks famously refused to give up her bus seat. There were stirrings, but civil rights advocates had yet to gel into a movement.

Russell, degree in hand, had few options. Selma had a train yard, a cigar factory, a couple of cottonseed oil factories, and a new nearby air force base. But the blacks who were lucky enough to get hired on at any of those places inevitably landed in the hardest and dirtiest jobs. And they were jobs without futures. The paths to promotions, more responsibility, and higher pay were reserved for whites. The other option was subsistence farming in the outlying regions, where those who worked the land made meager livings in a throwback to even worse times than the 1950s. "The blacks would drive horses and wagons into town on Saturday, and you'd see them parked," Russell recalled. It was a system of enforced stagnation, designed to limit the economic options for blacks. "When you're young, this is all you know. It was segregated but you understood your role in the system, and you understood the system and how it worked. And your parents made sure you didn't [violate the unwritten codes]. It was good as long as you knew your so-called place."[1]

But it wasn't good enough. Russell's father, unable to land a job that paid enough to support his family, had already moved north, first to Chicago, which he disliked, then to Detroit, where he eventually signed on at Ford. It was a marital separation driven by need, not a romantic break. Russell's mother was a teacher, and every summer she and her son would take the train north to Detroit to reunite with the senior Russell for a couple of months, then head back south for the school year. As Russell neared the end of his high school career, he knew that he, too, would be joining his father in the North.

Russell was in no particular rush to leave after graduation. He had spent the previous summer working with a friend in tobacco fields in Connecticut, so he had a pretty good sense of what life was going to be like. "I realized during that last month or so of school that you're getting out of high school and you're not coming back," Russell recalled. "Then you realize you're not going to see all these kids you've been seeing all your life, from grade school all the way through. You're used to seeing them every year and then all of a sudden you're not going to. And there are guys I have not seen since I graduated. This is it. You're going out into the world." He planned to hang around Selma for a week or so, whiling away some hours with his buddies for the last time, then make his way to Detroit. But on that first Monday after high school, Russell saw that, for the most part, the life he had known in Selma was already evaporating.

Like his classmates, Russell picked up his grades and diploma at the high school, and then walked around town. Everywhere he went, it seemed, he saw people with bags packed. "Everybody was leaving," he recalled nearly a lifetime later, sitting at a wooden dining room table in his house on Detroit's near west side. "The bus station. . . . The train station. Kids that you knew were leaving. I walked up to the Broad Street bus station and a lot of kids were waiting. They got their bags. I went home and told my mother, I said, I'm going to leave today. I went and told one of my best friends, and my mother drove me to Montgomery and I caught the Humming Bird train."

The Humming Bird train covered one of the main routes of the old Louisville & Nashville Railroad, making daily runs between Cincinnati and New Orleans through the heart of Alabama. The northbound train stopped in Montgomery in the late afternoon, and by the next morning, it had carried Russell to Cincinnati. There, he connected through on another line to Detroit, arriving late that afternoon at the massive Michigan Central Station, a Beaux Arts landmark with an eighteen-story office tower atop the cavernous depot and waiting room.

"That station," Russell said, "was beautiful." The depot had opened forty years earlier as a seed for business development nearly two miles west of downtown. The plan was to link international travel, via a rail tunnel under the nearby Detroit River to Canada, to the national network of rail lines, all fed by local trolley and light rail systems spider-webbing out into the city. The station itself was expected to generate spin-off development and businesses, expanding the beating economic heart of Detroit from the overcrowded (and thus expensive) downtown office district.

But the developments faltered shortly after Michigan Central opened, and then died during the Depression years. The depot remained busy

Henry Russell Jr. MICHELLE ANDONIAN

during World War II, but by the time Russell arrived in 1953 the station was already in financial trouble, a victim, in a sense, of the car culture that Detroit had created. Russell knew little of that on the June evening that marked the start of his own future in Detroit. He just knew his father lived in the city, had a good-paying job, and that as a young black man he could make his own mark in Detroit a lot more easily than in Selma. Russell wandered through the station until he found a row of pay phones and called his father to come pick him up.

A few days later Russell, armed with the name of a contact his father had given him, went to the employment office at the Ford Rouge plant to fill out an application. Ford had developed a reputation as a place willing to hire blacks while many of the other major employers refused to. Russell said he never encountered such rejection personally, but fellow workers with longer histories in Detroit—including his father—told him of being turned away at hiring offices while whites were handed applications to fill out.

How a black man was received depended to a large extent on the attitude of the hiring office. One plant might hire a lot of blacks; another might not, depending on the whims of the managers—all white in those years, and often from the South. Ford at the time maintained its own informal caste system. If there was a tough, dirty job to be filled, the black worker would get it. If an easier job opened up, like driving the finished cars off the end of the assembly line, it would go to a white worker. Much like the Jim Crow South, once you understood and accepted how the system worked, you could get by—an acquiescence that helped perpetuate the system itself.

All Russell wanted was to find a good, reliable job. He showed up early that morning and had to wait until the office opened at 8 AM. In a mark of the constant flow of southern blacks to Detroit, Russell ran into one of his Selma schoolmates and let him cut in front of him in line. It was a lucky act of generosity. The classmate was sent to fill an opening in the engine plant, where the work was easier but the shifts more prone to layoffs. Russell was sent to the assembly line, which had more job security.

The 1950s were a vibrant time in Detroit, for whites and blacks. Russell rented a room in a house off Clairmount Avenue and LaSalle Street on the near west side, close to where he lives now. It was a few blocks west of Twelfth Street, with its bustling pool halls, bars, and nightclubs catering to the growing black neighborhood—many of the residents transplants from Black Bottom. The landlady was from Selma. "She knew my parents and everything," Russell said. "She was just like a mother."

Russell's own mother moved north in 1954, reuniting with her husband, and a couple years later they bought a two-story pale-brick house on Atkinson Street, near where Russell was renting. Russell eventually moved in and stayed with them for seven years, until he married in 1969 and moved into the house next door. Without being aware of it, the family was part of the neighborhood changeover from mostly Jewish to all black. Russell's plan was for his wife, a hospital worker, to help Russell's mother tend to his father, who was ailing. Within a few years, though, Russell's own wife developed brain cancer, and Russell's mother helped care for her until she died in the late 1980s.

By then, Detroit had undergone some massive changes. In the Ford Rouge plant, Russell watched discrimination ebb. When he first started working on the assembly line, discrimination against blacks was part of the culture. "The women even had it worse," Russell recalled. "At that time, in the fifties, they weren't hiring women in the plants. Those that were there were from World War II, they were leftovers. . . . You saw a lot of discrimination going on. They didn't want blacks to drive the cars off the lines, because that was an easy job; you didn't work too hard and didn't get dirty."

Russell, though, had made himself more useful by learning a wide range of jobs. He was motivated by curiosity, he said, but an unforeseen benefit was that as layoffs came and went, the foremen kept Russell on, taking advantage of his versatility. He slowly moved his way up in seniority. As discrimination dissipated, black workers began winning jobs as foremen and supervisors, then as the all-important plant managers. As attitudes changed, and more blacks landed jobs, the internal politics of the plant changed, too. In 1969 Russell won election as UAW shop steward, a mark of acceptance and respect from his fellow autoworkers.

16

DEATH OF THE COVENANTS

In late 1944, D. Orsel McGhee, a black elevator operator (and eventual head custodian) in the *Detroit Free Press* building in downtown Detroit, and his wife, Minnie McGhee, a black Detroit public school teacher, decided to move four blocks north from their home at 6346 Ironwood Avenue into a thirteen-hundred-square-foot, two-story brick house at 4626 Seebaldt Street. The Ironwood Avenue neighborhood they were leaving was predominately black, part of a cluster of African American homes south of Tireman Avenue. Seebaldt Street, even though it was nearby, was all white. It's unclear whether that step over the racial line gave the McGhees much pause. But in early December, a few days after signing the deed to their new house, the McGhees moved in. A month later, one of their adjacent neighbors, a white man named Benjamin Sipes, flanked by members of the Northwest Neighborhood Association, showed up on the doorstep and explained to the McGhees that the house they had bought had a restriction on the deed barring the property's sale to black buyers. He asked the couple to move out.

The McGhees refused. The association sent them a couple of letters as a follow-up, and when the McGhees ignored those Sipes and the association sued. A Wayne County circuit court judge declared that the McGhees were, indeed, black, and as such were in violation of the deed restriction and so had to move. The court refused to grant a stay while the McGhees appealed. It's unclear how they managed it, but the McGhees remained in the house anyway, where they faced a steady stream of demonstrations and acts of harassment.

"Groups of people would walk by carrying guns," Orsel and Minnie's son Reginald McGhee recalled some forty years later. "Somebody burned a cross on the lawn one night, and another time somebody tried to break into the house. My father was a gentle person but all this turmoil really riled him up. Got his dander up. There were times when he would sit through the night in the front room with his gun."[1]

After the Michigan supreme court upheld the lower court's decision, the McGhees, by now represented by NAACP lawyer Thurgood Marshall, turned to the federal courts, and eventually to the US Supreme Court, which had in earlier decisions dating back decades affirmed the legal authority of deed restrictions on private property. Such covenants, the rulings held, were private agreements. But Marshall did not challenge the restrictions themselves. Instead, he challenged the court's authority to enforce them, saying that to do so meant the government would then be denying blacks access to property. And that, he argued, violated the "equal protection" clause in the post–Civil War Fourteenth Amendment that barred states from enforcing "any law which shall abridge the privileges or immunities of citizens of the United States; nor shall any State deprive any person of life, liberty, or property, without due process of law; nor deny to any person within its jurisdiction the equal protection of the laws." The McGhees' appeal was merged with a related case from Saint Louis by another black couple, J. D. and Ethel Lee Shelley, who had also been sued by their white neighbors for buying a deed-restricted house.

The case was argued before the Supreme Court over two days in January 1948, and the McGhees and the Shelleys had a surprise ally: the federal government. The US Solicitor General's office—essentially the house lawyer for the federal government—filed a "friend of the court" brief backing Marshall's argument. In May, the court ruled six to zero for the McGhees and the Shelleys and, by extension, for millions of African Americans who had been ghettoized by deed restrictions. (Three justices recused themselves without explanation, spawning speculation that they had lived in deed-restricted homes themselves.)

"The historical context in which the Fourteenth Amendment became a part of the Constitution should not be forgotten," the Court said in its opinion written by Chief Justice Fred M. Vinson. "Whatever else the framers sought to achieve, it is clear that the matter of primary concern was the establishment of equality in the enjoyment of basic civil and political rights and the preservation of those rights from discriminatory action on the part of the States based on considerations of race or color. . . . Upon full consideration, we have concluded that in these cases the States have acted to deny petitioners the equal protection of the laws guaranteed by the Fourteenth Amendment." The court decision angered whites but enthused open-housing advocates. In Detroit, and elsewhere, middle class and wealthy blacks began moving out of their overcrowded neighborhoods.

White home owners reacted to the new black mobility in two ways. In the years between 1943 and 1965, at least 192 neighborhood or home owners associations were formed in Detroit, aimed at preserving the status quo in neighborhoods. One telling flyer circulated in March 1950 summoned "all residents" of a sixty block area of northeast Detroit to an "emergency meeting." The subject: "Neighborhood Invaded by Colored Purchase on Orleans & Minnesota. Every resident asked to be present to vote on measures to be taken, sign petitions, and elect block captains."[2] Self-organizing soon gave way to the second reaction. The white home owners began putting up FOR SALE signs.

Significantly, black Detroit also began to split along the seams of class. For decades black Detroiters, barred by segregation from such white-dominated services as mortgages and quality healthcare, had created their own merchant and professional class. A. G. Wright had made a comfortable fortune as the owner and proprietor of the Hotel Gotham, where top-flight black entertainers stayed while in Detroit. The Diggs family handled most of the funerals for black Detroiters through their delightfully named House of Diggs parlor (Charles Diggs Jr., who grew up in the family business, went on to serve twenty-five years in the US House of Representatives before a 1980 corruption scandal sent him to prison). There were retailers and car dealers, publishers, and operators of small banks.

With more blacks getting jobs in the auto industry, where UAW-bargained wages were pushing the working class into middle-income lives, more black workers also were able to afford to move out of the slums around Hastings Street, Black Bottom, and the other traditional black zones, and into more comfortable and spacious homes in white neighborhoods.

Outlawing deed restrictions, though, was not the same as gaining acceptance by whites. Much like the black–white gap Kornhauser found in the 1951 survey of attitudes toward Detroit, how one viewed a neighborhood yawned widely by race. Later studies drawn from the 1976 and 2004 Detroit Area Studies surveys, conducted by the University of Michigan's Department of Sociology and the Survey Research Center of the Institute for Social Research, zeroed in on the difference. But the underlying attitudes were likely present in the 1950s and 1960s and became magnified over time with the city's deteriorating condition and rise in crime. Researchers showed different diagrams of racial balances in neighborhoods and asked whites and blacks into which neighborhoods they would be more likely to move, and less likely. The findings reveal the core propellant of the exodus from Detroit. In the 2004 study, three-quarters of the whites said they'd move into a neighborhood in which blacks accounted for less than 20 percent of the residents, but only half would move into a neighborhood if the black proportion rose to one-third. If a neighborhood was more than half black, less than a third of the whites said they would be likely to move in. Blacks, though, were most likely to move into a neighborhood that was evenly split, and less likely to move into predominately white or predominately black neighborhoods.[3]

So, in broad terms, black home owners were seeking new neighborhoods in which there was a racial balance. But once that balance was achieved, the neighborhoods became less attractive to whites who, one can presume, then began moving out. So as blacks sought stability and integration, whites would uproot in pursuit of what to them was a more comfortable level of segregation. But only after some initial resistance.[4]

The story of Detroit in the 1950s is studded with street-level showdowns between existing white residents and newly arriving blacks that were marked by arson, vandalism, parades of intimidation, and the occasional cross burning. Despite the mushrooming nighttime mobs, often egged on by white youths, there were few direct physical encounters. When the hurled stones and epithets didn't work—when black persistence overcame white resistance—the whites would begin drifting to other neighborhoods. And ever outward the expansion grew.[5]

Between the ambitions of black families and open-housing advocates and the fears of white home owners, opportunistic—and shady—real estate brokers found a strategy to get rich. White brokers dominated the real estate trade, many of them from offices in the ring suburbs, and they routinely solicited white home owners in Detroit neighborhoods near where black families were moving in, urging them to list their homes "before it was too late."

An April 21, 1966, report detailed four forces at play in Detroit's housing market. Despite a 1962 city Fair Neighborhood Practices Ordinance barring the practice, white residents of neighborhoods undergoing racial change were subject to repeated solicitations to sell their homes, which were then marketed exclusively to black buyers as white buyers were diverted to white neighborhoods. And blacks were never shown houses in the neighborhoods the white brokers were seeking to keep white. In many cases, white homes were sold on land contracts, with no banks involved, to blacks whose incomes shouldn't have qualified them for mortgages, a precursor to the practices that led to the 2008 housing collapse. When the black home buyers fell behind on the payments, they were booted out, losing their down payment and equity, and freeing the white owners—often, by now, real estate brokers or related investment groups—to resell the house on another land contract. Properties could be sold several times, with the owners pocketing the down payments, before a sale finally took root.[6]

The practice violated city codes and federal law alike, but the real estate agents often operated with impunity—and in the face of opposition from fair housing advocates and neighborhood associations. Jerry McDonald, head of the community relations commission for the community organization New Detroit Inc., summed it up in a letter in September 1968: "The real estate industry taken collectively forms a gigantic conspiracy which promotes and maintains segregated housing patterns. This is partly due to racist attitudes on the part of broker and the agents, but more importantly, it is because segregated housing markets are profitable for the industry. The real estate broker makes his profits from commissions paid on the selling price of the properties he sells. The more properties he can sell, the more commissions he collects. It is, therefore, obvious that panic selling in changing neighborhoods results in higher profits because more properties are sold. It is also clear that this kind of selling would not occur if the total market was racially integrated."

Brokers, of course, argued that they were merely the instruments of the market, "acting on behalf of homeowners and cannot be blamed for their clients' bigotry," McDonald wrote. "However, the facts of history do not substantiate this contention." The Michigan Real Estate Association, he pointed out, had been a major political player in fighting against a housing component of the 1966 US Civil Rights Act.

The problem embroiled the suburbs, too. McDonald cited revelations that brokers in the Grosse Pointes, well-to-do suburbs on Detroit's eastern boundary, had created a secret "points" system in which they assigned values to prospective customers based on race, ethnicity, and religion. If the would-be buyers didn't clear a certain threshold of WASPishness, they would be steered to houses elsewhere. In general, McDonald concluded, the Detroit metro area had two housing markets, separate and unequal. The pervasiveness of that racial divide persists today in informal ways. As middle-class blacks have moved into suburban enclaves from Southfield in the northwest to Eastpointe (formerly East Detroit), to the northeast, middle-class whites have moved out.[7]

Across the United States, the mid 1960s were plagued by excruciating urban violence. From 1964 through 1967 there were at least twenty-nine riots. Some were relatively nonviolent skirmishes, such as a protest in the Hunter's Point section of San Francisco in September 1966 after police shot and killed a black teen. Others were catastrophic, such as the thirty-four deaths in an August 1965 riot in Los Angeles's Watts neighborhood. All the eruptions had racial overtones and grew out of long-simmering frustrations in black neighborhoods over housing conditions, job discrimination, and brutal and overtly racist tactics by white-dominated police departments.

None of the conflagrations, though, were as broad or as deep as the one that erupted at the corner of Twelfth Street and Clairmount Avenue in Detroit in the early morning hours of July 23, 1967. Over the next five days, forty-three people were killed—mostly young blacks shot by white police or Michigan National Guardsmen—and more than eleven hundred people were injured while some seven thousand people were arrested. Arson became the crime of choice, and two thousand buildings went up in flames. Unlike the 1863 riot, or the 1943 riot, the 1967 explosion was not a race riot, with whites and blacks battling each other in running street fights. Rather, it was a violent expression of frustration and rage by black Detroiters directed at anything within reach, and eventually quelled by military intervention. It was a revolt from below.

The origins of the 1967 Detroit riot could well be the most plumbed in history, from government commissions to academic treatises to journalistic dissections, such as John Hersey's *The Algiers Motel Incident*, about the killings of three young black men by Detroit police in the last spasms of the riot. Preriot police behavior, including summary beatings of blacks by special roving four-man police units known as Big Fours, was a key factor in the growing frustrations in Detroit's black neighborhoods. But the tinder was arranged by decades of discrimination formal and informal, stunted ambitions, and a lack of hope by the chronically poor that conditions would improve. The killings of the three unarmed black men by police at the Algiers Motel underscored the daily oppressions and indignities blacks suffered.

The riot began after what should have been a routine police raid on a blind pig packed with revelers for a welcome-home party celebrating two young black soldiers who had just returned from Vietnam. Not knowing about the party, police expected to find a handful of patrons inside; they found more than eighty. The police decided to arrest everyone, and as they waited for reinforcements and extra vehicles in which to cart away the illegal partiers, a crowd formed on the street. Residents began yelling at the police to let the detained partiers go. As the police finally left, some of the mob broke into a nearby store. Within hours, the looting and violence had spread, and the city burst into flames.

The riots raged for five days. Mayor Jerome Cavanagh, whose embrace of affirmative action and criticisms of police brutality had won him wide support among black voters, initially sought to quell the uprising with police units, but—given that most blacks considered the police the problem—the effort failed. Forty-eight hours later, Governor George Romney sent in the National Guard, and when they proved inadequate to the task, he asked President Lyndon Johnson to send in federal troops. The violence ended, though in truth it's just as likely the passion had, by then, burned itself out.

What happened after the riot is more significant than what happened during it. Commissions were established, including the National Advisory Commission on Civil Disorders, created by Johnson to determine the causes of the summer of fire across the country. The Kerner Commission, named after chairman and Illinois governor Otto Kerner Jr., blamed the riots generally on black response to white racism. It warned that the nation was descending into "two societies, one black, one white—separate and unequal." It pointed out the growing disparities in everything from access to livable housing to the deteriorating urban school districts, which in Detroit included the collapse of what had been one of the nation's marquee systems. At the time of the riot, Detroit was spending $500 less per student each year than was being spent in suburban school districts, and about half of the city's youth dropped out before graduating, consigning themselves, in most cases, to lives of poverty.

"What white Americans have never fully understood—but what the Negro can never forget—is that white society is deeply implicated in the ghetto," the report said. "White institutions created it, white institutions maintain it, and white society condones it." Critics argued that the Kerner Commission's conclusions were a simplification; that racism in the Deep South was much worse than in the North, yet cities like Birmingham, Alabama, had not burned, so racism could not have been the trigger.

But the difference between being black in the North and being black in the South lies in expectations. As Henry Russell Jr. had said about his decision to move to Detroit after growing up in Selma, Alabama, blacks could survive in the South by knowing "their place"; in the North, they expected to be able to define that place for themselves. And postriot analyses and surveys found that most of the blacks involved in rioting and looting were born in the North.

The 1967 riot—or rebellion, as local political progressives and many African Americans came to call it—was a pivotal moment in the modern trajectory of Detroit. Nearly a half-century later, areas destroyed during those five days remain undeveloped, and the clash between black frustration and white political and cultural domination continues to reverberate through the city and suburbs. It was a pivotal moment in image and self-perception as well, and seemed to confirm the worst racial fears of both whites and blacks. To whites, it affirmed racist perceptions of inner-city blacks; for blacks, it gave credence to perceptions that government institutions—including police—weren't concerned with their well-being.

While the riot didn't cause Detroit's white and middle-class flight, it was a powerful propellant behind already existing forces, exacerbating racial and class divides drawn by the national trend toward suburbanization, industrial decentralization by automakers and other industries, and local white reaction to housing desegregation.

In the aftermath, Detroit community organizations sprang up to seek ways to ameliorate the conditions that gave rise to the violence. Nonprofits such as FOCUS: Hope were created to provide the kinds of services the city failed to deliver, such as direct training in job and life skills for the chronically poor and unemployed. But in the end, nothing changed. In fact, white flight accelerated through the 1970s, as did the infusion of new black residents. Poverty spread as the white middle class left out of racism or fear of violence or declining property values, or to pursue the jobs that were moving farther away from the city core—or from the state altogether.

In 1966, the City of Detroit had lost twenty-two thousand residents, part of the inexorable slide that had begun in the 1950s. In 1967, with the riot occurring just after midyear, sixty-seven thousand people left. In 1968, some eighty thousand people left, and another forty-six thousand departed in 1969. Not just people were leaving; businesses were running away, too. In the decade after the riot Detroit lost more than 110,000 jobs. Detroit's population loss may actually have been slowing until the conflagration, only to pick up fresh energy from the fires and the killings. "The riot put Detroit on the fast track to economic desolation," Mayor Coleman A. Young, who was a state senator during the riot, said years later. "The money was carried out in the pockets of the businesses and the white people who fled as fast as they could." The number of manufacturing and retail shops dropped by half over the next twenty-five years.[8]

The drain continued as the years wore on, and the city's demographics changed significantly. In 1960, Detroit's black population totaled about 482,000 people, which grew to 660,000 by 1970, a gain of about 37 percent, as Southern blacks continued to see Detroit as a better alternative to the Deep South. But the white population shrank by a third from nearly 1.2 million in 1960 to 816,000. The racial balance was shifting as white Detroiters left at a higher rate than black migrants moved in. Segregation in the workplace was decreasing, but black workers were still being hired mostly for lower-wage positions and still remained in the minority on most job sites. The whites who moved out tended to be middle and upper-middle class, those with the financial wherewithal to buy new, and increasingly large, homes in outlying areas of Grosse Pointe, Bloomfield Hills, and the farmlands between Detroit and Ann Arbor. As the population shifted, so, too, did the economy. But it also changed in outlook. The city began to sour.

"The riot changed everything," says Carl S. Taylor, a Michigan State University sociologist who has written extensively about Detroit's criminal and economic underclass. Taylor grew up in the area near where the riots started, and believes those few days of violence marked Detroit's transition from a place of relatively mixed stability, with intact social institutions and viable neighborhoods, to what he refers to as the "third city." Detroit's mores turned upside down, and Detroiters began embracing what had been marginalized—the illicit economy of stolen goods, extralegal activities, the glorification of the violence, and the framing of the police and other governmental institutions as enemies.[9]

"Values have changed immensely," Taylor said, recalling a near west side of Detroit that was mixed racially and economically, with whites, blacks, and Jews, living in close proximity. Stores in the neighborhood were mostly owned by whites and Jews, and people still received milk and eggs via delivery trucks. There was a neighborhood ethic against illegalities. To buy something that had been stolen, for example, was to invite ostracism. After the riot, that changed. "There's a thriving economy going on, and some people have only worked that economy, and they have very strong antigovernment feelings," Taylor said. "I don't think we should be surprised by what we're seeing now."

Harder to measure is the impact of the assassination of Dr. Martin Luther King Jr. in April 1968, less than a year after the riots. King's murder sparked smaller uprisings and ventings of grief and rage in Chicago and Washington, DC. In Detroit, the emotions were no less acute, but the streets remained quiet. Still, the killing seeped into the city's soul and began to fester.

One collection of three surveys offers a telling shift in black attitudes. One was taken before King's assassination, one a week or so after, and the third in 1971. In the immediate aftermath of King's death there was limited change in black Detroiters' perceptions of race relations. But three years after the death, the percentage of those who said they didn't trust white people nearly doubled from 8.8 percent to 16.4 percent. And there was a related erosion in black perceptions of whether whites were willing to give blacks a break or try to keep them down. In 1968, 41.3 percent thought whites were willing to give them a break, and 24.4 percent thought whites wanted to keep blacks down. By 1971, the perceptions had flipped, with 28.4 percent saying whites were willing to give blacks a break and 40.9 percent felt whites wanted to keep them down. A fairly steady one-third across both studies believed that whites didn't care either way, which meant that a significant majority of black Detroiters believed their fellow white citizens were, at best, indifferent to them and, at worst, hostile to them.[10]

A cultural despair began to take hold. Before King's death, 70.9 percent of black Detroiters felt there had been progress made in ending racial discrimination of the previous fifteen years. That stayed about the same in the survey taken a few weeks after the assassination. By 1971, though, those who felt progress had been made had dropped to 67 percent, and those who felt there had been no change in racial discrimination had risen almost 5 percent. The attitudes played out in ways large and small. In the January 1968 survey, which came after the riot but before King's assassination, 23.6 percent of blacks felt downtown store clerks treated them less politely than they treated whites, a percentage that rose to 32.2 percent in the second survey. By 1971, 43.8 percent said they felt a difference in white politeness. This can be read as something of a mirror reading of white racial attitudes. After the riot, more whites likely found themselves uncomfortable with black customers, a sense that increased as time went on.

And then the bottom fell out.

DETROITERS IV

THE BALOKS

Linda Balok sits at the dining table of her comfortable ranch house in Macomb County's Shelby Township, some fifteen miles north of the Eight Mile Road divider between Detroit and the northern suburbs.

Balok was born in 1950 on McClellan Street, near Warren Avenue on Detroit's east side, then moved with her family in 1960 to a small and aging farmhouse on Greiner Street, a few blocks north of City Airport (now the Coleman A. Young International Airport). Balok, who is white, attended Catholic schools as a function of family faith. She got married and in the mid-1970s had a daughter, April, then a son, John, whom she and her husband, also named John, planned to raise in a large, two-story home on East Outer Drive near her mother's house in her home parish, Our Lady of Good Counsel. Soon the family was joined by another daughter, Hillary, in 1980.

Detroit was already struggling to save itself, but the neighborhood seemed stable. The Baloks lived, in effect, a suburban lifestyle in the city. They lived far from downtown; John Balok went off to work each morning as a salesman and Linda cared for the children, getting them breakfast and launching them on their day. "I took the kids to school one day and I came back home and looked into the kitchen and thought my husband had been home," she says. "The cupboard was open and all the papers were on the countertop, and I says, 'Boy, your father leaves such a mess.' Several hours later . . . I noticed we had been robbed. They cut a nice round circle in [the glass window of] the French doors in the back and reached in and unlocked the door."

The burglar had made off with some whiskey, which Balok says is about all there was in the house to steal. "But that upset me. You feel violated." There had been other break-ins in the neighborhood, including homes owned by Detroit police officers. "They didn't even call the police. They said there was no use." Balok began thinking that it might be time for the family to move. But interest rates were at record highs and the Baloks couldn't find a house they liked. The lure of family history, and neighborhood, overwhelmed the ebbing fear of another burglary.

The balance shifted in 1983, three years after that first break-in. Linda Balok heard a strange sound. "It was about one o'clock in the morning and I heard this, like a spring, and I was saying, 'Oh those kids, they're jumping on their beds." She peeked in on the children but found them motionless, seemingly asleep. She returned to her own bed and heard the noise again, and thought the kids were playing a trick on her. "I thought, I'm going to catch them." She went into the children's room and settled onto the floor between their beds. "I thought, Just move and I gotcha! And I heard the noise again, and I realized it wasn't that. We had a sunroom that had screens all around it. Somebody was trying to break into the house. We had the cars in the driveway. They knew we were home." She ran and woke up her husband, who ventured down the stairs turning on lights as he went, which scared the would-be burglar away.

"I got upset," Balok recalls. "It's one thing when they come during the day and break into your house when nobody's home. It's another thing when they see your cars, they know you're home, and they break in anyway. What was their intent? You would read newspaper stories where they would tie everybody up in the basement." Her husband had recently begun working as a field service engineer for Agfa, a photo products manufacturer and supplier, which had him on the road a lot and left his wife home alone with the children. They decided the risk of staying was too high, particularly for their children.

There were financial considerations, too. While Balok was educated in Catholic parochial schools as an expression of the family's religious faith, she and her husband were sending their kids to the nearby Our Lady of Good Counsel parochial school because they distrusted the safety and the caliber of the public schools, which were already in a steep and rapid decline. The couple was running out of reasons to stay, and the fears that had once ebbed rushed back in a flood tide. "We started seriously looking."

They joined the exodus of white families and moved into their new home, an exurban ranch house, a few months later. They got a deal. Few houses in the new subdivision were being sold because of high interest rates and a steep recession, this one spawned in part by a surge in oil prices, which dampened car sales—yet another economic contraction that had an amplified effect on Detroit. The Baloks talked the cash-strapped developer down from the $145,000 asking price to $85,000. "After he sold our house, he just got out of" the residential development business, she says. And the couple found what they were looking for: relative safety, a good public school system, and a deeper sense of happiness, though their faith in the caliber of the schools wavered over time. Their fourth and youngest child, Andrew, was born after the move to the suburbs and was sent to parochial schools.

Balok has had few regrets about the move, none of them substantial. "The houses in Detroit, you'll never find the workmanship that you do there out here," she says. "It was nice to be part of a neighborhood." She recalls with nostalgic warmth the days when, as a child, the door to the family home was never locked, a habit she followed into adulthood. "We moved out here and the back door was always left unlocked until my kids moved out."

The Baloks' daughter, Hillary Balok, is the reason Linda Balok's story stands out among the hundreds of thousands of people who decided to leave Detroit. In 2007, Hillary and her husband, Ben Brady, bought one of the condos in a restored Brush Park mansion near downtown Detroit, just a few weed-strewn lots away from the Taylor House renovated by art historian Michael Farrell. At first, Hillary kept the move a secret from her parents. "They probably knew we would be concerned, upset, so they didn't say anything until their deal was closed," Balok says.

And Balok did fear for her daughter, a child of the suburbs. "Because she grew up out here she didn't have the street smarts; she trusted everybody and everything," Balok says, adding that Brady, too, had "grown up in a structured environment. Now she's getting a little more street smart about things. I would worry if it was parents with children. What are you going to do, let them go out and play? But for their lifestyle, it's good for them. They like the activities, the football games, all the bars and restaurants. It's a good life for them."

The young couple's new home is one of four units in what is known as the Frederick Butler House, an eighty-four-hundred-square-foot, two-story, redbrick French Renaissance mansion with a high, sloping mansard roof. Butler was a banker, part of the early wave of Detroit's post–Civil War nouveau riche who made Brush Park the city's original neighborhood for the wealthy. Like much of the rest of Brush Park, his once-grand manor fell on hard times, and was eventually carved up into a series of single-room apartments with shared bathrooms. Unlike most of Brush Park, the building was never abandoned, and when the family-owned Renevatio redevelopment firm bought it in 2005 to restore it and remarket it as condos, people were still living there. So it still has original fixtures, including pocket doors and fireplaces, that otherwise would have been lost to scavengers long ago.

Hillary Balok and Ben Brady had been living across the river in Windsor, but wanted to move to Detroit for better job prospects for Ben and to cut down on the commute for Hillary, who was already working at Kautex, a division of the investment firm Textron. Ben eventually landed a job at Code Systems, which supplies keyless locks to Ford.

At first they looked in the Grosse Pointe suburbs, long a dream site for Hillary, but they didn't find anything they liked that they could afford or that didn't need expensive work, from a new roof to replacing leaky windows. Ben was ambivalent about buying a home in Detroit, but Hillary persuaded him to scout around some of the downtown lofts, ostensibly for design ideas. Then they saw the new condos in the restored Butler house within sight of the new Ford Field, home of the Detroit

Hillary Balok and Ben Brady. MICHELLE ANDONIAN

Lions, which is across the street from the ten-year-old Comerica Park, home of the Detroit Tigers. They bought one of the units.

Other than game days, it's a quiet neighborhood, with only seven people living on the mostly undeveloped street. "Today we're having people over," Ben says. "No one is ever going to complain about turning the radio down." But it can be a tough neighborhood to live in. There are a few small, relatively expensive grocery stores nearby (operated by the Spartan chain, based in Grand Rapids), and there are bars and restaurants in the nearby Cass Corridor, as well as downtown. Other items, such as clothing, require trips to the suburbs, only a slight inconvenience since they both work in the suburbs anyway.

They have had minor crime problems—a car was broken into, which led them to be more careful to park inside the building's garage. The bigger frustration comes with Detroit Tigers baseball games, when fans park for free along the neighborhood streets, dumping garbage as they leave and urinating in the streets and weed-covered lots. "They just treat it like a garbage can," Hillary says. "It makes me absolutely insane. If I were to walk by their yard and throw something, they'd have a coronary. But here it's OK, it's Detroit, so we'll just treat it poorly." But it's a "garbage can" with risks. During the games, the parked cars are targets for smash-and-grab thieves, and after the cars leave small piles of shattered safety glass glisten on the street like snow drifts.

Hillary recognizes the negative effect of the renovation of apartment buildings into condos. "We displaced people," she says, as the low-income renters were forced out to make way for the gentrification. But the spark of life such projects have brought to Brush Park and the other neighborhoods just north of downtown is worth the social costs, she believes, even though the spark has yet to turn into flame. When the Bradys bought, Detroit was in a small boom, with several renovation and new development projects underway and several others planned. The vast empty lot across the street from their condo was supposed to become new townhouses. But then the economy collapsed, the housing market dried up along with the commercial credit, and the projects died. The 1,680-square-foot, two-story condo was now worth a fraction of the $300,000 the Bradys paid six months earlier. In early 2011, the Bradys were able to get their loan modified, knocking $60,000 off the principal, but other, larger units in the area were selling for less than half what they owe. The couple had planned to own the condo as an investment, build some equity, then look to move. Those plans are in limbo.

"We believed in all the development that was supposed to happen down here, and that's why we paid so much for our property," Hillary says. "We were all like, OK, we buy this at like $300,000 and we stay for five years, we'll be able to sell it for that. But in three years, nothing has happened. Everything kind of fell through and we're on pause. I'm still hopeful. . . . God just wants us to stay longer."

1 7

THE OIL EMBARGO

At two o'clock on an early fall afternoon—October 6, 1973, the Jewish holiday of Yom Kippur—some six thousand miles east of Detroit, the Egyptian and Syrian armies launched a coordinated attack against the state of Israel. Egypt flooded troops into the Sinai Peninsula on Israel's southwest border, and Syria rolled into the Golan Heights in the northeast. While Syrian president Hafez el Assad argued that his nation was responding to a buildup of Israeli military units along the border, it quickly became apparent that the Arab states had started the war.

The attacks took Israel by surprise, as they were meant to. It was several days before the Israeli military regained its footing and began pushing back. For the first week or so the Egyptian and Syrian forces held the upper hand, but the Israelis—shored up by military resupplies from the United States—repelled the invaders, and nineteen days after the fighting started the United Nations brokered a cease-fire that held. In the end Israel wound up controlling more territory than it had at the start of the attacks, a persistent source of friction in the Middle East today.

The biggest impact for the United States was nonmilitary. In response to the American provision of arms to Israel, members of the Organization of Arab Petroleum Exporting Countries shut off oil deliveries to the United States, and kept the tap shut until March 1974.

The Arab Oil Embargo, as it came to be called, convulsed the American economy. Gasoline prices jumped, and low supplies led to long lines at neighborhood gas stations. People who previously thought of their cars in terms of horsepower and speed now began paying attention to how many miles they could drive on a gallon of gas. It changed what factors consumers considered when they went car shopping. In 1975, the federal government, which was simultaneously trying to find ways to cut air pollution, enacted fuel mileage standards for new cars, a change for which Detroit's automakers were unprepared. But Japanese car companies, which were already making smaller, more efficient cars, were ready, and the once seemingly unassailable market domination by American carmakers crumbled. More broadly, the nation entered a deep financial recession driven by the spike in fuel prices.

As the economy seized up, jobs disappeared even as consumer product prices rose, an economic quirk known as stagflation. And again, few places were hit as hard as Detroit. In 1973, the American automakers churned out 12,637,000 cars and trucks. Two years later, they sold 8,985,000 vehicles, a 29 percent decline, mostly in passenger cars. And fewer cars produced meant fewer people were needed to make them.[1]

Three weeks after the Arab countries began cutting oil exports to the United States, voters in Detroit went to the polls to elect a new mayor. It's a toss-up as to which ultimately affected Detroit more, the economic hit from the oil embargo or the victory in that election by a state senator named Coleman A. Young.

Young was born in Tuscaloosa, Alabama, in 1918 but moved with his parents to Detroit in 1923, part of that first migration of Southern blacks to the North. He grew up in Black Bottom, which was a multiethnic immigrant's ghetto when his family arrived. The neighborhood had become all black within a few years. Young's father worked first in clothing stores, where his light complexion led employers to presume he was white, and then at the post office, while running his own small tailoring business on the side. Young himself grew up working odd jobs in Prohibition-era speakeasies and gambling houses, doing a little street hustling (one gambit involved diving the Detroit River for bootleg whiskey dumped by runners avoiding the cops) and shoplifting. For a time he worked answering the Saturday lunchtime telephone for Ossian Sweet a few years after the doctor's gun and legal showdown with his neighbors.[2]

Young attended Catholic parochial school until eighth grade, but then was barred from advancing to a private Catholic high school. In his memoir, Young writes of watching the white religious brother in charge of admissions rip up his application. He enrolled in the public Eastern High School ("About ten or twelve black students had to raise hell even to go to Eastern, and after we left, the door was slammed on blacks and nailed shut") and graduated with honors in 1935.[3]

Growing up, Young encountered the fundamental, and demoralizing, array of white prejudice, from getting bounced from a Boy Scout excursion to being denied access to the Detroit River island amusement park, Bob-Lo, because he was black. He also lost out on a seasonal job as a retail clerk at Crowley's Department Store; the white applicants got those jobs while he was redirected to the janitorial staff in the basement.

After graduating high school, Young enrolled in an electrician's apprenticeship program and despite getting the top grade was passed over for the sole available job opening in favor of a less-qualified white man whose father was a foreman at the job site. "It was obvious to me that the workingman, black or white, had no strength, no security, no hope without unity. It was also obvious to me that the cause of the workingman and the cause of the black man were one in the same."[4] Young eventually landed a job at the Ford Rouge assembly line, but he was quickly identified by Harry Bennett's spies as a union sympathizer and fired after bashing one of the Service Department agents with a metal rod. (Young said it was in self-defense.)

Young moved around other jobs in Detroit "but my most important work was with a labor-oriented civil rights organization that was active in the thirties and forties," the National Negro Congress. Through it, he became involved in the Sojourner Truth public housing battle, but he was drafted into the US Army before that was resolved. Despite his chronic problems with pneumonia he was shipped off for training. Young resisted the deep segregation of the military, and also had his first encounter with the FBI, whose agents trailed him to a New Mexico training base to ask about leftist political meetings he had attended back in Detroit in the 1930s.

It was the beginning of a long and rancorous relationship, with the FBI eventually launching a series of investigations, though Young was never charged with any crimes. Young transferred to the air corps, and became a Tuskegee Airman, but was washed out of the program as a subversive at the last minute under secret orders from the FBI. He was among one hundred or so airmen arrested after challenging segregated social clubs at an Indiana air training base and went on to fight for desegregated housing and social quarters at military bases in Florida, where he was stationed.[5]

After the war, Young returned to Detroit and reconnected with both radical politics and city elections, working unsuccessfully to get Rev. Charles Hill Sr., his mentor, elected to the Detroit City Council. Young mounted his own unsuccessful run for a state senate seat in 1948 on the state Progressive Party line that included Henry Wallace as the presidential candidate. His political activism gave him a high profile, which got him blacklisted both from Reuther's UAW as a leftist and from the auto plants as a union radical. And it earned him a subpoena to testify before the HUAC when it stopped in Detroit in 1952 to plumb the depths of communism in the Motor City. The committee called in a number of local radicals, but met its match in Young, who defied the committee's authority to question him and needled the southerners on the committee for their unveiled racism.

Frank Tavenner, a Virginia lawyer serving as the committee's legal counsel, began the session by telling Young he wanted to know about some of the organizations with which the activist had been affiliated, then asked whether Young was, or had ever been, a communist. Young invoked the Fifth Amendment and went on to say he had no intention of naming names "since I have no purpose of being here as a stool pigeon." Tavenner, with his deep southern accent, asked Young if it was true he was "the executive secretary of the National Niggra Congress," but Young cut him off: "That word is Negro, not Niggra."

"I said Negro. I think you are mistaken."

"I hope I am,"Young countered. "Speak more clearly." Congressman John Wood of Georgia, the head of the committee, warned Young not to argue with the committee's lawyer. "It isn't my purpose to argue,"Young replied. "As a Negro, I resent the slurring of my race."

The committee members kept at him, but Young rebuffed their efforts, invoking the Fifth Amendment to any questions about his membership or association with radical groups or people engaged in radical politics, then shifting tactics to challenge the premise of other areas of inquiry. Tavenner again brought up the activities of the Communist Party in Detroit, and Young again said he had no intention of discussing that. Tavenner replied that he had been led to believe that Young was interested in helping the committee. "You have me mixed up with a stool pigeon," Young shot back. They went at each other for some time, with Young inflicting the deepest wound when he called Wood on the voting history of his congressional district. In another back-and-forth over the proper pronunciation of the word Negro, Wood said that he had the political support of all 122 blacks who had voted in the most recent election in his district. "I happen to know,"Young said, "in Georgia, Negro people are prevented from voting by virtue of terror, intimidation, and lynchings. It is my contention that you would not be in Congress today if it were not for the legal restrictions on voting on the part of my people."[6]

The exchange was a relative footnote against the broader background of the political abuses carried out by the HUAC, but it was significant for Detroit. The hearings were carried live over the radio, and a vinyl record of the exchange was later pressed and sold in Black Bottom, on Hastings Street, and elsewhere in Detroit. Blacks found themselves a new hero, a seemingly fearless man—one of them, part of their community—who openly and provocatively gave voice to the fears and angers they had harbored for generations. "It was a vicarious thing. I had said words that the people of Black Bottom had dreamed all their lives of saying to a southern white man. I had talked back to the plantation boss and gotten away with it. I had stood up to the landlord and told off the foreman. I had spoken for all of them, and they were standing a little taller."

It also sowed the seeds for a more successful foray into electoral politics. In 1960, Young ran for a seat on the Detroit Common Council, making police brutality against blacks a key issue, but was trounced in the primary. A few months later, though, he won election as a delegate to the state's first constitutional convention in fifty years, an experience that gave him the opportunity to show fellow Democrats and political movers and shakers that despite his radical beliefs, he could play well with others in a political setting. In 1964, Young won election to the Michigan state senate. Ten years later, after Mayor Roman Gribbs announced he would not seek reelection, Young became Detroit's first black mayor by fewer than twenty thousand votes—the only close mayoral race in what would eventually be five terms, totaling twenty years.

Young took over a city teetering on collapse. The recession caused by the oil embargo had already battered the nation, and particularly Detroit. Young ran on an antipolice platform built around the quickly filled promise to dismantle the city's violent and controversial STRESS units aimed at reducing street crime, which blacks viewed as police vigilantism. He embarked on a "fifty-fifty" hiring policy, dividing jobs between whites and blacks to desegregate city hall and its bureaucracy. He spoke in fiery terms and kept a placard in his home office desk that said MFIC—"Motherfucker In Charge." He disdained white racists—overt and covert—with a visceral hatred, and his willingness to point out racism by both individuals and institutions made him a lightning rod for whites fearing a "black takeover" of Detroit.

Detroit's newspapers fanned the flames by blowing up Young's comments into something akin to political causes. In his first inaugural speech, Young talked about crime and announced, in essence, that there was a new sheriff in town: "I issue a warning to all those pushers, to all rip-off artists, to all muggers: It's time to leave Detroit; hit Eight Mile Road! And I don't give a damn if they are black or white, or if they wear Superfly suits or blue uniforms with silver badges. Hit the road." It was a direct warning to the city's criminal element, including thuggish members of its nearly all-white police department, that the city would no longer be their playground, using Eight Mile Road as a metaphor for his directive that, in effect, the bad guys should get out of Dodge. By the time the media churn was done, white suburbanites were left with the impression that Young was sending hordes of street thugs to their quiet streets, and that the city they fled was being sent to chase them. Detroit's racial divide yawned wider, and Young's reputation among white suburbanites never recovered.

Young, though, made Detroit's economic underpinnings one of the main focuses of his five terms, often at the expense of its neighborhoods. He became both iconic and iconoclastic. "The only thing I find as contemptible as a conservative establishment bigot is a bleeding-heart, pansy-ass liberal," Young wrote in his memoirs. "Liberals talk as though they would change the world, but all of the things required to change the world are basically the things that liberals are not. Liberals are not radicals, by definition, and many of them are not capitalists, either. Liberals, whose currency is the impassioned harangue, nibble cheese and model the latest political fashions in front of each other while radicals and money are at work changing the world."[7]

Given the global economic pressures that began to erode the American manufacturing sector in the 1970s and 1980s, there was little that even a charismatic mayor could do to stop Detroit's decline. With the city schools already failing, Detroit's new entries into the workforce were undervalued in the new economic models of service and producer businesses (accounting services and the like). "Detroit simply has not been competitive in planning, management, financing, marketing, legal, and accounting services, in part because the city's economic elite have refused to recognize Detroit's potential for such activity," one analyst wrote in the late 1980s. "Industries that recruit heavily among college-educated twenty- to forty-year-olds have not seriously considered Detroit or its suburbs as a viable location."[8] Further, as factories closed, union, corporate, and government supported retraining programs were preparing displaced workers for jobs that didn't exist in meaningful numbers. And as Young recognized, without jobs a community cannot hold together.

Young oversaw landscape-changing developments in Detroit, from the building of the riverfront Joe Louis Arena in a bit of gamesmanship to keep the city's beloved Detroit Red Wings hockey team from following the Detroit Lions and Detroit Pistons to the suburbs, to Henry Ford II's Renaissance Center, the linchpin of what was expected to be a revival of the city's riverfront.

Young bulldozed the impoverished Poletown neighborhood near the Hamtramck border to make way for a new General Motors factory—it merged two Cadillac plants employing ten thousand workers into one plant with three thousand jobs, yet Young still saw this as a positive thing for Detroit—and another neighborhood on the far east side to accommodate Chrysler's expanded Jefferson Avenue plant in 1991. The latter project helped spawn a nearby residential development, Victoria Park, the first new subdivision in Detroit in a generation. And while these projects were undeniably good things for Detroit's economy, they were insufficient to stop the broader economic slide and further supported the belief that the city cared more about economic development than neighborhood health.

For white Metro Detroiters, particularly in the suburbs, the general perception of Young's tenure is that he drove a wedge between black Detroit and white Detroit. In retrospect, he didn't drive a wedge so much as he openly acknowledged that the divide existed, and tried to get the metropolitan region to confront it. Young developed close and productive working relationships with the region's dominant white power brokers, from Republican governor William G. Milliken to Henry Ford II and other local corporate and business leaders such as Max Fisher, Max Pincus, A. Alfred Taubman, Peter Stroh, and Charles Fisher III. And his economic polices, which focused on large-scale corporate development, including trying to develop a convention industry, won him the support of Detroit's white business community.[9] But for the average white suburbanite who looked nostalgically at Detroit, Young personified the demographic changes that had occurred as the whites abandoned the city—or, from their perspective, had been forced out. And Young didn't care whether he ruffled feathers while pointing out the inherent racism behind the white flight. It was not a recipe for mending fences.

Young also couldn't counter the tide pulling away from Detroit's core economic strength, its skilled and unskilled labor force. Even as Young engaged in the bidding process—whichever local government offered

the best deals got the new projects—he complained that government
policies that allowed localities to compete for domestic development
ultimately hurt the communities while enriching the private businesses
and shareholders. He referred to it as "federally assisted industrial reloca-
tion" that began with the spreading out of the defense industries, which
Young recognized as militarily prudent but economically dangerous to
core cities like Detroit.

Young also saw racism behind it, though he may have put more
weight on that motive than it deserves. "The breaking up of Detroit
represented a powerful and multifaceted social movement that served to
strand the black community in a city of endangered resources," Young
said. "I'll never accept the notion that the federal government wasn't
aware of what it was doing to us." His reading of the situation is significant; through the prism of his own experience he was quick to see
conspiracies, a worldview that still permeates black Detroit. It seems just
as likely that federal authorities simply didn't think about the impact.
Given the little political capital available to poor black neighborhoods,
the victims of those policies had few mechanisms through which to
protest. Ultimately, with the industrial decentralization and the whip-
sawing tactics of industry and government (pitting factories against factories and municipalities against municipalities in a grotesque fight for
survival), went the jobs. "Of the four hundred thousand manufacturing
jobs that sustained and defined Detroit at its industrial peak, a staggering three hundred thousand have left in the ensuing forty years," Young
said in 1989. "A statistic that, by itself, goes a hell of a long way toward
explaining the city's economic troubles since World War II."[10]

Young, then seventy-five, chose not to run for reelection in 1993
and was succeeded as mayor by a former judge, Dennis Archer, who was
also black, and who continued to push for big-ticket developments in
Detroit, including new stadiums for the Detroit Tigers baseball team and
the Detroit Lions football team. He sought to reduce the racial divide
with the suburbs that Young had so persistently pointed out and, from
the white perspective, exacerbated. And he led the successful move to
gain voter approval for opening three casinos in Detroit. The casinos
were billed as job creators, and they have been that. In March 2007, some

twenty-six thousand people applied for an anticipated one thousand jobs at the new MGM Grand Casino at the northwest edge of downtown. But hopes that the casinos would make Detroit a major tourism destination fell flat. Standing outside the casino parking structures, one sees a steady parade of almost exclusively Michigan license plates.

So the exodus that began in the 1950s, when Detroit was led by a white pro-business Republican mayor, Albert Cobo, continued its inexorable slide through five subsequent mayors, both black and white, ranging from moderate to liberal—Louis Miriani, Jerome Cavanagh, Roman Gribbs, Young, and Archer. It's popular among political conservatives to look at present-day Detroit as the signal evidence of the failure of big-city liberal policies, and by those who view the world through a racial lens to see black incompetence. But as Young pointed out two decades ago, the storms that swept over Detroit were far larger than any single political figure could conjure, control, or counter. No matter the politician's party or race.

DETROITERS V

John Thompson

John Thompson sits at the island counter in his kitchen, a modern addition to the heart of an 1898 carriage house that backs up to a dock on a canal leading to the Detroit River. The building is three stories high, dominated by a castle-like battlement, and has been carved up, added to, and renovated so many times it feels like the warren of a well-heeled rabbit. It's a far cry—but only a few miles—from where Thompson was born in 1954 in Detroit's Cass Corridor, the local skid row and one of the toughest neighborhoods in a city of tough neighborhoods. How Thompson managed to climb from a hellish childhood to this oasis of comfort is, in many ways, the story of modern Detroit's resilience.[1]

Thompson opened his Honest ? John's Bar and Grill on Selden Street near Second in 2002 as something of a homecoming for himself. He'd already owned a successful predecessor of the bar on the east side of town, but he had always wanted to own a bar in the Corridor, a mix of dark irony and a desire to confront some personal demons. In the end, the demons won.

The bar is an island of sorts. At night soft lights warm the windows, drawing in a steady flow of regulars: students from nearby Wayne State University, downtown professionals stopping for a drink or a meal

John Thompson. MICHELLE ANDONIAN

before heading home, workers from the Detroit Medical Center and the Veterans Administration Hospital less than a mile away. There used to be an apartment building to the east of the bar, the Sylvia Apartments at 487 Selden, but it's long since been torn down.

There were other buildings across the street, but most of them are gone now, too, as are the buildings that lined Second Street, just to the west. The empty spaces are mostly given over to rough-hewn parking areas or overgrown and littered weed lots, with occasional mounds of trash and busted furniture surreptitiously dumped by people trying to avoid the cost of having it hauled away.

In the missing apartment building was the first home Thompson can remember, Apartment 208.[2] And they aren't fond memories. By the time Thompson came along, the Cass Corridor was already one of the city's most notorious drug zones, with robbery and rape and murder part of the daily drama. The tavern he now owns was more a home for his stepfather, Chester Thompson, than their small one-bedroom apartment next door. If the elder Thompson was awake, he was on a stool at the bar, which was called Elmer's back then. It also was one of several places where Thompson's mother, Margaret Ann Doesky, who often disappeared for weeks at a time, would turn tricks. Thompson recalls a childhood of regular beatings for himself and his sister, Linda, who was three years older, until Thompson, at age fourteen, reported the abuse to Catholic Social Services. Thompson was taken to Don Bosco Hall, a children's home. His sister, already turning tricks at age seventeen, disappeared into the streets.

It took a lot of therapy, which came after a lot of years of booze and cocaine, but Thompson slowly came to understand that the drunken beatings by his father, and the mother who slept with strangers for money, were the human failings of others, not his own. He has come to terms with the sense of abandonment. But he hasn't forgotten. In fact, that's why he bought the bar, a poetic move by a man who takes perverse pleasure in the ironies of life. And it is through such inscrutable motives, and such devotion to Detroit's past and present, that the city might actually rise.

Thompson eventually landed as a foster child in the home of the Reverend Lewis Redmond, whose Cass Community United Methodist Church still anchors the opposite end of the block from Honest ? John's Bar. In a sense, the young Thompson simply moved down the street from his parents. Redmond and his wife had a biological son, Robert, but raised at least eight more children—Thompson and other neighborhood castoffs. It was a large, boisterous family filled with the children of other failed families.

Many of the Redmonds' former charges remain in the area, and remain in touch, a surprisingly resilient bond forged among such tenuous lives. The Redmonds sought to give the youths the structure they missed in their original homes. School had to be attended. Grades had to be worked for. Sunday mornings were given over to church services, and during the week there was the constant impetus to help others, from checking on the elderly to serving free meals out of the church's basement kitchen.

Thompson took part, begrudgingly, in the church-related activities that were expected of him. But few of the behaviors that Rev. Redmond sought to instill took hold. Thompson was a difficult adolescent with a stubborn streak and a drive to taste the forbidden. Drinking. Drugs. Loose girls. And there was tragedy, too. Robert, at twenty-six, was shot and killed in a nearby apartment when he went to persuade the teenage boyfriend of one of the foster daughters to turn over an illegal handgun.

That death may have affected Thompson as much as his biological parents' abject failures. Rev. Redmond, in a very Biblical sense, sacrificed his son to do God's work, is how Thompson sees it. And that God so willingly took Redmond's son didn't reflect well on God. Thompson rejected faith as an answer to the world in which he was born, but he did absorb the lessons of generosity and of the responsibility to help others.

Such a welcoming hand had, in fact, saved him, though it was a long time before Thompson recognized that. For that matter, it was a long time before anyone could reasonably say Thompson had indeed been saved, and not in the religious sense. There were ruptures with the Redmonds. Thompson says he was sexually abused by a church employee, who promptly disappeared. When the employee resurfaced a year later, working at the church again, Thompson took off, squatting for a while in an abandoned hotel in the Corridor until the police picked him up. He refused to return to the Redmonds and finished out his minor years in a county home. He dropped out of school, but within months after being emancipated he earned his high school equivalency diploma. He was still a young man with a lot of anger to burn through. After years of bitterness—primarily from Thompson—he reconciled with the Redmonds, and in 1994 Thompson led an effort to name a local park across Second Street from the bar after the Redmonds' slain son.

Thompson survived his rambunctious childhood, and as an adult became a bartender (he co-owned a bar for a while in the Corridor) and eventually a hardware salesman. For a natural storyteller it was a good fit, spending his days trying to talk people into something. But Thompson was still drawn to the excitement of the night—the booze and the drugs and the women—like a character in a Charles Bukowski story.

By 1986, Thompson and a partner, a local doctor who shared Thompson's taste for the forbidden, went into business together and opened Honest? John's Bar and No Grill in a ramshackle building off East Jefferson, a block from the eastern end of Grand Boulevard and across from where the MacArthur Bridge connects the city to Belle Isle, where the vicious 1943 riot began. (Thompson and the partner eventually had an acrimonious falling out; Thompson retained the business.)

By the time Thompson opened the bar, the once grand east-side neighborhood was smothered by poverty. More than half the homes on the street had fallen to wrecking crews, or just collapsed under their own weight. Several of the remaining buildings were taken over by crack dealers. Few people held steady jobs. It was like the Cass Corridor without the hookers, or the legacy, but it was also the perfect spot to catch affluent commuters mid-drive from their downtown offices to their Grosse Pointe homes.

The bar quickly became a watering hole for journalists, lawyers, judges, and cops, including a few from the narcotics division—a connection that likely was not lost on the neighborhood drug dealers, who gave the place a wide berth. Thompson was already well-known in the city's bar culture as a customer; now he would become even better known as a bar owner. And he learned the trade by watching.

One of the classic watering holes in downtown Detroit is the Anchor Bar, which began in the mid-1950s as Leo's Grocery, owned by Leo Derderian, the son of Armenian immigrants. It was, in fact, a blind pig, a holdover term from Prohibition days. If you knew how to ask, you could go into Derderian's small grocery store at the western edge of downtown and order a few stiff drinks. "Leo's Grocery was a euphemism," his son, Vaughn, once said. "He sold a lot of beer and a lot of sandwiches and a lot of bets. I can recall going in there. I was four or five. He did have candy but I don't recall seeing a whole lot of grocery stuff on the shelves. Then he decided he could do all these things he liked to do better in a bar."[3]

The elder Derderian went legit, obtained the necessary licenses and, after a couple of other bar ventures, in 1975 opened his Anchor Bar on West Lafayette between the offices of the *Detroit News* and the *Detroit Free Press*. An inveterate gambler and drunk, a friend of bookies and pimps, cops and priests, journalists and politicians, Derderian hit on the perfect blend of clientele in a hard-drinking town. Part of his business plan was to become his own version of the gold-hearted hooker, sponsoring golf tournaments and other outings that raised hundreds of thousands of dollars for a local Catholic church through a fund he named after his close friend: the Monsignor Clement Kern Memorial Shakedown Fund. The Anchor Bar thrived. (The latest incarnation is now run by Derderian's son and grandson, both named Vaughn, a block away on West Fort Street.)

As he opened his own bar, Thompson had Derderian in the back of his mind. "It's the 'big wheel' approach," Thompson says. "You get the big wheels to come in, and the rest follow." Where Thompson differed from Derderian, though, was in his choice of locations. Derderian always sought to be in the heart of the action downtown. Thompson wanted to be in a neighborhood, and he wanted the bar to become both his livelihood and an agent to help the poor. He ran off customers who snorted coke or lit up joints in the bathroom, but infused the bar with a shrewd vibe of toughness laced with dark comedy. He custom ordered a blue neon light that beamed through the window, SOBRIETY SUCKS. A sign over the trough urinal in the men's room read, NO HECKLING. A poster-size mug shot from his own 1970s pot bust anchored a side wall, surrounded by framed copies of newspaper and magazine stories about the bar.

True to the bar's name, there was no kitchen, but there was a microwave and frozen White Castle sliders for the drunk and desperate. The jukebox spun old 45s; the selection of obscure soul and blues earned it a spot in journalist William Bunch's *Jukebox America: Down Back Streets and Blue Highways in Search of the Country's Greatest Jukebox*. Through the jukebox, Bunch wrote, a corner of Detroit found racial harmony. "I turned around, and Al Green, slow and sexy, came on the jukebox. A tall man, an African American in a yellow baseball cap, led a short white woman—she couldn't have been more than four-and-a-half feet tall—out into an open space in front of the jukebox. The woman wrapped her arms around the man's hulking waist, and they swayed, slowly, unevenly to the record."[4]

Thompson adapted Derderian's model of using fundraising to propel the business. Over a span of ten years he raised more than one million dollars through such annual events as the polar bear club–style Dipps for Toys, in which regulars collected pledges and jumped in the frigid Detroit River on the first Sunday in December. The money was spent on toys, at least one for each child in three neighborhood elementary schools. The bar was then turned into a gift-wrapping center with regulars packaging up presents for strangers—while buying drinks at the bar.

Other holidays became marketing moments, too. On Easter Sunday, Thompson held "Bunny Roasts" to raise money for seniors living in subsidized housing across the street. On Thanksgiving, regulars donated hundreds of whole turkeys that were passed along to families, and others cooked turkeys in home ovens and brought them to the bar on Thanksgiving morning to anchor a free feast for hundreds of people in the neighborhood. As the good deeds were done, Thompson's business flourished.

There were two problems with Thompson's business, though. First, Thompson didn't own the building; he was renting, which limited the work he could do on the place and meant part of every month's outlay went to someone else. And it wasn't in the Cass Corridor, which was where Thompson ultimately wanted to be. When Elmer's Bar, the shot-and-beer joint in which his stepfather drank himself to death, and where his mother once turned tricks, came up for sale in 2000, Thompson bought it, gutted it, installed a kitchen, and moved, SOBRIETY SUCKS sign and all, back home.

The new bar has become an economic spark. Thompson brought the fundraising model with him, though children in different schools, and empty bellies in different apartments, now received the benefits. While most of the other scant, but growing, businesses in the Cass Corridor operate from behind grated windows—if they have windows at all—Honest ? John's bar is a fishbowl and glows at night like a beacon in a neighborhood of shadows and broken glass. A fenced lot in the back has video cameras to protect cars in an area in which auto theft is considered a part-time job. Early on, on the busiest nights Thompson would stand sentinel on the sidewalk out front, steering away the hard-core drunks and addicts and asking the drug dealers to pick a different corner, not to mess with a good thing. Or, looked at another way, he was staking out his own corner in a turf-conscious neighborhood.

That all changed in June 2010 when Thompson's wife, Irene, who had become the bar manager, suffered a brain hemorrhage. Though she recovered, Thompson sped up his retirement plans and turned the bar over to two suburban-raised employees—Jeff Fontecchio, a former autoworker, and Kelly Rossi, an aspiring performer who studied theater at Wayne State—under a no-cash-down agreement in which they pay Thompson a regular dividend.

The new owners don't have the outsized personality that marked Thompson and his bars—nor his volatility (the number of customers Thompson has banned could support a bar/restaurant all by themselves). But they have the same drive to make the business succeed. Where Thompson in his last two years was pulling away from daily involvement in the business, they have fully embraced it. "We both had been here for a long time and enjoyed being here, enjoyed the people," Fontecchio says. Rossi had worked in different bars and restaurants while going to college and found she enjoyed the work and the environment. "It's more of a community bar than you think," Rossi says. "We do get a lot of people from outside and new faces, but you do see a lot of the same people, which is good. That is definitely what we are trying to do. . . . We're not looking to make millions. We just want to keep the doors open and keep that part of Detroit. It's important for the city."[5]

Since Thompson opened his bar, other small businesses have set up shop in nearby buildings, trying to build on the vibe of recovery. Unlike most of the rest of Detroit, the Cass Corridor, ironically enough, has some stability, with the growing Wayne State University to the north and the similarly expansive and expanding Detroit Medical Center (DMC) and the nearby US Veterans Hospital to the east.

In early 2011, Wayne State and the DMC joined with Henry Ford Health System, which operates another hospital to the northwest, and began offering cash incentives to employees who relocated to the midtown area, which encompasses the Cass Corridor, hoping the lure of subsidies would help overcome reticence about moving into a neighborhood with a long and troubled history. At the same time, the closing of tenement-style apartment buildings (many used by drug dealers and hookers) and the shuttering of the crime-ridden Brewster-Douglass housing project east of Brush Park radically slashed the area's crime rate. Streets that a decade before would be dangerous to walk at night were, in early 2011, making a comeback. New small businesses, like Honest ? John's, are both propelling and benefitting from the changes. There's Curl Up and Dye, a retro-themed hair salon that quickly racked up a steady client base of fifteen hundred customers who formerly had to drive miles to get hair treatments. A former French teacher, Torya Blanchard, followed with Good Girls Go to Paris, a creperie. Next door another former teacher opened a bookstore, Leopold's (after James Joyce's Leopold Bloom character in *Ulysses*). In the fall of 2009 an art movie house even opened, albeit on shaky legs, in the former Burton International School on Cass Avenue. "Nobody could comprehend why we'd start a theater," one of the investors, twenty-five-year-old Nathan Faustyn, told the *New York Times*. "But when you live in Detroit, you ask, 'What can I do for the city?' We needed this. And we had nothing to lose. When you're at the bottom of the economic ladder, you have nowhere to look but up."[6]

Together they form a small flicker of entrepreneurial life in a place that has been beaten to an economic pulp. Whether it survives or not is the key to Detroit's entire future. Large-scale industry will not lead whatever comeback might be possible. It will take the spiderwebs of small businesses, and the drive and devotion of people like Faustyn, Blanchard, Fontecchio, and Rossi, to slowly bring back some of these neighborhoods.

But the future is uncertain. In December 2009, as the aftershocks of the auto-industry meltdown and the broader Great Recession were still shaking the city's foundation, Thompson made a painful but realistic decision. For the first time in more than twenty years, he canceled the annual Dipps for Toys. People, he said, were too broke to give. But in early 2011, Fontecchio and Rossi were making plans to revive it, a passing of both a torch and a sense of faith.

18

WHEN THE JOBS GO AWAY

There is a significant difference between a neighborhood of the working poor and a neighborhood of people who can't find work. The latter
communities tend to lack the kind of social cohesion that offers a buffer
against crime and blight. It's not a function of selection by the residents.
Few people choose to be poor, to be undereducated, to be socially and
economically isolated, to live in places where violence and hunger are
endemic. Such neighborhoods—which account for much of Detroit—
are what's left when the rest of society breaks down. When jobs move
out of neighborhoods, whether they are well-paying union factory jobs
or minimum wage janitorial work, those financially capable of moving
go with them, or at least go somewhere else to find new work.

Left behind are the financially isolated and immobile—the uneducated and undereducated and those with pressing medical, psychological,
or drug problems. Without access to reliable transportation, they also
lose access to suburban jobs. In Detroit, the problem is compounded
by the spread of its geography and an inadequate public transportation
system. It can take a couple of hours in each direction, depending on the
bus lines, to get from parts of Detroit to different suburban sites. Given
the option of a minimum wage job in a suburb where they feel unwel-
come, and that involves adding a four-hour round-trip commute to an

eight- or nine-hour workday, most people choose not to work (and the hurdle is even higher for workers with children).[1]

Crime travels hand in hand with joblessness, and when Detroit's economic foundations softened, then collapsed, Detroit's reputation morphed once again. As the car industry rose in the 1910s and 1920s, Detroit was the City of Tomorrow. With World War II, it was the Arsenal of Democracy. In the 1960s it was Motown, the musical heartbeat of America. But in the 1970s and 1980s, it became Murder City, and it was a title well earned. The murder rate peaked in 1987, with 686 homicides, or a rate of about 63 per 100,000 residents. The same year, New York City—the place where many Americans feared to tread—had 1,672 homicides, or a rate of 22 per 100,000. In its worst year, 1990, New York City had 31 murders per 100,000 residents, half of Detroit's peak rate.[2]

The most vicious crimes grew out of the rise of Detroit's drug culture. In the 1970s, heroin became an epidemic. Black drug dealers who formerly were little more than retail outlets for Detroit's Mafia families began cutting out the middlemen, establishing their own gangs and organizations. The goal was money, but also thrills and a level of respect in a world that afforded little to young black men.

Greg Mathis, the one-time Detroit judge who went on to an entertainment career with the *Judge Mathis Show*, wrote about his own early experiences growing up poor on the city's west side, including the Prairie Street neighborhood and the Herman Gardens housing project, and about sliding into the street life despite the presence of a loving and religious mother. Mathis was born in 1960, so he was a child when the riots broke out. By the time he was a young teen he had developed a romanticized view of the excitement of the street despite the brutality of police patrols, who would arrest and beat black males for infractions real or presumed. From the outside, it can be hard to understand the power of that relationship between police and young black men, but it has been incredibly influential on behavior. The police were the face of authority, and of society. To walk down the street in fear of what the police will do cemented expectations of what to expect from the normal configurations of society.

In Mathis's case, he made a personal decision to become a thug, but it was not a decision made in a vacuum. "Practically everyone detested the junkies, but I found them fascinating just because they ignored all of Prairie Street's unwritten rules, including the ones saying that you slaved from nine to five every day, moaning constantly about bills, and spent Sunday sitting in a boring-ass church for hours on end. They didn't give a shot what society said or thought about their drug-addled lifestyle. So I didn't see the junkies as pitiful people bumbling around in a narcotic stupor—I saw them as independent souls to be admired."

In the end, the streets were a bigger lure than family. "Our house was a sanctified bastion of spirituality, but just outside its walls lurked a Wild West Detroit in all its sinful, secular glory. In my early years I bounced back and forth between those incredibly different worlds, barely tolerating one and lusting for the other with all my heart." The lure was money, excitement, recognition. Prostitution was omnipresent, and so were pimps with their flashy cars, pockets of cash, and pretty women on their arms. "The husbands and fathers of Prairie Street provided a jarring contrast that I never aspired to: They'd trudge home after a grueling day's work in some dirty factory, lugging a lunch pail, looking tired and bent down and smelling like machine oil."[3]

Mathis eventually fell in with the Errol Flynns street gang, so named for their flash, and their audacity. Mathis was part of a small army of Flynns who descended on an August 1976 Cobo Hall concert by the disco-playing Kool and the Gang and the Average White Band, and beat and robbed customers row by row. They were an intimidating crew, some elevated by four-inch Plexiglas heels and wearing fur Borsalino hats and double-breasted suits, with handguns tucked into their belts. Through a quirk in jurisdiction, Detroit police remained outside the building while the overmatched Cobo security force tried to handle the gang, and they didn't begin to make arrests until the violence spilled outside with gang members chasing the panicked audience. Two women were raped in the melee, and nearly two dozen gang members were arrested.[4] But others got away. Mathis and his crew, once reaching the doors, blended in with the panicked throng then reunited a few blocks away where, with the police distracted by the bedlam outside Cobo Hall, they looted several blocks worth of stores before returning to their neighborhood. "Feeling like a kid on Christmas morning, I eagerly make my way back to the 1968 Camaro that my five-man crew and I parked several blocks from Cobo Hall. I can't wait to divvy up the booty we've lifted from the Average White Band crowd and I'm looking forward to seeing how the eleven o'clock news covers our audacious heist. My boys and I have just ripped off several thousand Detroit concertgoers located mere blocks from police headquarters."[5]

Mathis left the gang life while still in high school, after his mother had moved the family to suburban Wayne and he got caught in school with drugs and a gun. He had a bit of a personal epiphany when his mother was diagnosed with cancer at the same time. A suspended sentence and requirement that he obtain a GED coincided with his first reading of the *Autobiography of Malcolm X* and hearing a speech by Jesse Jackson. Together, they propelled him into the law—from the other side. But few veterans of Detroit's drug culture can claim such good outcomes. Most are dead, imprisoned, or still trolling the streets, dealing and using.

Carl S. Taylor, a sociologist, saw the rise of the Errol Flynns as a conversion in Detroit's permanent underclass. Their flamboyance drew the same street kids that the pimp culture once drew, that the Hastings Street bars, whorehouses, and gambling halls had drawn before that. Kids like Mathis, who saw more upside than downside in pursuing crime and life on the streets instead of the increasingly unstable and hard-to-find legitimate jobs that sent you home smelling of machine oil. The romanticization of the drug world exploded, and descendants of the Errol Flynns became even stronger and more violent.

In the early 1980s, the west side was dominated by Young Boys Inc., or YBI, which was a sophisticated network of remarkably canny street dealers who brought the organization, marketing, and violence of the drug world to new heights. Beyond the wide swath of ruined lives and neighborhoods left in their wake, the leaders of these gangs in many ways represent Detroit's biggest loss. With their intelligence and daring, had these young men grown up in a different place, or a different time, and had they been educated in a more effective school system that tracked them into business or government, they could easily have become generational leaders. Instead, they ended up dead or imprisoned.

The key figure in the Young Boys was Milton "Butch" Jones, who was brought into the drug trade at age fourteen by a brother-in-law when the main business was selling "dime caps," one-dollar doses of heroin. Jones started as a security guard of sorts at drug houses. "You gotta realize, I grew up in the '70s when movies like *Superfly*, *The Mack*, and *Hell Up In Harlem* dominated the screen," he said in a later memoir. "So far as I was concerned, this was my big chance to be what I saw, and I wasn't about to blow it."[6]

He made the most of the opportunity—much to the detriment of the city in which he was born. "I killed my first person when I was fifteen. It was cold-blooded murder. And basically, after the first time I did it, killin' became second nature to me. . . . If you kill somebody and you tossin' an' turnin' all night, then you know you ain't got the stomach for murder." The victim was a street thug with a reputation for robbing drug houses and killing all the witnesses. Jones saw him at the door of a drug house he was protecting, grabbed a shotgun, and blew the perceived threat off the porch, an act that immediately vaulted the fifteen-year-old into the ranks of the feared.

Over the next few years, Jones, with a handful of close associates, created a heroin business that grossed more than $35 million a year by selling small packets stamped with brand names like C.B.S., Hoochie Con, and Murder One. He also helped establish the legal career of a young public defender named W. Otis Culpepper, making him in essence the YBI's corporate defense lawyer, handling the cases of dealers caught up in police raids or murder raps.[7]

YBI's genius, for lack of a better word, was using minors as their prime drug runners, which meant that if they were caught they received minimal sentences through juvenile court. Local news media covered the gang's exploits with fervor.[8] There was a certain prurient interest, and more than a little sense of awe, at the sheer audacity of the drug culture and the wealth it generated. And it was a flabbergasting amount of money. Jones, in his memoir, describes a personal crossroads. "By October of 1982, I had saved $5 million," he wrote. "At that point, I began to seriously think about goin' into retirement." He was, at that point, about twenty-five years old. (He didn't retire; in May 2008 he was sentenced to thirty years in federal prison for running a continuing criminal enterprise. His guilty plea removed the possibility of receiving the death penalty for his involvement in murders through YBI.)

One tactic that law enforcement used to try to crack the gangs was federal drug-forfeiture laws, which allowed police to confiscate large amounts of cash, cars, and houses, and force the owners to go to civil court and prove they were not bought with drug money. Drug dealers often walked away from $100,000 in cash rather than expose themselves to perjury charges if they falsely claimed they were the gain of legitimate business. Bling became the drug dealer's personal showcase. One necklace worn by a key YBI member was a gold map of the United States, with an embedded diamond marking each city where the gang had connections.[9]

It was an era of lawlessness that overwhelmed law enforcement, both local and federal, and was reminiscent of the Prohibition-era gang wars. Street-level dealers were shot and killed with abandon, and power struggles at the top led to high-profile hits, which became even more prevalent with the rise of crack cocaine in the 1980s. The Chambers Brothers, on Detroit's east side, created a drug business model to rival the YBIs, drawing young dealers from their hometown of Marianna, Arkansas, north to work their network of crack houses. It was a highly sophisticated corporate organization that relied less on violence, which the Chambers Brothers saw as not worth the risk of drawing more serious police investigations. Depending, of course, on the nature of the provocation. Petty thefts and incursions brought proportional punishments, such as beatings and expulsion. A more serious infraction shifted the equation, and killings were authorized. What's significant is that there was a subtle shift from macho shoot-outs to preserve street reputations to more targeted and considered uses of violence. The Chambers Brothers' enterprise, like YBI, eventually collapsed under the weight of internal blood feuds and prosecutions.

As the drugs and the bullets flew, Detroit's reputation as a pit of violence grew. In 1987, Detroit's murder rate had risen to sixty-three per one hundred thousand residents, by far the highest among the nation's major cities. And the true rate was likely even higher: the 686 reported homicides were divided into the 1980 census data, which set the population at just under 1.1 million. By 1987, the population was closer to one million, given the pace of white and middle-class flight.

The killings were primarily targeted. Innocent and not-so-innocent bystanders lost their lives, but by and large the killings came in turf wars or disputes over bad debts among the drug dealers. Armed robberies downtown were relatively rare, though African Americans unlucky enough to have to wait for a bus out in the neighborhoods ran the risk of being mugged by young hoods or drug addicts looking for cash. There was an average of nearly 1,500 rapes and nearly 14,400 robberies reported over the last half of the 1980s—figures that have dropped by two-thirds in recent years.[10] Yet the ethos of violence then seeped into younger age brackets. Teenagers—and younger—began shooting each other for their designer coats or sneakers, often the chosen emblems of different street gangs. Ironically, as the violence within the drug world tapered off, the effects picked up among young black males (reminiscent of the white schoolchildren who, emulating the Black Legion, tried to hang a schoolmate because he did better in school). Even the college bound were arming themselves, risking mandatory jail sentences if caught. And given how heavily Detroit had armed itself, domestic violence often quickly escalated into murder.

White flight turned into class flight. Young professional adults, white and black, who wanted to remain in the city and try to stem the slide reconsidered their decisions once they began having children.[11] Many of those with the economic means moved out, and some of the segregation patterns that had marked 1950s Detroit began replicating themselves in the suburbs in the 1980s and 1990s. The adjoining cities of Oak Park and Southfield, across Eight Mile Road from Detroit's northwest neighborhoods, had been white (and in the case of Oak Park, heavily Jewish) since the original subdivisions began cropping up in the 1950s and 1960s. In 1990, Oak Park was 35 percent black and Southfield was 30 percent black. By 2000, Southfield had a black majority and Oak Park was split about evenly, even though both suburban cities' total populations remained stable. (Southfield had grown by about five thousand people, or 7 percent.) In 2010, some 70 percent of Southfield's residents and 57 percent of Oak Park's residents were African American. In a sense, the people who had long resisted fleeing Detroit on grounds of race and job loss finally were driven out by crime. And as they moved into suburbs, whites again fled. Southfield had 30,406 white residents in 2000; ten years later only 17,876 remained.

Lack of jobs drives Detroit's illicit economy. The loss of private-sector jobs has hit at every industrialized urban center in the nation, and in each it has had the most pronounced effect on African Americans. In 1973, three out of every eight black men living in an urban environment held a manufacturing job. By 1987—fourteen years later—the proportion had dropped to one in five. There was a related increase in the number of black males working in the retail and service industries, which offered much lower wage and benefits packages.[12] Nowhere has the impact been worse than in Detroit, with its overlapping stresses of generations of racism, formal and informal segregation, class division, and the mushrooming growth of the permanent underclass.[13]

All of those issues are symptoms of the long-gestating problems that might not have been easily avoided but that certainly were seen coming. Conventional and politically palatable solutions, such as federal enterprise zones and tax abatements to lure investment, were for naught. Industries left anyway. So did people. Nearly 250,000 people left the city in the decade ending in 2010, and while clear data is not available, it seems a large portion of them left during the economic and housing crisis. The 2010 census count of 714,000 people was at least 100,000 fewer than the most conservative precensus estimates.

In 2008, Detroit had 101,000 vacant housing units, up from 81,754 before the recession, accounting for more than one in four of all available units. And that was after years of steady demolition of vacant buildings, which meant Detroit houses and apartment buildings were being abandoned faster than the city could tear them down. The housing bubble was significant in Detroit, too, and when it collapsed, the foreclosures propelled the federal Department of Housing and Urban Development onto the list of the city's ten biggest property taxpayers. The average

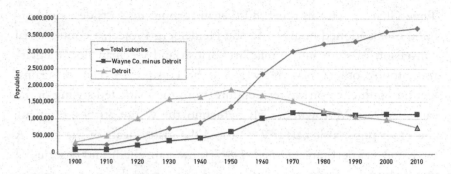

The emptying of Detroit began in the 1950s. SCOTT MARTELLE

home price dropped from $97,847 in 2003 to $12,439, and those who still owned homes and businesses began petitioning the city for reductions in tax assessments on properties that were, from a marketing standpoint, virtually worthless. Conditions have become so bad that more than half of Detroit residents with jobs traveled to the suburbs to get to work. The urban hub is that in name only.[14]

Yet Detroit remains a place of surprising—if often misplaced—optimism. While the 2008 recession had the feel of a death blow, with two of the three major auto companies filing for bankruptcy, hope was still resurgent in some quarters. And in countless small ways, changes have begun. There has been a much-noted move by urban farmers to convert vacant lots into community gardens, and at least one entrepreneur has proposed commercial farming on a corporate scale, much to the annoyance of the small neighborhood enthusiasts. Some speculate that the proposal is little more than an attempted land grab, allowing the firm to amass and farm city lots that could become valuable if the city does recover. As of this writing, not a seed from that project has been planted. And while the neighborhood gardens are positive developments—from improving access to affordable healthy food to helping strengthen neighborhood cohesion—they'll do nothing to help counter the economic collapse.

Artists have also settled in the city, drawn by its openness, its cheap cost of living, and the sense of romance attached to being an urban pioneer. They add a cutting-edge vibe to Detroit, following in the steps of

Tyree Guyton, who in the 1980s began turning his eastside neighborhood of abandoned houses into the Heidelberg Project, a controversial
conversion of slum into public art. British and German documentar-
ians, among others, have recently set the collapse of the city against
Detroit's influence on western culture, from the marketed styling of the
cars it built to Motown, the MC5, techno, the White Stripes, Eminem,
and other pop music acts that captured the gritty heart of the place. A
television crime drama *Detroit 1-8-7* (now cancelled) and a series of
movies have been filmed in and around Detroit, while art photography
books have been published depicting Detroit's collapsing and abandoned
buildings. *Time* magazine bought a house and staged a year-long project
to cover the city, an effort that failed to deliver little more than clichés
about the place and that failed to get at the roots of the city's crisis.

There have been other semivoyeuristic media accounts and personal
websites detailing the breadth and depth of the collapse of the city's
industrial heart. The best of them, though heavy on nostalgia, are infor-
mative, offering somewhat dispassionate accounts of what once was, and
what's left. Locals dismiss the worst of them as "ruins porn," with all that
that implies. Degradation. A sense of victimization. Shame.

These incremental flickers of life, though, do nothing to address the
city's core problem: disinvestment and abandonment propelled by corporate decisions framed and aided by government policies, from housing
to free trade, with an overlay of stubbornly persistent racism. And the
city can't expect much help from the state of Michigan, which between
2000 and 2007 lost fifty-four hundred businesses with employees (as
opposed to the self-employed), a decline of about 3 percent, compared
with a national growth rate of 7 percent.[15] And this was before the
economic collapse and gutting of the Big Three automakers, and the
financial crisis that has swept local and state governments with massive
drops in tax revenues. So severe is the crisis that in 2011 Governor Rick
Snyder persuaded the state legislature to grant him broad and unprec-
edented powers to take control of fiscally unstable local governments,
and to abrogate union agreements, a highly controversial maneuver that
smacks of malevolent paternalism more than sound public management.

The first government targeted, the Lake Michigan city of Benton Harbor, is predominately black.

Adding a few urban farms within Detroit might create some seasonal jobs, and they would be good use of abandoned land. They also are good for morale, offering a sense of progress in some direction, at least. But they will not save Detroit, let alone revive it. They are more in the "when you have lemons, make lemonade" category. At best, these efforts form small pieces of the solution in that they form fresh ways of envisioning the new Detroit. At worst, they are opportunistic moves by people motivated by the collapse of land values. Consider it modern homesteading.

At the same time, there is a subtle crosscurrent among some black Detroiters who, while they appreciate and support the flickers of life, fear that the return of whites to the city could signal an effort to retake political control of a place they had once abandoned. Of Detroit's many barriers to self-improvement, the lock that old fears and traditions—good and bad—have on the collective mind-set could well be the most significant, and potentially the most lethal. As is the delusion that what once was can be again. Because it cannot. Detroit's industrial past will never roar back to life; the national and global economies have undergone too drastic a transformation for it to be possible.

Even if the auto industry stages a comeback, most of the work, and the riches, will go elsewhere. Early in 2011, for instance, Ford, GM, and Chrysler all announced that they would be adding jobs as the consumer demand—frozen during the recession—began to pick up. While hailed as good news, buried in the announcements were the details that the bulk of the jobs would be added elsewhere, and those in Michigan would be mostly outside Detroit. Ford's Michigan Manufacturing plant in Wayne for instance, about twenty-five miles west of downtown Detroit, was one of the beneficiaries. The new jobs were a tiny counter tide to the hundreds of thousands of previously lost jobs. And even then, many of the new factory hires came in as second-tier employees making around $15 an hour, or $31,000 a year. It was clear the past, with its middle-class wages for blue-collar work, is dead.[16]

There is some progress, though. In early summer 2011, Detroit native and Quicken Loans mogul Dan Gilbert bought the downtown land-mark Dime Building, adding it to a personal fold that already includes three other downtown properties, where by fall of 2011 four thousand of his employees were working. He has said he wanted to create some-thing of an incubator for new businesses in Detroit that, if successful, could at least propel a revival of the downtown district begun in 2003 with the opening of the sixteen-story Compuware headquarters near the site of the former Hudson's department store. How those projects and developments would help the dead and dying neighborhoods in outlying sections of Detroit is unclear, but any job addition is bound to be good for the city.[17]

Detroit's leaders—in government and private industry—have known Detroit's troubles were looming. In 1966, the year before the riot and fifteen years after Detroit began shrinking, Mayor Jerome Cavanagh appointed the Committee on Community Renewal, which produced a report that compared Metro Detroit's sputtering growth with that of other cities. Of the fifteen largest metropolitan areas, Detroit—which in many ways was the engine that propelled the nation's phenomenal twentieth-century growth and wealth—was already falling behind the pack, dragged down in part by its lack of economic diversification. As the auto industry decentralized, nothing of significance replaced it.

Yet looking ahead, the report predicted that metropolitan Detroit would have a population of 4.4 million by 1970 with nearly 1.6 million jobs, and by 1980 a metro population of just over 5 million with 1.85 million jobs. It didn't work out that way. By 2010, the entire metropoli-tan area held about 1.7 million jobs (after years of seesawing), which amounted to stagnant growth during a time when jobs nationwide grew by about 44 percent. The nation simply left Detroit behind.[18]

DETROITERS VI

SHELLEY

On a snowy Saturday morning in January 2011, Shelley, a nineteen-year-old African American mother, sat down at a conference table in a neighborhood office of a social services agency working to feed and find jobs for the hungry and the homeless.[1] She's slightly built, with an infectious smile, but she is wary in an awkward way.

Shelley was born in northwest Detroit in August 1991, at the tail end of the crack epidemic, the only girl and the youngest of seven children in her family. Her father worked for the City of Detroit Water and Sewerage Department, and he apparently suffered from mental illness, filling his house with old newspapers and other collections of the worthless. Her mother, a former nurse, suffered from crippling alcoholism and would disappear for days or weeks at a time as Shelley was growing up. Sometimes her mother was off on a bender; sometimes she was in jail; sometimes she was in rehab. When she was home, each day ended with a violent argument between Shelley's father and mother. "He was just very abusive. He would break her arm sometimes."

When Shelley was eight years old, welfare authorities took her and her minor siblings from the home after what she describes as "some lies" one of her brothers told Child Protective Services. "He was staying with us at the time and my daddy didn't want him in the house so my brother end up telling some lies saying that my parents were using crack cocaine," she says. "At the time the lights was out" because the electric bill was unpaid "so Child Protective Services wound up taking me and my youngest brother away."

Shelley spent the next eight years running away from foster homes, invariably trying to return to her parents. Sometimes she made it. "My mom would be drunk. She ended up turning me in once because she was scared she would get in trouble." Most often, though, she was caught, or gave up, lost and hungry and unable to navigate the city. Each runaway resulted in a reassignment, adding to her disorientation. "I was just basically just moved around a lot." Shelley said she smoked the occasional joint but otherwise stayed out of direct involvement with the drug life that seems to be the most sustaining part of Detroit's economy. (Her mentor at the agency, who has watched over Shelley for several years, said she has seen no signs that the young woman has been involved with drugs.)

Shelley's drive to reunite with her parents hit an abrupt end when she was fifteen. During one visit home to celebrate her father's birthday, she wound up staying overnight at the apartment of one of her brothers. He raped her. "I didn't say anything to nobody." But the violence, and the humiliation, festered. "A few days later I was talking with this one lady, she was a church-going lady, and I was trying to explain to her, you know, was it sick for me not to be saying anything. She told me no, and she ended up telling the lady that I was staying with and they ended up taking me to the police station to file a police report" but "I haven't heard anything since." A week later Shelley tried to kill herself "because of that and because I was just thinking of everything that was going wrong in my life. I counted out ninety-two pills and probably took at least fourteen Tylenol PMs, little yellow pills, I found in one of the ladies' bathrooms" at the group home she had been assigned to. She threw up then told the caregivers she had taken the pills and they took her to the hospital.

Shelley eventually told her parents about the rape; they chose not to believe her. When the rapist showed up at family gatherings, Shelley hid away in a room until he left. "They would invite him over like nothing had happened." She received counseling in the different group homes as she was shuffled around the system. She told one counselor, "I wish he was dead. I was telling her I was going to kill him and myself. I used to just sit there and plot on it, a lot." The counselor said she understood, but that "she hoped I learned a lot through therapy. They ended up discharging me." She has not had any continuing therapy.

The pain is still raw, a spot in her memory that she tries not to touch. "My family, they either didn't care what happened or they just didn't want to believe it. That made me feel very angry. Even if this is your son, I'm telling you what he did to me, and you still want to let him around. It's like, it hurt a lot." Yet she still kept her parents in her life. "I really have no other place to go."

In 2008 Shelley ran away yet again from a foster home, and at the urging of a lawyer assigned to watch out for her interests, declared herself an independent minor and left foster care at age seventeen. In the process, she signed away any claims to medical or other government services. Shelley left school after the tenth grade and eventually, facing no other options, moved back in with her father, who was by then separated from her mother, and got a part-time job. "I just wanted to be home. I was tired of being in foster care."

But life at home wasn't any easier than foster care. Despite a pension as a thirty-year city employee and monthly Social Security checks, her father lived as though he were penniless. "We would always have to eat at the soup kitchen and go to churches for food. Or wait for my mom to come around with her food stamps so we could go shopping. She was still an alcoholic and didn't want to come around." The living conditions were spartan. "The house is very old. The furniture is old and dusty. Paint chips are off the walls, there are stains on the walls. It's just really old. He's got boxes of old stuff, his old clothes, old tapes. They're pretty much everywhere. On the dining room table. Near his TV. Behind the couch. In my room my window broke out one day" during a violent storm "and my father still hasn't got that window fixed to this day. There's no dresser in my room so all my stuff was in bags." Drugs surrounded her daily life. "My father's landlord was a drug dealer. There are drug dealers up at the liquor store—basically, everywhere."

Of her six brothers, two are dead (one death was apparently drug related, the other from AIDS, likely drug related as well), one was adopted by another family, one still lives and works temp jobs in Detroit, and the other two—including the rapist—dropped out of sight. One, last she heard, was selling drugs in another city. Shelley has worked some part-time jobs, but none has lasted (some have been working for the social service agencies through which she was receiving help). Then in the spring of 2010, no longer on birth control because she had signed away her access to health care, Shelley became pregnant. Once pregnant, as an indigent, she again qualified for heath care services for the unborn baby.

It was Shelley's second pregnancy. A year earlier she had miscarried, a turn of events that in retrospect she was thankful for. "I was with this guy. I thought I loved him. . . . I wanted to really be with this person and start a family with him. . . . When I got pregnant, he ended up dissing me and stuff. He basically just wanted money. . . . He ended up cussing me out that I better not tell that baby anything about him, that it wasn't his, and all of that stuff." After the miscarriage, she fell into depression. "I stayed in my room for four days straight. Didn't take a shower or anything, just was sitting there in my room." She eventually came out of the shell and resumed her life and began hanging around with a twenty-five-year-old man she knew through the agency where we met to talk. The baby's father is somewhat active in the baby's life, but she was uncertain about whether they might have a future together. "I don't truly know where his mind is. It's hard to explain."

After Shelley gave birth at Henry Ford Hospital in late December 2010, she realized she had to move out of her father's house or face severe social isolation. "He's a guy that really likes his privacy, so no one can come over to help me with the baby. The nurse couldn't even come over to do the home care visit" two days after she was released from the maternity ward "so I had to go to someone else's house so we could meet." She moved in with a friend from one of her foster home stays, a few miles from her father's house. The friend had recently been fired from her job at a McDonald's restaurant. Shelley was receiving $306 a month in welfare benefits for the care of her daughter, though she didn't know how long she would qualify for that support. The friend was receiving unemployment. The friend's boyfriend also lived there, but he wasn't working. "She was telling me she was getting tired of taking care of a grown man. He's got a lot of potential. He can fix things but he don't want to do anything with it." But she also acknowledges jobs in Detroit are rare things. "They are very hard to find."

Still, Shelley has a sense of optimism about the future, though she also has trouble articulating a plan of action for improving her life. She has to travel to a library or a support agency to get online access to look for jobs and, in many cases, to apply for them. She knows she needs to get her GED but is uncertain how to go about doing that with an infant daughter. Yet she sees a future for herself in which "hopefully I'll have a decent job, so that I can be able to support my baby more. I don't plan on staying with my foster sister forever. It was just she offered me a place to stay and I took it. Hopefully, I'll have my own place, a good job, and just be able to support me and [the baby.] . . . I know it's going to be a lot of work. Hopefully, I can get my GED and get a trade and hopefully become a medical assistant or something. Otherwise, the only jobs here in Detroit is working at McDonald's or a waitress or something. The job opportunities here in Detroit really suck."

19

PITTSBURGH,
A DIFFERENT CASE

The natural place to seek comparisons to Detroit is Pittsburgh, the former steel city built around the peninsula formed at the head of the Ohio
River, a waterway that, like the Great Lakes, played a significant role in
the early development of the interior of the country. And there are simi-
larities—but also vast differences. Pittsburgh, too, was a single-industry
city whose economy stalled under the weight of foreign competition,
in this case from steel manufacturers. In the 1970s and 1980s the city
and region lost population as unemployment skyrocketed and young
families moved out. Much of that came from the collapse of the steel
industry, but corporate mergers also robbed the city of key white-collar
employers, including Gulf Oil and Rockwell International. Unemployment in the region peaked at over 16 percent in the spring of 1983.

After struggling to find ways to revive the steel industry—a quix-
otic quest, as it turned out—Pittsburgh leaders looked elsewhere for
solutions. They focused on three stable cores: the heath care industry,
higher education, and finance. By 2010, more than one in five jobs in
the region were in education and health care services, a nearly 18 percent increase from 2000 to 2009, while manufacturing jobs ebbed by a
third. Pittsburgh also missed the national run-up in housing prices, so

when that collapsed in 2008–09, local real estate values remained stable and affordable. In the Great Recession, the Pittsburgh area unemployment rate reached 9.6 percent in February 2010, and in the city of Pittsburgh it topped out at 9 percent in May and June 2010. Tellingly, the worst unemployment rate in the urban core was lower than that of the overall region, suggesting an urban core with some vitality.[1]

In Detroit, the reverse has long been the case, with unemployment in the old core city far exceeding that of the metropolitan region it anchors. And it is differences like that—economic, demographic, sheer scale—that make it unlikely Detroit will find a Pittsburgh-style rebound. The Metro Detroit area (excluding the adjoining Ann Arbor metro area) holds 4.3 million people, compared with 2.4 million for metro Pittsburgh. The city of Detroit's population, which peaked at around 1.85 million in 1950, dropped to 714,000 in 2010. Pittsburgh, by comparison, had 677,000 residents in 1950, and shrank to 305,704 in 2010. So Detroit's current population is still larger than Pittsburgh at its peak. Crafted another way, the number of people living in poverty alone in Detroit at the present time is about equal to Pittsburgh's total population. And Detroit's 140 square miles dwarfs Pittsburgh, at 55.5 square miles.

The second major difference is the creation and persistence of sustaining institutions. Pittsburgh's most-famous industrial baron, Andrew Carnegie—as honored and reviled in his time as Henry Ford would be later—donated chunks of his fortune to create the ancestor of Carnegie Mellon University, now a key part of Pittsburgh's educational heart, which also includes the quasi-public University of Pittsburgh and the Catholic Duquesne University. In Detroit, Ford and his auto-making peers did little to create or nurture local institutions of higher learning. There is no Ford University, or Chrysler College. The city, despite its size and history of wealth, has one significant public university—Wayne State University—and a handful of much smaller private schools, including Marygrove College and the University of Detroit-Mercy. Pittsburgh is home to at least eleven universities and colleges, with a few more than that in the suburbs. Together, they draw a fairly stable student population of around one hundred thousand—so sizable that the mayor of Pittsburgh in 2009 raised, then abandoned under political opposition, plans to tax the students to help balance the city's budget. And the universities themselves are significant local employers.[2]

Both Pittsburgh and Detroit have large medical centers. Expansion of Detroit's main health care complex near Wayne State, and the growth of the university itself, are two positive and significant forces in the city. Michigan State University, based in East Lansing, about ninety miles northwest, has also recently staked out a presence near Wayne State. As has the University of Michigan, which began in Detroit but moved to Ann Arbor in the 1830s—another opportunity for economic diversity that got away. One can only imagine what Detroit would look like today if the University of Michigan, with its forty thousand undergraduate and graduate students, its nearly forty thousand employees, and its business spin-offs, had stayed put.

But the biggest differences between Pittsburgh and Detroit are history and demography. While Pittsburgh saw an influx of southern blacks during the Great Migration years, it was nothing like the scale that swept into Detroit. At its peak, in the 1970s and 1980s, Pittsburgh's black population was just over one hundred thousand, a little more than a quarter of the total. Though there have been racial frictions, Pittsburgh has never suffered the kind of neighborhood-shifting violence that has marked Detroit's racial history, or the mass white flight that drained Detroit beginning in the 1950s. And it has not endured Detroit's staggering joblessness and poverty. In 2009, about 15 percent of Pittsburgh families and one in five of all Pittsburgh residents were living on incomes below the federal poverty line. In Detroit, more than 28 percent of families and one in three residents were living in poverty. Pittsburgh's median household income was almost $36,000, compared with just under $30,000 for Detroit, both well below the national median of about $50,000. Ultimately, Detroit's population is much larger, much poorer, and less educated than Pittsburgh's.

Powerful forces built Detroit into one of the nation's, and the world's, great industrial centers and cities. Similarly powerful forces have led to its collapse. The result is a national problem, not a local one, both from a moral and a financial standpoint. The long-term stability and viability of a society depends on its cohesion. Hundreds of thousands of people living in close proximity to each other who have lost a sense of connection with the broader society is a political crisis in the making. Less dramatically, unless the cycle of poverty in Detroit and other urban cores is broken, future generations become recipients of government spending rather than contributors to the common weal. On a more humane level, it is morally reprehensible to look away while so many fellow citizens live in misery, and without hope.

There is plenty of blame—and responsibility—to go around. Racism, those who commit crimes, corporate policies, failure of government to plan regionally, housing policies, banks, and realtors—all played critical roles in Detroit's collapse. It's important to understand these culpabilities but distracting to focus on them. The path to solutions is hard enough without wasting time and energy on recriminations.

Racism could well be the most difficult hurdle for Detroit to overcome and makes it all the harder to change other factors, from business reinvestment to home sales. Significantly, nearly a third of Detroit's households are headed by single women, compared with 22 percent nationally. And men tend to live alone in Detroit at a higher percentage than in the nation as a whole and than in most other urban centers.

It is a place of fractured relationships, with children being raised by young, undereducated, and often unemployed mothers, and men living in social isolation, also often undereducated and unemployed.[3] There is a common thread, particularly in conservative circles, that the urban poor should pull themselves up by their own bootstraps. But to be born in Detroit is to face imposing restrictions on one's ability to become an educated, productive, and contributing member of society, from dysfunctional families as the norm to a failed school system to a crime-driven underground economy to an aboveground economic structure incapable of supporting itself.

Some Detroiters do manage to carve out rewarding lives for themselves, but the failures dominate. And the successes tend to leave, either for careers, or safety, or to give their own children a better educational foundation than they received. It's telling that in the 2010 census, the African American populations in the five counties that surround Wayne

County, with Detroit as its heart, increased, while Detroit lost some 185,000 black residents. More blacks, in fact, left Wayne County than whites. In a sense, white flight was followed by black middle-class flight, which left behind a city dominated by people caught in the cycle of poverty that social critic (and socialist) Michael Harrington identified in 1962 in *The Other America: Poverty in the United States*. A half-century later, the urban socioeconomic crisis that Harrington defined has, if anything, become worse.

Detroit's toughest hurdle is likely its own divisions. In January 2011 there was a revealing unplanned online debate primarily among white, mostly suburban Detroiters, on Facebook. Neither the host nor the prime debater will be identified here because it took place within a limited audience of the host's circle of friends. The topic began with a posting about new 2010 census data showing a radical difference in poverty levels between Detroit and its suburbs. It drew a forceful opinion from a white male suburbanite (edited for clarity and to clean up misspellings): "Detroit is a city run by an administration that has WANTED to be segregated for the last 50 years, sans the brief period when former Mayor Dennis Archer tried to clean it up (and he was hated for it and called an Uncle Tom). What did you expect the border to look like? . . . There is one reason why Detroit is what it is. The 'minorities' took over in this 'Entitlement' city and here is where we stand. Show me one productive black community. Don't even think of blaming it on Whites. Now all of their crap that ruined Detroit is quickly moving North. I don't know about you but I am tired of losing on my investments, tired of not feeling safe, and tired of being called a racist when all I do is pay taxes and believe in an honest living. Nothing comes for free. That is the problem here. Detroit is the pits and I don't see it coming back. Now the suburbs are going to die with this influx. I have seen the border move from Outer Drive, to 7 mile to 8 mile and now it is 20 mile road. (Note: Outer Drive is within Detroit; 8 Mile Road is the northern border; 20 Mile Road is twelve miles north of the city line). All of the homes in this area are a quarter the value of what they once were. I get around the country. There is definitely a reason why and one common factor as stated above."

The anger and the racism were reflected by other posters in the thread, too (a few, it should be noted, condemned the racism and broken logic). Together, though, the anti-Detroit comments clearly displayed the endemic racism that still defines the region. And it cuts both ways: many black Detroiters are derisive of what they perceive life to be in the white-dominated suburbs. Decades of social agency work, of regional coalitions, of union efforts to try to bridge the racial divide here, have all failed. Until the sharp barbs of racism are dulled, Detroit will not revive.

There's a perception among whites—not just in southeast Michigan—that African American residents of Detroit created the problems of crime and poverty that define the city today. After all, they are the ones committing the crimes, and they are the ones who "do nothing" to climb out of poverty. But that misreads the reality and is little more than a rationalization for white Americans to do nothing. Detroit was crippled by forces far beyond the ability of most individuals to counter in their own lives. When a child is born to a teenage high school dropout who lacks the skills to either raise the child or become a productive, employed member of society, that child's future is just as bleak as the parent's. And it is no fault of the child that he or she is being raised in those circumstances. It is the moral responsibility of all of us to find remedies. If we can find a way to shore up the financial well-being of corporations, Wall Street financiers, and banks that gambled and lost, then we have no excuse for letting Detroit—or Newark, New Jersey, or Gary, Indiana, for that matter—wither and die.

Similarly, unless Detroit's current population finds a way to move away from the "Third City" economy Carl Taylor talked about, and integrates itself into the legitimate economy, Detroit will continue to deteriorate. Where racism created the crevasse, it has been crime, widespread poverty, and the abject failure of government—from the schools to the city to the state to the federal level—amid an abrogation of community responsibility by corporations that has made the divide unbridgeable. And that makes a better future harder to obtain.

Kim Trent, a politically connected African American woman, lives in the downtown Millender Center residential complex across Jefferson Avenue from the towering Renaissance Center, with her husband, Ken

Coleman, and their toddler son. Trent is a former journalist and worked, for a time, as a key aide for former governor Jennifer Granholm.[4] She was also on the board overseeing the development of the Detroit river-front into recreational space. She's lived in the city nearly her entire life, and Detroit has no bigger, or more consistent, booster. Coleman, too, is a major supporter of Detroit—in 2010 he was elected to the Charter Commission, whose members are tasked with updating the city's "con-stitution." He, too, has a journalism background as a former senior editor of the *Michigan Chronicle*, the local African American newspaper, and as the host of radio and television public affairs shows.

In January 2011, Coleman attended a meeting about youth inter-vention in a community center in northwest Detroit, near Seven Mile and Greenfield. As Coleman walked out of the building, a young thug knocked him to the ground and, at gunpoint, robbed him. For the first time, Trent began talking about abandoning her city. "I love it so much, but the thought of raising a son here really frightens me," she said. "I'm not sure I'm up to it. Every time he walks out the door, I think I'll be worried sick. I actually feel a little guilt [discussing this publicly] because I don't want to add to the city's dangerous reputation. But I am just so outraged that the good guys are being victimized when they're trying to do the right thing."

20

AN EPILOGUE

The emptying of Detroit was the result of a million individual decisions. And how those decisions were made gets at the heart of Detroit's most difficult challenges.

There is a tendency to blame executives of the Big Three auto companies and other corporate leaders for abandoning the Detroit workforce upon which their fortunes were made, and there is some merit to that. Decisions to decentralize from Detroit, and then to globalize, put the interests of profits and shareholders ahead of those of the communities that gave rise to the industry in the first place. Yet those decisions were framed under US laws. Executives and policy makers for publicly traded companies are required to act in the best interests of their shareholders—i.e., seeking profits—and not in the best interests of the communities in which they exist. Those executives and policy makers are richly rewarded for their close attention to the shareholders' return on investment (and punished when they fall short), which puts executives' self-interest ahead of the interests of their workforces, and their communities.

Corporate decisions that destroy communities—a major component of Detroit's collapse—are deeply lamentable and at a significant level immoral. But railing against them does no good. It's like blaming a dog for being a dog. To lead a corporation to make different decisions—

decisions that would maintain or strengthen communities, not destroy them—American society must change the environment in which such decisions are made. We need to retrain the dogs. That requires a fundamental shift in how we view the role of business in society. For years our political and social culture has put the interests of corporations ahead of the interests of individuals and community stability. That has led to the decimation of the middle class, and well-paid working-class jobs, as US-based corporations shifted production overseas to keep up with the global drive for the lowest possible production costs. In theory, that is good free-market economics. But in practice, those production costs are, on the local level, individual jobs and neighborhoods. So as a matter of policy, we have traded our social and economic stability for higher profits for corporations, which has exacerbated the nation's income divide and gutted the urban centers of our industrial cities and countless small manufacturing towns across the nation. These are the effects of national policies, and until those policies are changed to put the needs of people and communities ahead of corporations—or to tie the fates of corporations to the communities in which they work—there is no real answer to the troubles afflicting places like Detroit.

Another theme that courses through assessments of Detroit and Michigan—particularly among conservative Republicans—is that the economy is crippled by onerous taxes and regulations. Yet in 2010, *Forbes* ranked Michigan, and by inclusion Detroit, fourteenth in the nation for its business climate based on criteria that "measures regulatory and tort climate, incentives, transportation, and bond ratings." The state ranked forty-seventh overall among the "best states for business," dragged down by low ratings for the state's economic vitality and prospects for growth and the "educational attainment, net migration and projected population growth" of its labor force—not its taxes or regulations. The state was in the middle of the pack, ranking thirtieth, on a measure of the quality of life. Louisiana, with Republican governor Bobby Jindal, ranked last in quality of life, which would seem to counter the argument that the problems of weak economies and standards of living were the faults of one party or the other.[1]

Looking at all these factors, the business climate in Michigan was poor not because regulations and taxes were a disincentive but, in a chicken-or-egg conundrum, because of the general ill health of the regional economy—which remains dominated by the auto industry. The solutions won't be found in partisan bickering or in such antidemocratic actions as the new Michigan law that allows the governor to, by fiat, seize control of lower-level governments that he finds not up to the task of governing.

Significantly, the outflow of residents from Detroit has been a function mainly of individuals reaching similar conclusions to those reached by corporate executives. They put their own interests ahead of community. The area has a large and vibrant base of political progressives (many of whom are my friends) who decry the outsourcing and profiteering decisions by Detroit industries and businesses and believe at an organic level in the power and necessity of communal action and of neighborhood. Yet many, if not most, of those people live in the suburbs, having forged their own decisions to leave Detroit—or not move into Detroit in the first place—in a crucible of factors: concerns over personal safety, financial security (at least in home values), better educational systems for their children, and a general desire for a more stable and satisfying daily existence. They have, in effect, made the same decisions for themselves as the corporations did, opting for relative financial stability and security. White racism clearly was a propelling factor for much of Detroit's early 1950s and 1960s population drain, and it remains one of the area's most intractable and lamentable problems. But not every white resident who left was a racist. Many, much like middle-class black Detroiters with children, made personal or family decisions within the context of specific circumstances, be it the pursuit of jobs, a shorter commute, schools, or a flight from crime. Stated less obliquely, in recent years there have been fewer reasons or incentives to stay—for all residents—than there have been to leave.[2]

As the residents and businesses go, so goes the tax base. The city government, which is responsible for basic civic services, is collapsing along with the neighborhoods and local industry. Dave Bing, a wealthy

Detroit-area businessman and member of the National Basketball Association's Hall of Fame, became mayor in a special election in May 2009 during a scandal that sent the former mayor, Kwame Kilpatrick, once a rising star in the Democratic Party, to federal prison for lying under oath about a sexual affair with his female chief of staff.[3] At the time, Detroit's economy was hitting Depression-like lows, with an official unemployment rate peaking at 27.4 percent in July 2009.

In late December 2010, Bing released the city government's annual financial report, the first time in five years and second time in thirteen years that it had been submitted to the state on time (it's due within six months of the end of the fiscal year, June 30).[4] That itself marked an improvement, but that's where the good news ended. The city, with a $3.1 billion budget for 2010 to 2011, had a $155 million overall deficit in the general fund and a mind-boggling $1.6 billion in debt, plus more than $5 billion in unfunded retiree obligations after pension accounts lost value in the economic collapse. While the city sought to slash spending, anticipated revenues failed to materialize as mounting layoffs cut into city income taxes—some $24.3 million disappeared with the GM and Chrysler bankruptcies alone—and as property values eroded. Cuts in the state budget threatened to lop another $175 million in revenues for the city. In November 2011, Bing announced the layoff of one thousand city workers, and the news that the city could run out of cash by spring.

"When I was elected, I thought I knew what was going on, but I got here and found out [that] in the short term, things were way worse than I ever imagined," Bing said less than two years into his term. "Financially. Ethically. From a policy standpoint. We were on the brink of a financial calamity."[5]

The Detroit public school system faced a similar fiscal crisis, and early in 2011 was contemplating a plan to close half of the city's schools and increase high school class sizes to sixty-two. This is in a system from which three out of four students already walk away without a degree, and whose seventy-four thousand students set low national benchmarks for educational achievement. Key to the problem: getting the students in their seats. On the opening day of the 2011–12 school year, only 55 percent of students expected to be enrolled showed up.[6]

Both the city and school governments—now the two biggest employers in Detroit—have resorted to deep staffing cuts, which adds significant pressure on the already high unemployment rate, not to mention the delivery of key services, and in turn the income taxes those city-based workers were paying. In April, using the controversial powers granted by the Michigan state legislature that allows the state executive branch to usurp local government, the school district's state-appointed emergency financial overseer, Robert Bobb, announced that he would be sending layoff notices to all of the city's nearly fifty-five hundred schoolteachers, the first step in abrogating union contracts. The move added yet another layer of turmoil and confusion to a system already collapsing in crisis. By September, Bobb's successor, Roy Roberts, proposed a four-year budget under which the teaching staff would be cut by more than a third, reflecting the dwindling number of students enrolled in the district. Of 140,000 school-age Detroiters, nearly half have been siphoned off by charter schools or attend suburban school districts—an exodus of the best and the brightest that consigns the low-performing students, and those with limited parental support, to the ineffectual city district.

Fixing the schools is where the cycle of poverty can best be broken, since that is where the new generation gets trained to forge a new kind of life. And that has proven to be as difficult as keeping business and industry from leaving. When schools fail, the political solution is to blame the teachers, when in reality the biggest hurdle to improving educational results lies with the students—and their families. The best teachers in the world can't teach students who aren't in the classroom and supplied with the proper textbooks and other material. Blaming the teachers for broken educational systems is like blaming a ship's crew for not being able to keep a rust bucket from sinking.[7]

The cumulative effect of all this on Detroiters' outlooks about their own lives has been pronounced. In a survey in early 2010, a year after the federal bailouts of GM and Chrysler, two of every five Metro Detroit residents reported having trouble keeping up with their bills at some point in the previous year, and a slightly higher ratio admitted to having credit card or personal-debt problems, or facing large outstanding medical bills. The troubles extended to meeting mortgages or rents, with 17 percent saying they were behind. And 14 percent said they were struggling to keep food on the table. Those troubles led to regional sour feelings, with the majority pointing to the economy as Metro Detroit's single biggest problem. An even higher proportion, 59 percent, felt the national economy was equally as poor off, and two-thirds felt it was only getting worse.

Incongruously, six of ten felt optimistic about the region's future, and nearly two out of three, looking ahead ten years, believed the quality of their lives would be better than it was at the moment. Unfortunately, the survey did not break out data for City of Detroit residents, where one can presume the economic stresses were significantly higher. But that sense of optimism, at least based on interviews and talks with scores of Detroiters, seems to hold in the city as well, regardless of how desperate the straits in which individuals might find themselves.[8]

In that environment, small counter tides are welcomed as possible game changers. General Motors, Quicken Loans, and Blue Cross Blue Shield have all moved operations, or announced moves, to downtown Detroit, bringing eight thousand mostly white-collar jobs (primarily shifted in from suburbs or other parts of the city; few were new jobs). Five companies—including Quicken and Blue Cross Blue Shield—in the summer of 2011 began offering incentives to their combined sixteen thousand employees to buy or rent homes or apartments in downtown and its surrounding neighborhoods, including a $20,000 forgivable loan for buying a home. And the Big Three announced in 2011 they would add several thousand new autoworker jobs after three years of deep cuts—good news, but not a step toward the diversification Detroit really needs. Plans were in the works for building a long-sought $500 million light-rail system down the middle of Woodward Avenue, though how that might improve job and economic development once the construction project ends is unclear.[9] If these steps and the program by the medical complex and Wayne State to offer incentives to their employees to move to the area work, the core area of the city could reach the kind of critical mass to make the light-rail system workable—and help Detroit end its population collapse.

The bigger challenge, though, will be reversing the fortunes of Detroit's vast and empty neighborhoods, which account for the majority of the city's 140 square miles. A range of nonprofit foundations have moved to fill in some of the social-program void, including the Skillman Foundation, Kresge Foundation, and others, focusing on education, neighborhood preservation, and political engagement. Other organizations, from the Capuchin Brothers and their soup kitchen to such long-standing independent services agencies as Crossroads of Michigan and FOCUS: Hope, try to help individual Detroiters. In February 2011, the Michigan Restaurant Opportunity Center announced it would open a worker-owned restaurant and training center in downtown Detroit to train up to 150 Detroiters a year for jobs in the growing service industry.

But the most radical change could be yet to come. As part of his mix of proposals to try to grab control of Detroit, and to find ways to stabilize and then build, Bing embraced a long-gestating idea that the way to deal with Detroit's collapsing population base would be to close off sections of the city. The suggestion was first seriously discussed, then quickly mocked, in 1993, when it was raised by then ombudsperson Marie Farrell Donaldson. Bing proposed enticing stragglers in mostly depopulated areas to leave their homes for more populous neighborhoods, building a critical mass of people in the new areas that could, much like the birth of galaxies after the Big Bang, coalesce into pockets of vitality. The seeds, perhaps, of a new Detroit. The plan also would save the city money by concentrating its police, fire, garbage, and other services in fewer areas of the city.

In a sense, Bing was admitting the obvious: the city could no longer continue to perform its duties. "There are areas in the city that are totally depopulated," Bing told the *Detroit Free Press*. "For those people who are there, it's going to be a job trying to persuade them to move. But that has to happen. We can't afford to continue to give them the services they need." A few weeks later, he announced plans to accelerate the disassembly of Detroit, ordering three thousand vacant and dilapidated houses to be razed, part of a program that would bulldoze ten thousand empty buildings by the end of his first term in 2013.

It was a watershed moment in the evolution of Detroit. More than three hundred years after Cadillac's entourage pieced together the first makeshift houses on the grassy north bank of the straits, Detroit's top elected official argued that the city's survival would require turning large swaths of the city that helped build America back into uninhabited meadows.

AFTERWORD

October 2013

Seats on the second tier of Comerica Park, home of the Detroit Tigers professional baseball team, offer an impressive view of the downtown Detroit skyline. Tall buildings shoulder their way skyward beyond the center field fence. Some have the clean lines of modern architecture, but most are much older, dating back to the 1920s, and have been dirtied by time, with a patina of gray covering ornate cornices and other architectural details that exude a sense of history. And despite a surge in purchases in recent years, many remain shuttered and empty.

This is the cradle for the potential rebirth of Detroit, which has endured continued troubles since *Detroit: A Biography* was first published in April 2012. A lot has changed since then, not the least of which was Governor Rick Snyder's decision to install an emergency manager for the city, effectively trumping local democracy. But much remains unchanged, particularly the quality of daily life for most of Detroit's dwindling population.

As I write this, the emergency manager, bankruptcy expert Kevyn Orr, has already filed for federal bankruptcy protection for the city government—the largest municipal bankruptcy in US history—as he recalibrates its finances and debt. It's difficult for now to say much about his ultimate plans, which still evolve as I write this. But the solutions Orr has been contemplating include slashing pension payouts for the city's retired workers, possibly selling off some artwork from the collection of the world-renowned Detroit Institute of Arts (there are legal questions about whether the city has that authority), and the privatization of some city services. Since that narrative remains without an end at this point, I'll leave the specifics alone, other than to point out that cutting the pension payments to city retirees—many of whom still live in the city—will only exacerbate Detroit's problems by further reducing the money flowing through the local economy. And there's something inherently unfair in a scenario in which employees who worked hard over the years, with commitments in hand to an eventual pension, would take a backseat to investors, who, by definition, know they are taking a risk when they invest.

The most important thing to note is that even if Orr manages to balance the city budget, he will have done little to improve the broad circumstances of life in Detroit. As I mentioned earlier in this book, the collapse of the city education system is a function, not a cause, of the city's problems. And the same goes for the city government. Governments are not places; they are institutions that reflect the economic vitality of the place they govern. And without stabilizing neighborhoods and getting people jobs, Detroit's problems will remain.

Still, there are positive developments. In the two years since *Detroit: A Biography* was published, more middle-class housing—most in the form of converted lofts—have opened in the midtown area, between the Wayne State University/medical center complexes and downtown, about a two-mile stretch along Woodward Avenue. Despite the bankruptcy filing, a quasigovernmental development agency announced plans this summer for a new hockey arena north of Interstate 75 for the Detroit Red Wings franchise. If it's built—and there is no reason to think it won't, given the public/private partnership at work—that will mean three of the city's four major professional sports franchises will play their home games within walking distance of each other and downtown and within close proximity to some already gentrifying neighborhoods. Usually new sports stadiums don't have much impact on a neighborhood's vitality, in part because of the relative light usage. Ford

Field, for instance, hosts only eight professional football games a year. But with professional hockey, baseball, and football stadiums drawing people to the same general neighborhood, the opportunity for a critical mass of retail and residential development becomes much stronger. Among the three teams, there will be 130 home games over the course of a year. Even if most of the primarily suburban (and white) audiences don't patronize nearby retail businesses, those who do will provide a lot of economic drive.

It's not a solution. It's one part of what must become a broad mix of developments. Some of it is already happening. As of early August 2013, Dan Gilbert, the billionaire owner of Quicken Loans, had bought at least thirty properties in downtown Detroit encompassing 7.6 million square feet.[1] Other investors have bought up lesser numbers of parcels, and most—including Gilbert—seem intent on renovating the properties and renting space out, rather than mothballing them in hopes of better days ahead. As I write this, two landmark buildings in downtown—the Detroit Free Press Building and the David Stott Building—have been sold at auction for a combined $14 million, and not to Gilbert, which suggests a broadening of the investment appeal. The sputtering economic energy reaches down to the small-business level. On any given evening, the bar and most of the tables at Honest ? John's (see "Detroiters V: John Thompson," page 215) are busy, as are other bars and restaurants in the area. Parking, in fact, has become hard to find at times in parts of midtown and downtown, a positive development in a place that five years ago echoed with emptiness. New hotels have reclaimed spaces in once-shuttered buildings. There is a pulse to streets that not so very long ago felt abandoned. It's no Times Square, but it is several giant steps forward, and still moving.

All these developments are commendable and should be supported. There is some local backlash to the emergent "hipster" culture in Detroit, a kind of "Park Slope moves west" vibe. But communities are people, and for Detroit to rebound in any meaningful way, it needs to become much more diversified—racially, ethnically, politically, economically, and by family composition and age. Yet such diversification can create friction. Gentrification of Cass Corridor, where Honest ? John's is located, has made the area much safer, but has also reduced available housing for the underclass that has made the area home for generations. Similarly, gentrification of Corktown, the city's oldest neighborhood, nestled between downtown and the empty Michigan Central train depot, has led to backlash from longtime residents. And new residents have been complaining about the high number of homeless who frequent nearby soup kitchens, which have existed for, in some cases, decades. But friction comes from interaction, and that Detroit, after years of decline, is experiencing growing pains can be read as a good sign.

The problem, though, is these changes remain limited to the core downtown and midtown areas, which account for just a sliver of Detroit's 140 square miles. At the end of July 2013, my wife and I spent a few days in Detroit—including the visit to Comerica Park mentioned earlier—and drove through some of the worst affected neighborhoods. As an imprecise measure, we decided to drive out Mack Avenue eastward from midtown to the border with Grosse Pointe Park, the nearest suburb. We started at Interstate 75, which divides midtown from an industrial area north of the Eastern Market (one of the city's gems), and covered 5.8 miles of what was once a thriving commercial and residential artery. We counted 58 open businesses, 26 churches, one school, one senior-citizen housing complex, two apartment buildings, and 13 apparently lived-in houses. That's 101 occupied buildings along both sides of nearly six miles of urban street. Splitting it in half (north side and south side), that's about nine occupied, in-use properties per mile on each side of the street. In places, Detroit's urban population density rivals that of rural communities.

This is the real crux of Detroit's current condition and efforts to revive the city: its emptiness, lack of jobs, and deep intergenerational poverty. A balanced budget would help, especially if it meant an end to siphoning off vital tax dollars to pay debt and using them instead to restore basic services. The average police response time earlier this year, for instance, was 58 minutes. Some 40 percent of streetlights didn't work, and many residents had stopped paying their property taxes in protest of the lack of services.[2]

But at heart, this is a crisis of community, not government. How does the nation address that? And yes, it does need national involvement.

When *Detroit: A Biography* came out, it was met with overwhelmingly positive reviews, which is gratifying for any author. Bloggers picked up on it, urban policy advocates dissected it, and after Detroit fell into bankruptcy, I was interviewed by fellow journalists and invited to write op-eds for a variety of outlets. (Some of those thoughts are incorporated in this Afterword.) But there was also a consistent undercurrent of vicious negativity and racism among online comments. The vast majority of them were, as seems the norm in this digital era, offered anonymously, which unleashes a sense of freedom to espouse deeply hateful views.

As I mentioned in an earlier chapter, racism remains Detroit's most intractable problem. It comes predominately from whites on the outside looking in—a pervasive theme is "African Americans wanted their own city and now they can rot in it." Unions, Democrats, and liberal public policies were vilified, too; cogent arguments were rare. Most of the comments were preset conclusions channeled through racial and political prisms, not detached analyses of the forces that have come to bear on Detroit (or any of our other cities, for that matter). The racial prism changes a bit from the other perspective, with blacks resentful of young white hipsters treating their troubled hometown as some sort of urban playground, as though they were European colonizers discovering an "empty" continent. And there is also some black resentment of white suburbanites who, from a black historical perspective, abandoned the city and thus helped create the economic morass that exists today. Many black residents are loath to welcome back the people they feel already spurned them once.

Those are high emotional hurdles to overcome, though there are some indications that a thaw might be in the works. In August 2012, voters in Wayne County as well as the two biggest suburban counties, Macomb and Oakland, passed an initiative establishing a tax in all three counties to support the Detroit Institute of Arts (DIA). Without that tax initiative, the DIA faced severe curtailments in operating hours and programming, and the support for the new tax among suburban voters signaled a sense that, at least when it comes to the DIA, a regional solution was possible. But after Detroit entered bankruptcy, Orr, the emergency financial manager, decided to inventory the DIA collection and invited Christie's to assess the collection in the event of an art sale to help pay down the city's staggering debt. The entire collection has been loosely pegged at $1 billion, with significant individual pieces, including Van Gogh's *Portrait of Postman Roulin*, Pieter Bruegel the Elder's *The Wedding Dance*, and Giovanni Bellini's *Madonna and Child*, expected to sell for $150 million each at auction.[3] But as word circulated of Orr's plans, the Oakland County Art Institute Authority, which handles that county's portion of the tricounty financing agreement, quickly voted to back out if the art is sold or if money from the initiative is used for nonmuseum purposes.

Still, it's an all-too-rare spirit of urban-suburban cooperation that needs to be nurtured. For Detroit to survive, let alone rebound, that wall of distrust must be breached, and the cycle of poverty that has come to define the city needs to be disrupted. In what is sure to become a landmark work, Patrick Sharkey's *Stuck in Place: Urban Neighborhoods and the End of Progress toward Racial Equality* (University of Chicago Press, 2013) makes the case that since the effective banning of racial segregation in the 1960s, the economic well-being of African Americans has not changed. In fact, in recent years there has been a downward shift in economic mobility as the current generation comes of career age only to find jobs that pay less and offer fewer chances for advancement than those held by their parents' generation. Much of that is attributable to the disappearance of middle-income, blue-collar jobs, as well as government jobs that, amid pervasive segregation in private sector hiring, became a more accessible career path for African Americans seeking stable jobs.

More significantly, and picking up on an observation that dates back to Michael Harrington's *The Other America: Poverty in the United States* (MacMillan, 1962), poverty often is rooted in a specific place, and the spread of impoverished neighborhoods in urban centers, and inner-ring suburbs, serve as an infrastructure for poverty. "Over seventy percent of African Americans who live in today's poorest, most racially segregated neighborhoods are from the same families that lived in the ghettoes of the 1970s," Sharkey writes. "I do not mean that children grow up and remain in the same physical space, but rather that children grow up and remain in the same type of environment. The level of poverty and racial composition of families' neighborhood environments remain incredibly similar across generations of family members."[4] In other words, economic mobility for many poor African Americans—Detroit's predominant population—is a myth. Poverty begets poverty, and a community cannot thrive when the economic system is choked by lack of jobs.

Another popular target for Detroit's critics is corruption. It's a legitimate issue. After *Detroit: A Biography* was written in mid-2011, former mayor Kwame Kilpatrick—already convicted on perjury charges—was convicted anew on racketeering and other corruption charges based on a scheme to divert municipal contracts to a friend. Kilpatrick was sentenced in October 2013 to 28 years in federal prison. Separate investigations have found suspected corruption among city building inspectors and a handful of Detroit Public Schools employees; these are the kinds of stories that feed preset narratives about urban bureaucracies in general and Detroit in particular.

Despite his breach of the public trust, Kilpatrick's corruption did not sink the city of Detroit. Neither did Democrats, black political leadership, unions, or liberal federal policies and the welfare programs—all of which have been cited in some of the more caustic reactions to Detroit's filing for bankruptcy. Make no mistake, corruption is corrosive and should be rooted out. But corruption did not cause Detroit's collapse. It's done nothing to improve things, and in fact may have exacerbated the city government's fiscal crisis because it was a massive local distraction at a time when the city sorely needed strong leadership. But, in the broad world of Detroit's problems, it is an ancillary issue. New Jersey and Louisiana have elevated corruption to an art form, yet both states are still standing. Wall Street's corruption is endemic—it's hard to avoid it in a system built on greed—yet Wall Street has recovered from the Great Recession even as most Americans have not. When it comes to discussions of Detroit, corruption is used as a red herring. Fight corruption, disrupt it wherever it can be found—it perverts the political process and taints residents' views of their government—but corruption is neither an explanation for Detroit's collapse nor a defensible excuse to turn our collective back on those who live there.

Bureaucratic ineptitude is another matter. Small business owners routinely complain about byzantine processes to deal with city permits and other requirements. In his optimistic look at Detroit's future *Revolution Detroit: Strategies for Urban Invention, Detroit Free Press* journalist John Gallagher relates the stories of people seeking to establish large-scale urban farming ventures in the city. But after a century of industrialization, Detroit does not have a zoning category for farming, which has posed a Kafkaesque problem that so far has been insurmountable. Tellingly, a simple and expedited addition of a new zoning category seems to be beyond the city's capabilities. While it is unlikely urban farming will do much to alleviate the city's massive poverty and joblessness, it would be a small and positive development. And the city's inability to adapt quickly does not bode well for broader business development and innovation.

This type of small-scale reinvention is Detroit's best shot at regaining its footing. For decades, as the city hemorrhaged both jobs and people, city leaders focused on large-scale, big-budget developments, most of which either failed to launch or did not deliver what was expected. I wrote in an earlier chapter of the city refusing to sell individual plots in the historic Brush Park neighborhood, hoping to keep the crumbling buildings in one package to offer to a large-scale developer. That big deal never materialized, and grand late-19th century homes that could have been saved instead crumbled and rotted beyond the point of recovery. So it will take a radical reinvention of city bureaucracy to create the kind of flexibility and adaptability that shepherds innovation.

As economist Enrico Moretti points out in *The New Geography of Jobs* (Mariner Books, 2013), innovation is the job creator of the present, and the future. Despite perceptions that the internet allows people to work from any physical location, researchers have found that physical proximity does make a difference and that regions with clusters of innovators tend to attract more innovators. In fact, that has helped feed a new and growing divide between innovative—and thriving—cities with good-paying, high-skills jobs, and cities like Detroit that are still attached to dead or dying industries in which jobs require fewer skills and produce lower wages (particularly in nonunion worksites). Moretti believes—correctly—that this innovation divide has created a geographic fragmenting of the nation along socioeconomic fault lines, exacerbating income inequality. Finding ways to reconnect those splintering communities is crucial not just for places like Detroit, but for the nation.

In Detroit's case, smart and creative public investment in targeted neighborhoods can spark local renaissances, which in turn become the building blocks for a new Detroit. Universities can help if there is an infrastructure to nurture academic research and invention into sustainable businesses. To that end, Wayne State University is one of several local backers of TechTown, a business incubator located in an Albert Kahn–designed building in Midtown that, when opened in 1927, was a Pontiac service department. In the summer of 2013, it accepted four teams of business entrepreneurs into its incubator program, three into its "Labs Venture Accelerator," and provided advice to 32 entrepreneurs. It also helped three would-be retailers open stores and provided advice to 29 small businesses. While one would hope for a more productive list of nestlings to emerge from an incubator program, it remains a significant potential force for business development.

Jumpstarting a city requires an educated populace and workforce, savvy leadership, long-term public investment (particularly in infrastructure and sustaining institutions), and a clear public sense of livability. One or two of those factors alone isn't enough. Currently, Detroit suffers from low educational achievement among its residents (one in four adults lack even a high school diploma) and a national reputation for being unlivable (lack of basic services, a dysfunctional public education system, dilapidated housing stock, pervasive poverty and crime, etc.). So there's a chicken-and-egg aspect to this. Detroit needs to vastly improve its educational system and the effectiveness of the city bureaucracy; reduce unemployment and crime; revive impoverished neighborhoods; and break the cycle of poverty among the intergenerational poor to attract the kinds of residents who can help improve the educational system, elevate the caliber of the city government, create jobs, and revive the local economy. How to do that? With an influx of jobs across the economic spectrum targeting the unemployed and changing the local mindset to find more economical and effective ways to handle local governance. Some of that might come to pass under the emergency-manager reforms, though the presumed cuts in pensions and privatization of services seem likely to do more damage than good.

But the sprouts of growth in the downtown and midtown areas are a start. As are grassroots efforts in neighborhoods, some of which are receiving help from nonprofits such as the Skillman Foundation. Those efforts will require sustained assistance to blossom and spread. The key, as Sharkey argues in *Stuck in Place*, is to envision and adopt urban policies that make a sustained difference in the lives of people living in chronically impoverished neighborhoods. This is different from sustenance support, like public assistance programs. These are transformative programs like Head Start, which, studies show, has had an effect on children's preparedness for entering school and, to a lesser extent, on their long-term educational outcomes. Conservatives have sought to kill the program, citing what they perceive to be minimal or even negative outcomes (according to some poorly constructed studies). But what places like Detroit need are expanded Head Start–style programs to parallel and shore up the educational system through twelfth grade. Among the key hurdles affecting education in Detroit is a general lack of parental support, another legacy of intergenerational poverty. To break the cycle of poverty, we need programs that will get inside the cycle. And not programs limited to three- and four-year-olds. Charter schools are not the answer, nor are vouchers. Families that are vested in their children's education yet separating themselves into charter schools simply distill the core problem into a more concentrated nut that will prove even harder to crack. And it creates yet another form of segregation, this time along lines of educational engagement.[5]

The same goes for business development policies. Short-term tax abatements and the like are inducements whose lure diminishes once the time limit ends. There needs to be long-term policies that are both broadly conceived—portable among different municipalities—but also target specific. In the case of Detroit, one approach could be providing city-owned property—there are tens of thousands of acres of it—to businesses for free for as long as they remain at the site. When the business moves, or closes, the property gets paid for at then-market price. Tax breaks should be tied to workers' proximity to the site; the closer they are, the bigger the break. Similarly, the city could offer forfeited properties near the job site to employees currently renting, with covenants attached to ensure long-term tenure, such as a sliding percentage of equity based on length of time the resident lives in the house. The state and federal governments must help by bankrolling jobs programs that focus on improving the physical aspects of a place. These would include upkeep of local parks, sidewalks, and streets as well as performing simple tasks such as keeping trees and ground cover in public and abandoned spaces trimmed and instituting accelerated programs for razing unrecoverable structures. (Detroit is already engaging in that.)

Ultimately, all this comes down to a change in basic approach, and attitude. The collapse has occurred. Our options are to step in with new energy and vision and work to revive the revivable, or to continue to gawk like motorists slowing for an accident scene. The latter really isn't an option. Detroit's story may be sui generis, with its checkered history of race and class divides and its meteoric rise and fall on the back of a single industry. But its core problems reappear from Newark to Buffalo to Gary to countless small towns dotting the former manufacturing-centric Midwest. A wide range of national, regional, and corporate policies have helped create the problems, and it will take fresh policies and energies to work with the residents of these troubled urban cores to find a way back from segregation—racial and economic—and social isolation. The question is, are we a society that is willing to acknowledge these failures and assume the responsibility for righting them? So far, we are not.

ACKNOWLEDGMENTS

This book has been brewing for so long I can't recall exactly when I first started mapping it out in my mind, which also means I can't clearly recall all of the people whose conversations, assistance, and support helped me navigate its completion. Some are already mentioned in the book, particularly the people who shared their life stories with me, tales that helped put flesh-and-blood details on occasionally arcane elements of history. I am grateful for their generosity, born in each case of a desire to help others understand what their lives, and Detroit, are about.

Special thanks are due to Mike McBride, a former *Detroit News* colleague who provided a place to crash during my summer trip to Detroit. Writer, singer, and cultural professor M. L. Liebler offered steady support for this and my other projects, including inviting me to speak before his Detroit history class at Wayne State University, where I first presented this arc of narrative to other ears. Janine Lanza, also at Wayne State, let me discuss the project with her class, too. Both outings helped me solidify in my mind some of the ideas and perspectives that inform the work. Others whose ears I bent, and whose perspectives helped me frame the project, include Cathy and Toby Anderson, Bob Ankeny, Steve Babson, Bob Berg, Al Bradley, Jim Carney, James Chambers, Ann K. Crowley, Darrell Dawsey, Betty DeRamus, Vaughn Derderian (both father and son), Serena Donadoni, Prentiss Edwards Jr., Elena Herrada and her father, Fred

Herrada (who died before this book was finished), Kate DeSmet Kulka, David Elsila, Bill Hanson, Barb and Bob Ingalls, Brian Kidd, Thomas Klug, Rochelle Lewis Lavin, Joseph McGlynn, Francine Parker, Becky Powers, Kimberly Simmons, Kim Trent, Alex Uhl, and Anora and Walter (who also passed away during the project) Zeiler. Marc Herrick went to unusual lengths—including trudging through a cemetery on a chilly damp spring afternoon—to help nail down details for me. And the usual caveat applies here: any errors in fact or interpretation lie with my work, not with their input. A note of thanks is also due to Adam Hochschild, whose work as a writer and teacher, and whose generous conversations as a friend, are a source of continuing inspiration.

Libraries and archives are the wellsprings for any good history project, and I am indebted to the staff at the Walter P. Reuther and Purdy/Kresge libraries at Wayne State University, and the staff at the Burton Historical Collection at the Detroit Public Library (particularly librarian Ashley Koebel, who helped me find elusive details and photographs). I also am indebted to the staff at the Leatherby Libraries at Chapman University and at the University of California-Irvine's Langston Library.

My wife, Margaret, and longtime friend Robin Mather both read drafts of the book, and their sharp eyes saved me from embarrassments untold. My sons, Michael and Andrew, endured endless dinner table conversations about the city of their birth, which they left while still too young to have many memories of their own. My parents, Walter and Dorothy Martelle, also sat through long and mostly one-sided conversations about this project. Thanks, also, to my editor, Jerome Pohlen, for our shared vision of what this book should be, and to project editor Michelle Schoob for helping steer me around disasters of phrasing and grammar. And to Jane Dystel and her literary partner Miriam Goderich at Dystel & Goderich, my key sounding board on all projects. Their honest assessments and unflinching support make this work possible, and for that I am indeed thankful. But most of all I'm grateful to Margaret, without whose love and support I would not be able to pursue this all-consuming way of engaging the world.

SELECTED BIBLIOGRAPHY

DATABASES, ARCHIVES, AND STATISTICAL SOURCES

Burton Historical Collection, Detroit Public Library
Purdy/Kresge Library, Wayne State University
Walter P. Reuther Library, Wayne State University
Statistical Abstract of the United States
US Census Bureau

NEWSPAPERS AND PERIODICALS

American City
Michigan Chronicle
Christian Science Monitor
Detroit Free Press
Detroit News
Harper's
Heritage: A Journal of Grosse Pointe Life
The Liberator
Michigan Historical Review
Michigan History Magazine
Michigan Quarterly Review
The Nation
New York Times
Pittsburgh Post-Gazette
Political Science Quarterly
Survey
Washington Post

ARTICLES AND DISSERTATIONS

Amann, Peter H. "Vigilante Fascism: The Black Legion as an American Hybrid." *Comparative Studies in Society and History* 25, no. 3 (July 1983).

Baskin, Alex. "The Ford Hunger March—1932." *Labor History* 13 (Summer 1972).

Bledsoe, Timothy, Michael Combs, Lee Sigelman, and Susan Welch. "Trends in Racial Attitudes in Detroit, 1968–1992." *Urban Affairs Review* 31, no. 4 (March 1996): 508-528.

Brown, Earl. "Why Race Riots? Lessons from Detroit." Pamphlet (New York: Public Affairs Committee, 1944).

Capeci, Dominic J. Jr., and Martha Wilkerson. "The Detroit Rioters of 1943: A Reinterpretation." *Michigan Historical Review* 16, no. 1 (Spring 1990): 49–72.

Chandler, Lester V. "The Banking Crisis of 1933." *Reviews in American History* 2, no. 4 (Dec. 1974): 558–563.

"The Colored People of Detroit: Their Trials, Persecutions and Escapes." Reprinted from *Daily Post* (January 1 and February 7, 1870): copy in the Burton Collection.

Dowd, Gregory Evans. "The French King Wakes Up in Detroit: 'Pontiac's War' in Rumor and History." *Ethnohistory* 37, no. 3 (Summer 1990): 254–278.

Ernecq, Jean Marie. "Urban Renewal History of Detroit, 1946–70," PhD diss., Center for Urban Studies, Wayne State University.

Glaeser, Edward L., and Matthew E. Kahn. "Decentralized Employment and the Transformation of the American City." *Brookings-Wharton Papers on Urban Affairs* (2001): 1–63.

Goodspeed, Robert C. "Urban Renewal in Postwar Detroit: The Gratiot Area Redevelopment Project: A Case Study." History honors thesis, University of Michigan, 2004.

Halpern, Martin. "'I'm Fighting for Freedom': Coleman Young, HUAC, and the Detroit African American Community." *Journal of American Ethnic History* 17, no. 1 (Fall 1997): 19–38.

Hayes, George Edmund. "Negro Newcomers in Detroit." Reprinted in *The American Negro: His History and Literature* (New York: Arno Press and *New York Times*, 1969).

Heale, M. J. "The Triumph of Liberalism? Red Scare Politics in Michigan, 1938–1954." *Proceedings of the American Philosophical Society* 139, no. 1 (Mar. 1995).

Hyde, Charles K. "The Dodge Brothers, the Automobile Industry, and Detroit Society in the Early Twentieth Century." *Michigan Historical Review* 22, no. 2 (Fall 1996): 48–82.

Jones-Correa, Michael. "The Origins and Diffusion of Racial Restrictive Covenants." *Political Science Quarterly* 115, no. 4 (Winter, 2000–2001): 544.

Klug, Thomas. "Stories That Employers Tell: Employment Managers and Black Workers in Detroit, 1916–1929." Presented at the North American Labor History Conference, October 22, 2010.

Krysan, Maria, and Michael Bader. "Perceiving the Metropolis: Seeing the City Through a Prism of Race." *Social Forces* 86, no. 2 (Dec. 2007).

Lumpkin, Katherine DuPre. "The General Plan Was Freedom: A Negro Secret Order on the Underground Railroad." *Phylon* 28, no. 1 (1st Qtr. 1967).

"Making Migrants an Asset: The Detroit Urban League-Employers Alliance in Wartime Detroit, 1916–1919." *Michigan Historical Review* 26, no. 1 (Spring 2000).

Maloney, Thomas N., and Warren C. Whatley. "Making the Effort: The Contours of Racial Discrimination in Detroit's Labor Markets, 1920–1940." *Journal of Economic History* 55, no. 3 (Sep. 1995): 465–493.

Marger, Martin. "Ethnic Succession in Detroit Politics, 1900–1950." *Polity* 11, no. 3 (Spring 1979): 340–361.

Mason, Gregory. "Americans First: How the People of Detroit Are Making Americans of the Foreigners in Their City." *Outlook* (September 27, 1916): 193–201.

Merry, Ellis B. "Bank Reorganization and Recapitalization in Michigan." *Michigan Law Review* 32, no. 2 (Dec. 1933): 137–170.

Metzger, Kurt, and Jason Booza. "African Americans in the United States, Michigan and Metropolitan Detroit." *Working Papers Series*, no. 8 (2002): Center for Urban Studies of Wayne State University.

Mirel, Jeffrey. "The Politics of Educational Retrenchment in Detroit, 1929–1935." *History of Education Quarterly* 24, no. 3 (Autumn 1984): 323–358.

Mueller, Eva, and James N. Morgan. "Location Decisions of Manufacturers." *American Economic Review* 52, no. 2, Papers and Proceedings of the Seventy-Fourth Annual Meeting of the American Economic Association (May 1962).

Potter, Ryan A. "Enforcing National Prohibition Along the Detroit River, 1920–1933." Unpublished master's thesis, Eastern Michigan University (2000).

Reps, John W. "Planning in the Wilderness: Detroit, 1805–1830." *Town Planning Review* 25, no. 4 (Jan. 1955): 240–250.

Schneider, John C. "Detroit and the Problem of Disorder: The Riot of 1863." *Michigan History* 58, no. 1 (Spring 1974).

Sugrue, Thomas J. "Crabgrass-Roots Politics: Race, Rights, and the Reaction against Liberalism in the Urban North, 1940–1964." *Journal of American History* 82, no. 2 (September 1995).

BOOKS

Adler, William M. *Land of Opportunity: One Family's Quest for the American Dream in the Age of Crack.* Boston: Atlantic Monthly Press, 1995.

Babson, Steve. *Working Detroit: The Making of a Union Town.* Detroit: Wayne State University Press, 1984.

Babson, Steve, Dave Riddle, and David Elsila. *The Color of Law: Ernie Goodman, Detroit, and the Struggle for Labor and Civil Rights.* Detroit: Wayne State University Press, 2010.

Bairlein, Edward R., and Harold W. Moll. *In the Wilderness with the Red Indians.* Translated by Anita Z. Boldt. Detroit: Wayne State University Press, 1996.

Belfrage, Cedric. *A Faith to Free the People.* New York: Dryden Press, 1944.

Bergmann, Luke. *Getting Ghost: Two Young Lives and the Struggle for the Soul of an American City.* New York: New Press, 2009.

Bernstein, Peter L. *Wedding of the Waters: The Erie Canal and the Making of a Great Nation.* New York: W. W. Norton, 2005.

Birdwell, Michael E. *Celluloid Soldiers: The Warner Bros. Campaign Against Nazism.* New York: New York University Press, 1999.

Bluestone, Barry, and Bennett Harrison. *The Deindustrialization of America: Plant Closings, Community Abandonment, and the Dismantling of Basic Industry.* New York: Basic Books, 1982.

Borus, Daniel H. *These United States: Portraits of America from the 1920s.* Ithaca, NY: Cornell University Press, 1992.

Boyle, Kevin. *Arc of Justice: A Saga of Race, Civil Rights and Murder in the Jazz Age.* New York: Henry Holt, 2004.

Boyle, Kevin. *The UAW and the Heyday of American Liberalism, 1945–1968.* Ithaca, NY: Cornell University Press, 1995.

Bunch, William. *Jukebox America: Down Back Streets and Blue Highways in Search of the Country's Greatest Jukebox.* New York: St. Martin's, 1994.

Burton, Clarence M. *The City of Detroit, Michigan.* 5 vols. Detroit: S. J. Clarke, 1922.

Capeci, Dominic J., Jr. *Race Relations in Wartime Detroit.* Philadelphia: Temple University Press, 1984.

Chalmers, David M. *Hooded Americanism: The First Century of the Ku Klux Klan, 1865–1965.* New York: Doubleday, 1965.

Chafets, Ze'ev. *Devil's Night: And Other True Tales of Detroit.* New York: Random House, 1990.

Clark, Charles F., Henry H. Chapin, James Edmund Scripps, and Ralph L. Polk. *Michigan State Gazetteer and Business Directory for 1875.* Detroit: R. L. Polk, 1875.

Conot, Robert. *American Odyssey: A Unique History of America Told Through the Life of a Great City.* New York: William Morrow, 1974.

Darden, Joe T., Richard Child Hill, June Thomas, and Richard Thomas. *Detroit: Race and Uneven Development.* Philadelphia: Temple University Press, 1987.

DeRamus, Betty. *Forbidden Fruit: Love Stories from the Underground Railroad.* New York: Atria Books, 2005.

Dowd, Gregory Evans. *War Under Heaven: Pontiac, the Indian Nations, and the British Empire.* Baltimore: Johns Hopkins University Press, 2002.

Dray, Philip. *There Is Power in a Union: The Epic Story of Labor in America.* New York: Doubleday, 2010.

Dunbar, Willis F., and George S. May. *Michigan: A History of the Wolverine State*. Grand Rapids: William B. Eerdmans, 1965.

Farley, Reynolds, Sheldon Danziger, and Harry J. Holzer. *Detroit Divided*. New York: Russell Sage Foundation, 2000.

Farmer, Silas. *The History of Detroit and Michigan, or The Metropolis Illustrated: A Chronological Cyclopedia of the Past and Present*. Detroit: Silas Farmer, 1884.

Fine, Sidney. *Frank Murphy: The Detroit Years*. Ann Arbor: University of Michigan Press, 1975.

Fine, Sidney. *Violence in the Model City: The Cavanagh Administration, Race Relations, and the Detroit Riot of 1967*. Lansing: Michigan State University Press, 2007.

Finkelstein, Sydney. *Why Smart Executives Fail: And What You Can Learn from Their Mistakes*. New York: Portfolio, 2003.

Ford, Henry. *My Life and Work*. New York: Doubleday, 1923.

Fuller, George Newman. *Economic and Social Beginnings of Michigan: A Study of the Settlement of the Lower Peninsula During the Territorial Period 1805–1837*. Lansing, MI: Wynkoop Hallenbeck Crawford, 1916.

Greeley, Horace, et. al. *The Great Industries of the United States*. Hartford: J. B. Burr & Hyde, 1873.

Hartigan, John, Jr. *Racial Situations: Class Predicaments of Whiteness in Detroit*. Princeton: Princeton University Press, 1999.

Hersey, John. *The Algiers Motel Incident*. New York: Knopf, 1968.

Hill, Eric J. and John Gallagher. *AIA Detroit: The American Institute of Architects Guide to Detroit Architecture*. Detroit: Wayne State University Press, 2003.

Holli, Melvin G. *Reform in Detroit: Hazen S. Pingree and Urban Politics*. New York: Oxford University Press, 1969.

Hyde, Charles K. *Storied Independent Automakers: Nash, Hudson, and American Motors*. Detroit: Wayne State University Press, 2009.

Ingrassia, Paul. *Comeback: The Fall and Rise of the American Automobile Industry*. New York: Simon and Schuster, 1994.

Johnston, James Dale. *The Detroit City Directory and Advertising Gazetteer of Michigan for 1855–56*. Detroit: James Dale Johnston, 1855.

Jones, Jacqueline. *American Work: Four Centuries of Black and White Labor*. New York: W. W. Norton, 1998.

Jones, Milton "Butch," and Raymond Canty. *Y.B.I. Young Boys Inc.: The Autobiography of Butch Jones*. Detroit: H. Publications, 1996.

Katzman, David M. *Before the Ghetto: Black Detroit in the Nineteenth Century*. Urbana: University of Illinois Press, 1973.

Keeran, Roger. *The Communist Party and the Auto Workers Unions*. Bloomington: Indiana University Press, 1980.

Kennedy, Susan Estabrook. *The Banking Crisis of 1933*. Lexington: University Press of Kentucky, 1973.

Kornhauser, Arthur. *Detroit as the People See It: A Survey of Attitudes in an Industrial City*. Detroit: Wayne State University Press, 1952.

Lay, Shawn. *The Invisible Empire in the West*. Champaign: University of Illinois Press, 1992.

Leake, Paul. *The History of Detroit: A Chronicle of Its Progress, Its Industries, Its Institutions, and the People of the Fair City of the Straits*. Chicago: Lewis Publishing, 1912.

Lee, Alfred McClung, and Norman Daymond Humphrey, *Race Riot*. New York: Dryden Press, 1943.

Lewis, David L. *The Public Image of Henry Ford: An American Folk Hero and His Company*. Detroit: Great Lakes Books Publication, 1987.

Lichtenstein, Nelson. *The Most Dangerous Man in Detroit: Walter Reuther and the Fate of American Labor*. New York: Basic Books, 1995.

MacCabe, Julius P. Bolivar. *Directory of the City of Detroit, with Its Environs, for the Year 1837*. Detroit: R. L. Polk, 1837.

Mathis, Greg, and Blair S. Walker. *Inner City Miracle*. New York: Ballantine Books, 2002.

Maynard, Micheline. *The End of Detroit: How the Big Three Lost Their Grip on the American Car Market*. New York: Doubleday Business, 2003.

McFeely, William S. *Frederick Douglass.* New York: Touchstone Books, 1992.

Meier, August, and Elliott Rudwick. *Black Detroit and the Rise of the UAW.* New York: Oxford University Press, 1979.

Mirel, Jeffrey. *The Rise and Fall of an Urban School System: Detroit, 1907–81, Second Edition.* Ann Arbor: University of Michigan Press, 1993.

Moran, J. Bell. *The Moran Family: 200 Years in Detroit.* Detroit: Alved of Detroit, 1949.

Mowitz, Robert J., and Dail S. Wright. *Profile of a Metropolis: A Case Book.* Detroit: Wayne State University Press, 1962.

Mueller, Eva. *Location Decisions and Industrial Mobility in Michigan, 1961.* Ann Arbor: Institute for Social Research, University of Michigan, 1961.

Neimark, Marilyn Kleinberg. *The Hidden Dimensions of Annual Reports: Sixty Years of Social Conflict at General Motors.* New York: Markus Wiener Publishing, 1992.

Parkins, Almon Ernest. *The Historical Geography of Detroit.* Port Washington, NY: Kennikat Press, 1918.

Parris, Guichard, and Lester Brooks. *Blacks in the City: A History of the National Urban League.* Boston: Little, Brown, 1971.

Perloff, Harvey S. *Regions, Resources, and Economic Growth.* Baltimore: Johns Hopkins Press, 1960.

Report of the Pioneer Society, State of Michigan, Together With Reports of County, Town, and District Pioneer Societies, Vol. VII. Lansing: Thorp & Godfrey, State Printers & Binders, 1886; 1904 reprint.

Rich, Wilbur C. *Coleman Young and Detroit Politics: From Social Activist to Power Broker.* Detroit: Wayne State University Press, 1989.

Roberts, Robert E. *Sketches and Reminiscences of the City of the Straits and Its Vicinity.* Detroit: Free Press, 1884.

Russell, Nelson Vance. *The British Regime in Michigan and the Old Northwest, 1760–1796.* Northfield, MN: Carleton College, 1939.

Schuman, Howard, and Shirley Hatchett. *Black Racial Attitudes: Trends and Complexities.* Ann Arbor: Survey Research Center, Institute for Social Research, University of Michigan, 1974.

Smith, Page. *America Enters the World: A People's History of the Progressive Era and World War 1, Volume 7.* New York: McGraw-Hill, 1985.

Squires, Gregory D. *From Redlining to Reinvestment.* Philadelphia: Temple University Press, 1992.

Stolberg, Mary M. *Bridging the River of Hatred: The Pioneering Efforts of Detroit Police Commissioner George Edwards.* Detroit: Wayne State University Press, 1998.

Sugar, Maurice. *The Ford Hunger March.* Berkeley: Meiklejohn Civil Liberties Institute, 1980.

Sugrue, Thomas J. *The Origins of the Urban Crisis: Race and Inequality in Postwar Detroit.* Princeton: Princeton University Press, 1996.

Taylor, Carl S. *Dangerous Society.* Lansing: Michigan State University Press, 1989.

Thompson, Heather Ann. *Whose Detroit? Politics, Labor, and Race in a Modern American City.* Ithaca, NY: Cornell University Press, 2001.

Trachtenburg, Alan. *The Incorporation of America: Culture and Society in the Gilded Age.* New York: Hill and Wang, 1982.

Villard, Oswald Garrison. *John Brown, 1800–1859: A Biography Fifty Years After.* Boston: Houghton Mifflin, 1910.

Watts, Steven. *The People's Tycoon: Henry Ford and the American Century.* New York: Knopf, 2005.

White, Walter, and Thurgood Marshall. *What Caused the Detroit Riots?* New York: National Association for the Advancement of Colored People, 1943.

Wildick, B. J. *Detroit: City of Race and Class Violence.* New York: Quadrangle Books, 1972.

Wilson, William Julius. *The Truly Disadvantaged: The Inner City, the Underclass, and Public Policy.* Chicago: University of Chicago Press, 1990.

Wilson, William Julius. *When Work Disappears: The World of the New Urban Poor.* New York: Knopf, 1996.

Young, Coleman, and Lonnie Wheeler. *Hard Stuff: The Autobiography of Mayor Coleman Young.* New York: Viking, 1994.

Zunz, Olivier. *The Changing Face of Inequality: Urbanization, Industrial Development, and Immigrants in Detroit, 1880–1920.* Chicago: University of Chicago Press, 1982.

NOTES

PREFACE

1. "Chaos Erupts at Cobo as Thousands Jockey for Aid," *Detroit News*, October 8, 2009.
2. "Mayoral Debate Tackles Crime," *Detroit News*, January 8, 2009.
3. US Census data and Bureau of Labor Statistics
4. Annie E. Casey Foundation, Kids Count Data Center, http://datacenter.kidscount.org.
5. Digest of Education Statistics, National Center for Education Statistics, August 2010, www.nces.ed.gov/programs/digest/d10/tables/dt10_116.asp.
6. Geoffrey T. Wodtke, David J. Harding, and Felix Elwert, "Neighborhood Effects in Temporal Perspective: The Impact of Long-Term Exposure to Concentrated Disadvantage on High School Graduation," *American Sociological Review* 76, 2011, 713.
7. Scott Martelle, "The Collapse of Detroit," *Los Angeles Times*, March 27, 2011.

CHAPTER 1: A DIFFICULT CHILDHOOD

1. Letter from Cadillac to Louis XIV, October 18, 1700, translated and reprinted in *Historical Collections: Collections and Researches Made by the Michigan Pioneer and Historical Society* (Lansing: Robert Smith Printing, 1903), 99.
2. Silas Farmer, *The History of Detroit and Michigan, or The Metropolis Illustrated: A Chronological Cyclopedia of the Past and Present* (Detroit: Silas Farmer, 1884), 331–333.
3. C. M. Burton, *In the Footsteps of Cadillac* (Detroit: Wolverine Printing, 1899), unnumbered pages. Also, Burton paid to have Cadillac's papers in France translated, and they were published in *Collections and Researches Made by the Michigan Pioneer and Historical Society, Vol. XXXIII* (Lansing: Roger Smith Printing, 1902).
4. Farmer, *The History of Detroit and Michigan*, 231. Bourgmont would later become the commandant of the fort, but his behavior led to complaints and his eventual recall.
5. Marcel Giraud, *A History of French Louisiana: Volume Two, Years of Transition, 1715–1717*, translated by Brian Pearce, (Baton Rouge: Louisiana State University Press, 1993), 80–84.

CHAPTER 2: THE BRITISH DECADES

1. See the 1763 map reproduced in *The City of Detroit, Michigan, Vol. I*, Clarence M. Burton, editor in chief (Detroit: S. J. Clarke Publishing Company, 1922), 115.
2. Burton, *The City of Detroit, Michigan, Vol. I*, 118.
3. Silas Farmer, *The History of Detroit and Michigan, or The Metropolis Illustrated: A Chronological Cyclopedia of the Past and Present* (Detroit: Silas Farmer, 1884), 222.
4. Burton, *The City of Detroit, Michigan, Vol. I*, 114–116, and Nelson Vance Russell, *The British Regime in Michigan and the Old Northwest, 1760–1796* (Northfield, MN: Carleton College, 1939), 16–20.
5. Gregory Evans Dowd, *War Under Heaven: Pontiac, the Indian Nations and the British Empire* (Baltimore: Johns Hopkins Press, 2002), see pages 118–120 for details of the failed attack.
6. Farmer, *The History of Detroit and Michigan*, 173.
7. In some histories, Wyley was given her freedom.
8. The following is drawn from Farmer, *The History of Detroit and Michigan*, 489–491; Burton, *The City of Detroit, Michigan, Vol. 1*, 304–309; and Jean Dilhet, *Beginnings of the Catholic Church in the United States*, trans. Patrick W. Brown (Washington: Salve Regina Press, 1922) 110–114.

DETROITERS I: THE MORANS

1. Details on the Moran family history, unless otherwise noted, are from J. Bell Moran, *The Moran Family: 200 Years in Detroit* (Detroit: Alved of Detroit, 1949).
2. "Abstract of Title, Plat of the Sub'n of the C. Moran Farm, between Gratiot and Indiana Sts.," copy in the Burton Collection: E&M, B.A., P.C.5.
3. "Best of Detroit" issue, *Metro Times*, October 17, 2007.

CHAPTER 3: DETROIT AND THE CANAL OF RICHES

1. Details are drawn from Peter L. Bernstein, *Wedding of the Waters: The Erie Canal and the Making of a Great Nation* (New York: Norton, 2005), 308–321; William L. Stone, "Narrative of the Festivities Observed in Honor of the Completion of the Grand Erie Canal Uniting the Waters of the Great Western Lakes with the Atlantic Ocean," 1825, available at www.history.rochester. edu/canal/bib/colden/App18.html; "Proceedings at the Celebration of the Canal," *New York Telescope*, November 12, 1825; and "Canal Celebration," *New York Evening Post*, Saturday, November 11, 1825.
2. "Sketches of the Upper Lakes," *Pittsburgh Post-Gazette*, May 1, 1819.
3. George Newman Fuller, *Economic and Social Beginnings of Michigan: A Study of the Settlement of the Lower Peninsula During the Territorial Period 1805–1837* (Lansing, MI: Wynkoop Hallenbeck Crawford, 1916), 49–52.
4. "Sketches of the Upper Lakes," *Pittsburgh Post-Gazette*, May 1, 1819.
5. Silas Farmer, *The History of Detroit and Michigan, or The Metropolis Illustrated: A Chronological Cyclopedia of the Past and Present* (Detroit: Silas Farmer, 1884), 769–770; Paul Leake, *The History of Detroit: A Chronicle of Its Progress, Its Industries, Its Institutions, and the People of the Fair City of the Straits* (Chicago: Lewis Publishing, 1912), 123–124; and Julius P. Bolivar MacCabe, *Directory of the City of Detroit, with Its Environs, for the Year 1837* (Detroit: R. L. Polk, 1837), 1–16.
6. Fuller, *Economic and Social Beginnings of Michigan*, 63–68 and 132.
7. Farmer, *The History of Detroit and Michigan*, 60–68.
8. *Report of the Pioneer Society, State of Michigan, Together With Reports of County, Town, and District Pioneer Societies, Vol. VII* (Lansing: Thorp & Godfrey, State Printers & Binders, 1886; 1904 reprint), 131–33; and Farmer, *The History of Detroit and Michigan*, 481.
9. Drawn from US Census records and MacCabe, *Directory of the City of Detroit*, 37.

10. Horace Greeley, et. al., *The Great Industries of the United States* (Hartford: J. B. Burr & Hyde, 1873), 998.
11. James Dale Johnston, *The Detroit City Directory and Advertising Gazetteer of Michigan for 1855–56* (Detroit: James Dale Johnston, 1855), 1–2.
12. Johnston, *The Detroit City Directory*, 243.
13. Charles F. Clark, Henry H. Chapin, James Edmund Scripps, and Ralph L. Polk, *Michigan State Gazetteer and Business Directory for 1875* (Detroit: R. L. Polk, 1875), 209.

CHAPTER 4: THE CIVIL WAR AND RACIAL FLASHPOINTS

1. Silas Farmer, *The History of Detroit and Michigan, or The Metropolis Illustrated: A Chronological Cyclopedia of the Past and Present* (Detroit: Silas Farmer, 1884), 344.
2. Chipman served on the Supreme Court of the Territory of Michigan until 1832, and was in private practice at the time of the Blackburn affair. Though he's identified in news accounts as the judge, it seems likely he was pressed into service due to an absence of the regular judge. See www.micourthistory.org/bios.php?id=8.
3. "The Colored People of Detroit: Their Trials, Persecutions and Escapes," a booklet of stories reprinted from the *Detroit Daily Post*, January 1 and February 7, 1870, 3–4, copy in the Burton Collection.
4. The true names of the Blackburns have been inconsistent over time—in some places they were identified as the Smiths, in others as Thorntons. I'm going with the name that appears most frequently in contemporary accounts. Details of the escape and riot, unless otherwise noted, are drawn from "The Colored People of Detroit"; "Slavery Record," *Liberator*, July 6, 1833; the *Detroit Courier Digest* entry for June 19 (held at Burton Collection); David M. Katzman, *Before the Ghetto: Black Detroit in the Nineteenth Century* (Urbana: University of Illinois Press, 1973), 9–12; and Betty DeRamus, *Forbidden Fruit: Love Stories from the Underground Railroad* (New York: Atria Books, 2005), 61–75.
5. "John Randolph's Will," *Liberator*, August 17, 1833.
6. Robert E. Roberts, *Sketches and Reminiscences of the City of the Straits and Its Vicinity* (Detroit: Free Press, 1884), 96.
7. Katzman, *Before the Ghetto*, 13.
8. Katzman, *Before the Ghetto*, 20. He puts the date at 1837 but other histories, including the National Park Service's description on the National Register of Historic Places, dates the split to 1836.
9. Katzman, *Before the Ghetto*, 13–16.
10. Katzman, *Before the Ghetto*, 32–42. Even Lambert and De Baptiste couldn't agree on what the name was.
11. For a full discussion of the problems in taking a close look at the group, see Katherine DuPre Lumpkin, "The General Plan Was Freedom: A Negro Secret Order on the Underground Railroad," *Phylon* 28, no. 1 (1st Qtr. 1967): 63–77.
12. "Annual Meeting of the Refugee Home society," *Detroit Free Press*, October 29, 1859, and "African Canadian Community," a Canadian government informational site, www.windsor-communities.com/african-organ-refugeehome.php.
13. Oswald Garrison Villard, *John Brown, 1800–1859: A Biography Fifty Years After* (Boston: Houghton Mifflin, 1910), 393–394.
14. Unheadlined report in *Detroit Free Press*, March 13, 1859.
15. "Our New Voters: Past History of the Colored People of Detroit," a reprint or articles from the *Detroit Daily Post*, January 1 and February 7, 1870, Burton Collection 74D4 325.26 C719; and Villard, *John Brown, 1800–1859*, 390.
16. "Took His Life," *Detroit Free Press*, April 29, 1890.
17. Contained in Lambert Files, Burton Collection, B L172 J62.
18. "Funeral of Late William Lambert," *Detroit Free Press*, May 1, 1890.

19. John C. Schneider, "Detroit and the Problem of Disorder: The Riot of 1863," *Michigan History* 58, no. 1 (Spring 1974).
20. "The Acting Mayor's Report on the Riot," *Detroit Free Press*, March 12, 1863.
21. Unless otherwise noted, details of the trial and aftermath are from "Justice at Last," *Detroit Daily Post*, January 1, 1870, contained in "Our New Voters: Past History of the Colored People of Detroit," a reprint of articles from the *Detroit Daily Post*, January 1 and February 7, 1870, Burton Collection 74D4 325.26 C719.
22. "Outrage," *Detroit Free Press*, February 27, 1863.
23. "Trial of the Negro Faulkner," *Detroit Free Press*, March 6, 1863, and "Trial of the Negro Faulkner," *Detroit Free Press*, March 7, 1863.
24. "Investigation Into the Case of the Negro, Joshua Boyd," *Detroit Free Press*, March 14, 1863.
25. "A Bloody Riot," *Detroit Free Press*, March 8, 1863.
26. "Riot Against the Negroes in Canada," *New York Times*, March 17, 1863.
27. "The Mob—Its Origin," *Detroit Free Press*, March 8, 1863.
28. Letter to Samuel Douglass, March 12, 1863, Burton Collection, MS/Samuel T. Douglass, January–June 1863.
29. Schneider, "Detroit and the Problem of Disorder"

CHAPTER 5: DETROIT TURNS INDUSTRIAL

1. Almon Ernest Parkins, *The Historical Geography of Detroit* (Port Washington, NY: Kennikat Press, 1918), 248–252.
2. "Annual Review of the Trade, Commerce and Manufactures of Detroit, 1860," Detroit Board of Trade, contained in a compilation it published in 1888.
3. Silas Farmer, *The History of Detroit and Michigan, or The Metropolis Illustrated: A Chronological Cyclopedia of the Past and Present* (Detroit: Silas Farmer, 1884), 70.
4. Charles F. Clark, Henry H. Chapin, James Edmund Scripps, and Ralph L. Polk, *Michigan State Gazetteer and Business Directory for 1875* (Detroit: R. L. Polk, 1875), 211.
5. "Fire an Added Torture for Many of the Victims," *Detroit Free Press*, November 27, 1901; "26 Killed in Explosion at Detroit," *New York Times*, November 7, 1895; *Twentieth Annual Report of the Bureau of Labor and Industrial Statistics* (Lansing, MI: Robert Smith Printing, 1903), 6–8.
6. "Obituary: Edmund A. Brush," *Detroit Free Press*, July 11, 1877, and "Hon. E.A. Brush," *Detroit Free Press*, July 13, 1877, the latter a lengthy, unsigned letter to the editor.
7. General Friend Palmer, *Early Days in Detroit* (Detroit: Hunt and June, 1906), 513.
8. Farmer, *The History of Detroit and Michigan*, 36.
9. "Terrible Accident," *Detroit Free Press*, February 22, 1872.
10. *The City of Detroit, Michigan, 1701-1922, Vol. V* (Detroit: S. J. Clarke Publishing, 1922), 46–50.

DETROITERS II: MICHAEL FARRELL

1. Berg's comments came in an interview with the author.

CHAPTER 6: THE AUTO ERA

1. Exactly what had been on display in Chicago is, surprisingly, in dispute. Although most accounts list the Benz import, Ford's biographer Allen Nevins makes note that *Scientific American*, which covered the exposition exhaustively, didn't mention a gasoline-powered vehicle. A journalistic omission seems a slight reason to doubt the other reports that one was indeed on display.
2. Henry Ford, *My Life and Work* (New York: Doubleday, 1923), 33.
3. Steven Watts, *The People's Tycoon: Henry Ford and the American Century* (New York: Knopf, 2005), 61.

4. *Twentieth Annual Report of the Bureau of Labor and Industrial Statistics*, (Lansing, MI: Robert Smith Printing, 1903), 10.

5. 1929 Census of Manufactures, Table 13, contained in the 1930 US Census.

6. Page Smith, *America Enters the World: A People's History of the Progressive Era and World War I, Volume 7* (New York: McGraw-Hill, 1985), 868–869.

7. Willis F. Dunbar and George S. May, *Michigan: A History of the Wolverine State* (Grand Rapids, MI: William B. Eerdmans Publishing, 1965), 494–496.

8. Ford, *My Life and Work*, 103.

9. Smith, *America Enters the World*, 867–873.

10. Steve Babson, *Working Detroit: The Making of a Union Town* (Detroit: Wayne State University Press, 1984), 30–34.

11. Douglas Brinkley, *Wheels for the World: Henry Ford, His Company, and a Century of Progress*, (New York: Penguin, 2004), 172–175.

12. "Police Repulse Ford Jobhunters with Icy Stream," *Detroit Free Press*, January 13, 1914.

13. Steve Babson, *Working Detroit*, 30–31; and Fourteenth Census of the United States, volume 8, 1920.

14. For a thorough and highly readable account of Detroit's labor history, see Babson's *Working Detroit*. Unless otherwise noted, details here of Detroit's early labor history are from Babson.

15. For an intimately detailed account, see Richard White, *Railroaded: The Transcontinentals and the Making of Modern America* (New York: Norton, 2011).

16. *Third Annual Report of the Bureau of Labor and Industrial Statistics* (Lansing: Thorp and Godfrey, 1886), 85–88.

17. Melvin G. Holli, *Reform in Detroit: Hazen Pingree and Urban Politics* (New York: Oxford University Press, 1969), 1–8, 12–19.

18. Holli, *Reform in Detroit*, 65–67.

19. See Holli, *Reform in Detroit*, "The Depression and a Commitment," chapter 4.

20. Some accounts list the cause as peritonitis. "Hazen S. Pingree Is Dead," *New York Times*, June 19, 1901.

21. Statistics of Unemployment and the Work of Employment Offices, Bureau of Labor Bulletin 109 (Washington, DC: Government Printing Office, 1912), 87–88; and Paul J. Leake, *History of Detroit: Volume III* (Chicago: Lewis Publishing, 1912), 1260–1261; and "Making Migrants an Asset: The Detroit Urban League-Employers Alliance in Wartime Detroit, 1916–1919," *Michigan Historical Review* 26, no. 1 (Spring 2000): 71–72; Gregory Mason, "Americans First: How the People of Detroit Are Making Americans of the Foreigners in Their City," *Outlook*, September 27, 1916, 200.

CHAPTER 7: A GREAT MIGRATION

1. Gregory Mason, "Americans First: How the People of Detroit Are Making Americans of the Foreigners in Their City," *Outlook*, September 27, 1916, 193–201.

2. "Making Migrants an Asset: The Detroit Urban League-Employers Alliance in Wartime Detroit, 1916–1919," *Michigan Historical Review* 26, no. 1 (Spring 2000): 72–76; and Guichard Parris and Lester Brooks, *Blacks in the City: A History of the National Urban League* (Boston: Little, Brown, 1971), 74–76.

3. These details are from Thomas C. Klug's unpublished "Stories That Employers Tell: Employment Managers and Black Workers in Detroit, 1916–1929," presented October 22, 2010, at the North American Labor History Conference in Detroit, and included here with my gratitude.

4. George Edmund Hayes, "Negro Newcomers in Detroit," reprinted in *The American Negro: His History and Literature* (New York: Arno Press and *New York Times*, 1969), 21–24.

5. Parris and Brooks, *Blacks in the City*, 89–91.

6. Hayes, "Negro Newcomers in Detroit," 14.

7. "Force 50 Negroes from Apartment," *Detroit Free Press*, August 23, 1917. It's unclear whether the African American tenants were renting one apartment or all four; regardless, the overcrowding was severe, and indicative. Parris and Brooks, as well as other sources, place the number of blacks involved at around two dozen. See *Blacks in the City*, 91.

CHAPTER 8: THE ROARING TWENTIES

1. "Another Fine Building," *Detroit Free Press*, July 27, 1902.
2. "Sky-Scraper to Rise," *Detroit Free Press*, March 10, 1906; "Edward Ford: Genius of Business," *Detroit Free Press*, August 19, 1906; "Ford Bdlg. Workers Sue," *Detroit Free Press*, March 22, 1907; "Caisson Men Go On Strike," *Detroit Free Press*, December 29, 1906; "Falls 100 Feet to Death," *Detroit Free Press*, June 1, 1907; "Killed at Ford Building," *Detroit Free Press*, September 7, 1907.
3. Leonard Lanson Cline, "Michigan: The Fordizing of a Pleasant Peninsula," *Nation*, November 1, 1922; "Cline Found Dead in Village Studio," *New York Times*, January 21, 1929.
4. Harvey S. Perloff, *Regions, Resources, and Economic Growth* (Baltimore: Johns Hopkins Press, 1960), 232.
5. Charles Evan Fowler, "Detroit's Struggle with the Traffic Problem," *American City*, June 1924, 612–615.
6. Steve Babson, *Working Detroit: The Making of a Union Town* (Detroit: Wayne State University Press, 1984), 50.
7. Marilyn Kleinberg Neimark, *The Hidden Dimensions of Annual Reports: Sixty Years of Social Conflict at General Motors* (New York: Markus Wiener Publishing, 1992), 63.
8. Monthly Bulletin, Detroit Department of Health, vol. 3, no. 5 (May 1920): 3.
9. Stuart Chase, "The Future of the Great City," *Harper's*, December 1929, 82.
10. "Enforcing National Prohibition Along the Detroit River, 1920–1933," unpublished master's thesis by Ryan A. Potter, Eastern Michigan University, 2000. See "Introduction."
11. "Wonderful Sweep of the Prohibition Wave," *Detroit Free Press*, November 10, 1907.
12. "Prohibition Fails, Speakers Assert," *Detroit Free Press*, October 21, 1916; "Drys Now Urge Ends of Bars by Statute," *Detroit Free Press*, November 11, 1916.
13. "Bennett Is Out as Rum Nabber," *Detroit Free Press*, November 14, 1918.
14. Philip P. Mason, "Anyone Who Couldn't Get a Drink Wasn't Trying," *Michigan History Magazine*, September/October 1994, 12–15; "Bootlegging Loses Romance and Glamor, Says Woodworth," *Detroit Free Press*, January 2, 1919.
15. *Detroit News* series summarized in "'The Collapse of Prohibition' in Detroit,'" *Literary Digest*, October 20, 1923, 52; "Major Faust Home; In Buzancy Attack," *Detroit Free Press*, November 5, 1918; "Resents Implied Charge of Underworld Backing," *Detroit Free Press*, October 24, 1920; "If You Must Bootleg, Do It at Night," *Detroit Free Press*, December 1, 1921, "Rum Raids 'Tips' Puzzle Police," *Detroit Free Press*, December 3, 1921.
16. Gary Freeman, "Bootlegging across the Border," *Heritage: A Journal of Grosse Pointe Life*, December 1985, 123.
17. "Liquor, Piled High, Is Found in Ecorse," *Detroit Free Press*, April 12, 1919.
18. "'The Collapse of Prohibition' in Detroit,'" *Literary Digest*, October 20, 1923, 52; "Rum Officers Nab Liquor 'Importers,'" *Detroit Free Press*, June 27, 1920.
19. "Battling the Rumrunners in Prohibition," *New York Times*, July 29, 1923.
20. "Nightly Rises the Tide of Border Rum," *New York Times*, June 5, 1927.
21. Mason, "Anyone Who Couldn't Get a Drink Wasn't Trying," *Michigan History Magazine*, September/October 1994, 19.
22. Quoted in "Bootlegging and Murder in Detroit," *Literary Digest*, September 29, 1923, 48.
23. Statistics available from the University of Missouri-Kansas City "Lynching in America" project at www.law.umkc.edu/faculty/projects/ftrials/shipp/lynchingyear.html. For a complete, and compellingly drawn, history of this shameful practice, see Philip Dray, *At The Hands of Persons Unknown* (New York: Random House, 2002).

24. For a detailed history of the Klan see David M. Chalmers, *Hooded Americanism: The First Century of the Ku Klux Klan, 1865–1965* (New York: Doubleday, 1965). The early history is in chapter two: "The Klan Rides, 1865–71."

25. Chalmers, *Hooded Americanism,* "The Klan Revival, 1915–21," chapter four; Christopher N. Cocoltchos, "The Invisible Empire and the Search for the Orderly Community: The Ku Klux Klan in Anaheim, California," in *The Invisible Klan in the West: Toward a New Historical Appraisal of the Ku Klux Klan of the 1920s,* ed. Shawn Lay (Bloomington: University of Illinois Press, 2003), chapter 4.

26. Melvin G. Holli, "Mayoring in Detroit, 1824–1985: Is Upward Mobility the 'Impossible Dream?'" *Michigan Historical Review* 13, no. 1 (Spring 1987): 6; Sidney Fine, *Frank Murphy: The Detroit Years* (Ann Arbor: University of Michigan Press, 1975), 102; "Report Finds Vice Rampant in Detroit," *New York Times,* July 11, 1926; "Klan Is Routed in Detroit," *New York Times,* November 5, 1925.

27. Suzanne E. Smith, "Where Did Our Love Go?" *Michigan Quarterly Review* (Fall 2010).

28. Reynolds Farley, Sheldon Danziger, and Harry J. Holzer, *Detroit Divided* (New York: Russell Sage Foundation, 2000), 148–149.

29. For a compelling and detailed retelling of the Sweet case, see Kevin Boyle, *Arc of Justice: A Saga of Race, Civil Rights and Murder in the Jazz Age* (New York: Henry Holt, 2004).

30. Farley, *Detroit Divided,* 147, and US Census records for 1930.

CHAPTER 9: GREAT DEPRESSION

1. For a fine and highly readable explanation of the complicated backdrop to the Great Depression bank crises, see Susan Estabrook Kennedy, *The Banking Crisis of 1933* (Lexington: University Press of Kentucky, 1973). This quote is from the Federal Reserve Bulletin, included on page 17.

2. For a recap of the lead-up to the crash and the wealth lost, see Claire Suddath, "Brief History of the Crash of 1929," *Time,* available online at www.time.com/time/nation/article/0,8599,1854569,00.html; and Harold Bierman Jr., "The 1929 Stock Market Crash," EH.net, the Economic History Association, www.eh.net/encyclopedia/article/Bierman.crash.

3. Stuart Chase, "The Nemesis of American Business," *Harper's,* July 1930, 129.

4. *Statistical Abstract of the United States, 1942* (Washington, DC: Government Printing Office, 1943), 470.

5. "Jerry Buckley Slain; City Offers Reward," *Detroit News,* July 23, 1930; "Underworld Here Raked for Three Assassins of 'Jerry Buckley,'" *Detroit Free Press,* July 24, 1930; "Killing of Buckley Arouses Detroit; Hint of Racketeer," *New York Times,* July 24, 1930.

6. Beulah Amidon, "Detroit Does Something About It," *Survey,* February 15, 1931; Maurice Sugar, *The Ford Hunger March* (Berkeley: Meiklejohn Civil Liberties Institute, 1980), 26; US Statistical Abstracts for 1930 and 1935.

7. Alex Baskin, "The Ford Hunger March—1932," *Labor History* 13 (Summer 1972): 334.

8. "Welfare Problem Perplexes Detroit," *New York Times,* May 3, 1931.

9. Baskin, "The Ford Hunger March—1932," 332–333.

10. Unless otherwise noted, details on the Ford Hunger March are drawn from Maurice Sugar, *The Ford Hunger March.* Sugar was an activist and socialist lawyer, and would become the longtime attorney for the United Auto Workers. He investigated the events surrounding the march after being hired to defend the arrested marchers. His account, contained in an unfinished autobiography, was split off and published posthumously as part of the Meiklejohn Case Studies on Law and Social Changes series.

11. "How orderly hunger march turned into bloody battle," *Detroit News,* March 8, 1932.

12. Any scene of street violence is prone to error, exaggeration, and conflicting versions by witnesses. This was drawn from newspaper accounts and affidavits in the Maurice Sugar papers, Part I, Box 53, Folders 6–10, Reuther Library.

13. The only African American to be killed; local lore has it that Williams was denied burial with the other four victims in segregated Elmwood Cemetery.
14. There is some confusion on this detail. Maurice Sugar, the defense lawyer, maintained the bullets were turned over to Dearborn police, but contemporary news accounts said Detroit police received the bullets and would seek to match them to the Dearborn officers' guns. Since no one was indicted, it seems a moot technical detail.
15. "Four Die in Riot at Ford," *Detroit Free Press*, March 8, 1932.

CHAPTER 10: THE BLACK LEGION

1. Unless otherwise noted, details are drawn from David M. Chalmers, *Hooded Americanism: The First Century of the Ku Klux Klan, 1865–1965* (New York: Doubleday, 1965), 308–311; Peter H. Amann, "Vigilante Fascism: The Black Legion as an American Hybrid," *Comparative Studies in Society and History* 25, no. 3 (July 1983): 490–524; and B. Kevin Bennett, "The Buckeye Lake KKK Rallies," *The Historical Times* 9, no. 3 (Summer 1995), Newsletter of the Granville Historical Society, Ohio.
2. Associated Press, "Dictatorship Reported Aim," *New York Times*, May 26, 1936.
3. Maurice Sugar papers, Part I, Box 18, Folder 18-5.
4. Alan Brinkley, "Comparative Biography as Political History: Huey Long and Father Coughlin," *The History Teacher* 18, no. 1 (Nov. 1984): 11–12.
5. The details were played out in the daily Detroit newspapers.
6. "Boys Copy Black Legion; Try to Lynch 'Scholars,'" *New York Times*, June 6, 1936.
7. The movie was part of Warner Brothers' effort to combat domestic fascism. See Michael E. Birdwell, *Celluloid Soldiers: The Warner Bros. Campaign Against Nazism* (New York: New York University Press, 1999), 43–56.

CHAPTER 11: HOUSING AND THE RACIAL DIVIDE

1. The complex would eventually expand to become the Brewster-Douglass Projects, now mostly closed and partially replaced by yet another generation of public housing.
2. "First Lady Starts a Housing Project," *New York Times*, September 10, 1935; "Today on the Radio," *New York Times*, September 9, 1935.
3. Karen Dash, "Slum Clearance Farce," *Nation*, April 1, 1936. The byline was a pseudonym, the true identity unknown.
4. Thomas J. Sugrue, *The Origins of the Urban Crisis: Race and Inequality in Postwar Detroit* (Princeton: Princeton University Press, 1996), 18.
5. Among other sources, see Earl Brown's pamphlet, "Why Race Riots? Lessons from Detroit," (New York: Public Affairs Committee, 1944), 9–11.
6. Steven Watts, *The People's Tycoon: Henry Ford and the American Century* (New York: Alfred A. Knopf, 2005), 454.
7. Nelson Lichtenstein, *The Most Dangerous Man in Detroit: Walter Reuther and the Fate of American Labor* (New York: Basic Books, 1995), 178–179; "UAW History," United Auto Workers' website, www.uaw.org/node/271.
8. For two good overviews, see Steve Babson, *Working Detroit: The Making of a Union Town* (Detroit: Wayne State University Press, 1984), and Nelson Lichtenstein, *Walter Reuther: The Most Dangerous Man in Detroit* (Urbana: University of Illinois Press, 1997).
9. Kevin Boyle, *The UAW: The Heyday of American Liberalism, 1945–1968* (Ithaca, NY: Cornell University Press, 1995), see "Introduction" for his overview.

CHAPTER 12: THE WAR YEARS

1. Statistical Abstract of the United States, 1942, Table 504; "Tank Production Faces Tools Lag; Priorities Called Key to Problem," *New York Times*, February 19, 1941.

2. Earl Brown, "Why Race Riots? Lessons from Detroit," pamphlet (New York: Public Affairs Committee, 1944), 5–6; Walter White and Thurgood Marshall, *What Caused the Detroit Riots?* (New York: National Association for the Advancement of Colored People, 1943), 4–6.

3. "Machine Shop for a War of Machines," *New York Times*, March 30, 1941.

4. "Detroit's Housing Shortage Acute," *New York Times*, August 9, 1942.

5. Mary M. Stolberg, *Bridging the River of Hatred: The Pioneering Efforts of Detroit Police Commissioner George Edwards* (Detroit: Wayne State University press, 1998), 48–52.

6. Nelson Lichtenstein, *The Most Dangerous Man in Detroit: Walter Reuther and the Fate of American Labor* (New York: Basic Books, 1995), 66–73 and 341–342; Sidney Fine, *Sit-Down: The General Motors Strike of 1936–1937* (Ann Arbor: University of Michigan Press, 1969), 131–133.

7. Marilyn Kleinberg Neimark, *The Hidden Dimensions of Annual Reports: Sixty Years of Social Conflict at General Motors* (New York: Markus Wiener Publishing, 1992), 67.

8. M. J. Heale, "The Triumph of Liberalism? Red Scare Politics in Michigan, 1938–1954," Proceedings of the American Philosophical Society, Vol. 139, No. 1 (Mar. 1995), 49.

9. Biographical details drawn from "Interviews with Michigan Supreme Court Justices," available at http://archive.lib.msu.edu/AFS/dmc/court/public/all/Edwards/ASP.html, and Lichtenstein, *The Most Dangerous Man in Detroit*.

CHAPTER 13: THE 1943 RIOT

1. Alfred McClung Lee and Norman Daymond Humphrey, *Race Riot* (New York: Dryden Press, 1943), 6. This is a remarkably detailed "tick-tock" recreation of the 1943 riot.

2. Earl Brown, "Why Race Riots? Lessons from Detroit," pamphlet (New York: Public Affairs Committee, 1944), 2; Walter White and Thurgood Marshall, *What Caused the Detroit Riots?* (New York: National Association for the Advancement of Colored People, 1943), 6.

3. Dominic J. Capeci Jr., *Race Relations in Wartime Detroit* (Philadelphia: Temple University Press, 1984), 21–33; August Meier and Elliott Rudwick, *Black Detroit and the Rise of the UAW* (New York: Oxford University Press, 1979), 88–90.

4. White and Marshall, *What Caused the Detroit Riots?*, 7; Robert Conot, *American Odyssey: A Unique History of America Told through the Life of a Great City* (New York: William Morrow, 1974), 403–404.

5. Capeci, *Race Relations in Wartime Detroit*, 7.

6. See Thomas J. Sugrue, *The Origins of the Urban Crisis: Race and Inequality in Postwar Detroit* (Princeton: Princeton University Press, 1996), see "Sojourner Truth," 73–75.

7. "Coughlin Weekly Ends Publication," *New York Times*, May 4, 1942; "Archbishop Mooney 'Gratified,'" *New York Times*, May 5, 1942, White and Marshall, *What Caused the Detroit Riots?*, 9.

8. White and Marshall, *What Caused the Detroit Riots?*, 7; Charles K. Hyde, *Storied Independent Automakers: Nash, Hudson, and American Motors* (Detroit: Wayne State University Press, 2009), 148.

9. Although the Eastwood incident is cited in much of the historical record, it's entirely possible the two incidents were not directly related, and the "two young blacks" exist as a chimera to try to pin blame for the violence on black instigators.

10. Lee and Humphrey, *Race Riot*, 28–30; Dominic J. Capeci Jr. and Martha Wilkerson, "The Detroit Riots of 1943: A Reinterpretation," *Michigan Historical Review* 16, no. 1 (Spring 1990): 52–53.

11. White and Marshall, *What Caused the Detroit Riots?*, 29–33.
12. Capeci and Wilkerson, "The Detroit Riots of 1943," 58–71.
13. From the decision: "The constitutional right of a Negro to acquire, own, and occupy property does not carry with it the constitutional power to compel sale and conveyance to him of any particular private property. The individual citizen, whether he be black or white, may refuse to sell or lease his property to any particular individual or class of individuals. The state alone possesses the power to compel a sale or taking of private property, and that only for public use. The power of these property owners to exclude one class of citizens implies the power of the other class to exercise the same prerogative over property which they may own. What is denied one class may be denied the other. There is, therefore, no discrimination within the civil rights clauses of the Constitution. Such a covenant is enforceable, not only against a member of the excluded race, but between the parties to the agreement." The court would reverse itself twenty years later.
14. Michael Jones-Correa, "The Origins and Diffusion of Racial Restrictive Covenants," *Political Science Quarterly* 115, no. 4 (Winter 2000–2001): 544.
15. Sugrue, *The Origins of the Urban Crisis*, 72–84.
16. Joe T. Darden, Richard Child Hill, June Thomas, and Richard Thomas, *Detroit: Race and Uneven Development* (Philadelphia: Temple University Press, 1987), 155–158.
17. For a detailed discussion of the Gratiot Redevelopment Project, to which the Detroit Plan gave rise, see Robert J. Mowitz and Dail S. Wright, "The Gratiot Redevelopment Project: Regenerating the Core City," *Profile of a Metropolis: A Case Book* (Detroit: Wayne State Press, 1962), 11–81; and Jean Marie Ernecq's 1972 dissertation, "Urban Renewal History of Detroit, 1946–70," Center for Urban Studies, Wayne State University.

CHAPTER 14: THE POSTWAR BOOM

1. Barry Bluestone and Bennett Harrison, *The Deindustrialization of America: Plant Closings, Community Abandonment, and the Dismantling of Basic Industry* (New York: Basic Books, 1982), 112–113.
2. Sugrue, Thomas J., *The Origins of the Urban Crisis: Race and Inequality in Postwar Detroit* (Princeton: Princeton University Press, 1996), 140–141.
3. Detroit Housing Commission, May 27, 1949, found in Box 64, UAW Political Action Dept., Roy Reuther, 1947–Aug 15, 1957, Reuther Library, WSU, Folder 64-7; also see Sugrue, *The Origins of the Urban Crisis*, 36–37.
4. Melvin G. Holli, "Mayoring in Detroit, 1824–1985: Is Upward Mobility the 'Impossible Dream'?" *Michigan Historical Review* 13, no. 1 (Spring 1987): 9–10.
5. Nelson Lichtenstein, *The Most Dangerous Man in Detroit: Walter Reuther and the Fate of American Labor* (New York: Basic Books, 1995), 271–273.
6. Campaign details are drawn from contemporary accounts in the *Detroit Free Press*, *Detroit News*, and *Detroit Times*.
7. "Edwards Brands Cobo B of C Man," *Detroit Times*, September 14, 1949; Edwards papers, Reuther Library, WSU, Series 1, Group 2, Box 16.
8. "4 Contenders Bandy Issues," *Detroit News*, September 2, 1949.
9. Edwards papers, Reuther Library, WSU, Series 1, Group 2, Box 15, Folder, "Campaign Literature."
10. I detailed that trial in *The Fear Within: Spies, Commies, and American Democracy on Trial* (Princeton: Rutgers University Press, 2011).
11. "George Edwards Beaten; Cobo Elected Mayor," *Michigan Chronicle*, November 12, 1949.
12. Meeting notes, Reuther Library, WSU, UAW Political Action Committee, Roy Reuther, 1947–Aug. 15, 1957, Folders 62-11 and 62-15.
13. "State's Top Vote Getter," *Detroit Times*, November 8, 1956. Edwards would leave that post in 1962 to become Detroit's police commissioner.

CHAPTER 15: RACE IN THE FIFTIES

1. Thomas J. Sugrue, *The Origins of the Urban Crisis: Race and Inequality in Postwar Detroit* (Princeton: Princeton University Press, 1996), 85–86.
2. Survey details drawn from Arthur Kornhauser, *Detroit as the People See It: A Survey of Attitudes in an Industrial City* (Detroit: Wayne State University Press, 1952).
3. See Kevin Boyle, *The UAW and the Heyday of American Liberalism, 1945–1968* (Ithaca, NY: Cornell University Press, 1998).
4. Eva Mueller, *Location Decisions and Industrial Mobility In Michigan, 1961* (Ann Arbor: Institute for Social Research, University of Michigan, 1961), 29.
5. Eva Mueller and James N. Morgan. "Location Decisions of Manufacturers," *The American Economic Review* 52, no. 2, Papers and Proceedings of the Seventy-Fourth Annual Meeting of the American Economic Association (May 1962): 207.
6. Harvey S. Perloff, *Regions, Resources, and Economic Growth* (Baltimore: Johns Hopkins Press, 1960), 460–461.
7. Steve Babson, Dave Riddle, and David Elsila, *The Color of Law: Ernie Goodman, Detroit, and the Struggle for Labor and Civil Rights* (Detroit: Wayne State University Press, 2010), 210–219.
8. See US Census of Manufactures for 1954 and 1958.
9. Detroit Commission on Human Relations, "Detroit Metropolitan Area Employment and Income, By Age, Sex, Color and Residence, 1963," 16–17; Detroit Housing needs report, 1973, New Detroit Inc., Box 18, Folder 8, Reuther Library, 21.
10. Barry Bluestone and Bennett Harrison, *The Deindustrialization of America: Plant Closings, Community Abandonment, and the Dismantling of Basic Industry* (New York: Basic Books, 1982), 112–113.

DETROITERS III: HENRY RUSSELL JR.

1. Quotes and details are from an interview with the author, July 19, 2010.

CHAPTER 16: DEATH OF THE COVENANTS

1. Neal Shine, "Orsel McGhee's Quiet Fight Opened Doors for Millions," *Detroit Free Press*, January 29, 1949; US Supreme Court, *Shelley v. Kraemer*, 334 US 1 (1948).
2. Thomas J. Sugrue, "Crabgrass-Roots Politics: Race, Rights, and the Reaction against Liberalism in the Urban North, 1940–1964," *Journal of American History* 82, no. 2 (September 1995): 557–560.
3. See Maria Krysan and Michael Bader, "Perceiving the Metropolis: Seeing the City Through a Prism of Race," *Social Forces* 86, no. 2 (December 2007): 699–733.
4. That 2004 study came after Detroit's crime problem skyrocketed, so although it is not directly applicable to 1950s Detroit, it is still a pertinent window into the differing perceptions.
5. For a nuanced look at the phenomenon of white resistance and black persistence, see Thomas J. Sugrue, *The Origins of the Urban Crisis: Race and Inequality in Postwar Detroit* (Princeton: Princeton University Press, 1996), chapter 8.
6. April 21, 1966, report from the New Detroit Inc. Housing Committee, New Detroit collection, Reuther Library, Series I, Housing and Economic Development, 1967–1975, Box 12, Folder 25: Blockbusting-open housing.
7. Letter from Jerry McDonald, New Detroit Inc. Commission in Community Relations, to James Streeter of the Model Neighborhood Program, September 19, 1968, New Detroit collection, Reuther Library, Series I, Housing and Economic Development, 1967–1975, Box 12, Folder 25: Blockbusting-open housing.
8. Coleman Young and Lonnie Wheeler, *Hard Stuff: The Autobiography of Mayor Coleman Young* (New York: Viking, 1994), 179–180.

9. Interview, January 15, 2011.
10. For a full analysis of the surveys and the shift in black attitudes, see Howard Schuman and Shirley Hatchett, *Black Racial Attitudes: Trends and Complexities* (Ann Arbor: Survey Research Center, Institute for Social Research, University of Michigan, 1974).

CHAPTER 17: THE OIL EMBARGO

1. United States Statistical Abstract, 1980, Table 1114, Motor Vehicles—Registrations and Factory Sales: 1950–1979.
2. Coleman Young and Lonnie Wheeler, *Hard Stuff: The Autobiography of Mayor Coleman Young* (New York: Viking, 1994), 16–25.
3. Young and Wheeler, *Hard Stuff*, 31.
4. Young and Wheeler, *Hard Stuff*, 40.
5. Young and Wheeler, *Hard Stuff*, 62–65.
6. Young and Wheeler, *Hard Stuff*, 122–124.
7. Young and Wheeler, *Hard Stuff*, 6.
8. Wilbur C. Rich, *Coleman Young and Detroit Politics: From Social Activist to Power Broker* (Detroit: Wayne State University Press, 1989), 183.
9. Rich, *Coleman Young and Detroit Politics*, 149–151 and 266–267.
10. Young and Wheeler, *Hard Stuff*, 149.
11. "26,000 Apply for 1,000 Casino Jobs," *Detroit News*, March 28, 2007.

DETROITERS V: JOHN THOMPSON

1. Unless otherwise noted, all details about John Thompson are from interviews with the author. As disclosure: Thompson has been a close friend since the early 1990s, when I got to know him while writing for the *Detroit News*, and I worked in the earlier incarnation of his bar. The compelling details of his life, though, outweigh our personal connection. I hope this doesn't burn any bridges.
2. Detroit City Directory, 1968 (Detroit: Polk, 1968).
3. "Anchor's aweigh: The bar that Leo built begins a new era, but memories linger of crooks, cops and camaraderie," *Detroit News*, December 11, 1993.
4. Will Bunch, *Jukebox America: Down Back Streets and Blue Highways in Search of the Country's Greatest Jukebox* (New York: St. Martin's Press, 1994), 269.
5. Interview with the author, January 2011.
6. "Detroit Entrepreneurs Opt to Look Up," *New York Times*, January 9, 2010.

CHAPTER 18: WHEN THE JOBS GO AWAY

1. William Julius Wilson, *When Work Disappears: The World of the New Urban Poor* (New York: Knopf, 1996), 23, 31, and 39.
2. The Federal Bureau of Investigation's Uniform Crime Reports.
3. Greg Mathis, with Blair S. Walker, *Inner City Miracle* (New York: Ballantine Books, 2002), 11–12.
4. "Black Gangs Terrorize Detroit Rock Fans," *New York Times*, August 17, 1976; "Motor City Fighting for Its Life Again," *Washington Post*, August 23, 1976.
5. Mathis, *Inner City Miracle*, 1–5.
6. Milton "Butch" Jones and Raymond Canty, *Y.B.I. Young Boys Inc.: The Autobiography of Butch Jones* (Detroit: H. Publications, 1996), 2.
7. For a graphic depiction of the rise and fall of Y.B.I., see Butch and Canty, *Y.B.I. Young Boys Inc.* Sylvester Murray, one of the Y.B.I.'s main heroin suppliers, and Culpepper, the lawyer, didn't respond to repeated requests for interviews. Convicted hitman Nathaniel "Boone" Craft, who emerged from the later gang culture on the east side, also declined to be interviewed.

8. I was among them. From 1986 to 1991 I was a general assignment reporter on the city desk of the *Detroit News* and covered more killings than I can remember.
9. For a dramatic depiction of the drug culture then, including detailed interviews with hitman Nathaniel "Boone" Craft, see the Alan Bradley's 2010 documentary, *Rollin': The Fall of the Auto Industry and the Rise of the Drug Economy in Detroit.*
10. The Federal Bureau of Investigation's Uniform Crime Reports.
11. My wife and I moved out of Detroit for the suburbs in 1990, when she was pregnant with our oldest son, after there was a shooting in our side yard, then part of a stable and multiethnic eastside neighborhood.
12. Wilson, *When Work Disappears*, 31.
13. For a compelling and close-to-the-ground look at the fate of one family within that underclass, see Luke Bergmann, *Getting Ghost: Two Young Lives and the Struggle for the Soul of an American City* (New York: New Press, 2008).
14. "The Fiscal Condition of the City of Detroit," Citizens Research Council, April 2010, executive summary.
15. 2011 Statistical Abstract, Table 720.
16. "Ford plans to fill 7,000 US jobs." *Detroit News*, January 10, 2011.
17. "Quicken Loans' Dan Gilbert Adds Dime Building to Downtown Detroit Holdings," *Detroit Free Press*, June 21, 2011.
18. US Census data.

DETROITERS VI: SHELLEY

1. Shelley is an assumed name. She asked that her real name not be used, a cloak of privacy I granted given the nature of her story. The agency, whose leader was the intermediary in setting up the interview with Shelley, also asked not to be identified.

CHAPTER 19: PITTSBURGH, A DIFFERENT CASE

1. Statistics are drawn from the US Bureau of Labor Statistics, US Census reports, and "Pittsburgh Today and Tomorrow," a 2011 report by *Pittsburgh Quarterly* and *Pittsburgh Today*.
2. "Pittsburgh's mayor drops tuition tax," *Pittsburgh Post-Gazette*, December 22, 2009.
3. US Census data tabulated in "The Fiscal Condition of the City of Detroit," Citizens Research Council, April 2010, 4.
4. We were colleagues at the *Detroit News* in the early 1990s. These details were drawn from a Facebook exchange over the events, which feels like some sort of watershed moment in interviewing sources for a book.

CHAPTER 20: AN EPILOGUE

1. Badenhausen, Kurt, "Best States for Business and Careers," Forbes.com, October 13, 2010, www.forbes.com/2010/10/13/best-states-for-business-business-beltway-best-states-table .html.
2. It's a decision that my wife and I also made. We left the region altogether in 1997 during a newspaper strike, when I was hired by the *Los Angeles Times* (neither of us is from Michigan originally).
3. Bing's staff did not respond to repeated requests for an interview with the mayor about his plans for the city.
4. Memo to Detroit City Council from Irvin Corley Jr., Fiscal Analysis Division, February 3, 2011.
5. "Crisis Turnaround Team: Executive Summary and Final Report," undated, 9–10; "With Detroit in dire straits, mayor invites big thinking," *Washington Post*, February 8, 2011.
6. "DPS Attendance 55% on First Day," *Detroit Free Press*, September 7, 2011.

7. "Robert Bobb Plans to Use New Powers to Modify Union Contracts," *Detroit Free Press*, April 15, 2011; "As Students Leave, Detroit Public School Teachers Must Follow," *Detroit Free Press*, September 21, 2011.

8. "Health and the Economy in the Detroit Area," April 2010, by the *Washington Post*, Harvard School of Public Health and Kaiser Family Health Foundation, available at www.kff.org/ kaiserpolls/upload/8062.pdf.

9. Mayor Dave Bing's "State of the City" speech, February 22, 2011, www.ci.detroit.mi.us/ departmentsandagencies/mayorsoffice/stateofthecity.aspx.

AFTERWORD

1. "Database: Who owns downtown?" *Crain's Detroit Business*, http://www.crainsdetroit.com/ article/20130806/NEWS/130809931/database-who-owns-downtown#; David Muller, "Dan Gilbert and affiliates now control 7.6 million square feet of real estate in Detroit," MLive, June 18, 2013, http://www.mlive.com/business/detroit/index.ssf/2013/06/dan_gilbert_and_ affiliates_now.html#incart_river_default.

2. Scott Martelle, "Five Myths About Detroit," *Washington Post*, July 26, 2013, http://articles .washingtonpost.com/2013-07-26/opinions/40864923_1_auto-industry-uaw-detroit-news; Christine MacDonald and Mike Wilkinson, "Half of Detroit property owners don't pay taxes," *The Detroit News*, February 21, 2013, http://www.detroitnews.com/article/20130221/ METRO01/302210375.

3. "Christie's to Value Detroit's $1 Billion Art-Institute Holdings," Bloomberg via MoneyNews .com, August 6, 2013, http://www.moneynews.com/FinanceNews/Detroit-bankruptcy-art-institute/2013/08/06/id/518972#ixzz2gPH4z7zS.

4. Patrick Sharkey, *Stuck in Place: Urban Neighborhoods and the End of Progress toward Racial Equality* (Chicago: University of Chicago Press, 2013), 9–10.

5. Patrick Sharkey, "Toward a Durable Urban Policy Agenda," chap. 7 in *Stuck in Place*,; W. Steven Barnett, reprinted in "Does Headstart Work for Kids? The Bottom Line," *Washington Post*, March 5, 2013, http://www.washingtonpost.com/blogs/answer-sheet/wp/2013/03/05/does-head-start-work-for-kids-the-bottom-line.

INDEX